Leaf and Branch

Trees and tall shrubs of Perth

Robert Powell

Illustrated by Margaret Pieroni and Susan Patrick
With a foreword by George Seddon

Department of
Environment and Conservation

Our environment, our future

Publisher Department of Environment and Conservation, 17 Dick Perry Ave, Kensington, Western Australia, 6151

Editor Samille Mitchell

Design and production Tiffany Taylor

Cartography Promaco Geodraft

Illustrations Margaret Pieroni and Susan Patrick

Front cover and title page leaves and fruits of quandong, illustrated by Margaret Pieroni
Back cover (top) modong, (bottom) tuart longicorn, painted by Margaret Pieroni

Set in Bembo Regular and Avant Garde Gothic

Printed in Western Australia by Scott Print

ISBN 978-0-7309-3916-0

Foreword

By Professor George Seddon[1]

This is a book that tries to change the way we see the world around us, on the south-western edge of this dry land. How and what we see depends on what we value, so to see differently is to behave differently. Seeing is culture-laden, so it is hard for older people to see afresh what they have learned to ignore, reject, despise. It is easier for children and young adults to take in what this book has to teach, and it will enrich their lives. Perhaps they can then help their elders and worsers (well, not betters, in this case).

Judging from their behaviour, especially as shown in their parks and gardens, most people in Perth are profoundly alienated from their natural environment. Almost any new housing estate, even the prestigious ones, will show this very clearly, but it is equally clear in most long-settled areas. To take one of many possible examples, the grounds of the John Curtin High School[2] in Fremantle still show remnants of the original trees and shrubs, the moonahs and Rottnest cypresses, so strong and clear on their limestone hill against bleached rock and blue sky. But they are totally neglected, infested with fennel and wild oats, living on borrowed time, while the immediate surrounds of the school have buffalo lawn and rose-beds. The educational message must be very clear — reject your local heritage; strive for an alien one.

This book should help change that. It is full of the kind of information that helps not just identification, putting name tags on things, but understanding and appreciation. I had never stopped to ask myself why marri has wiggly branches; you will find out on page 94, and not forget.

Other books by Robert Powell (with Jane Emberson) show how much we have already lost. *An Old Look at Trees* is a book of photographs taken between 1890 and 1930, showing a beauty that is now much less common. The tuarts have suffered greatly. So have the jarrahs, often low and spreading on the coastal plain, but massive in girth. After an absence from Perth for twenty years, I drove across the coastal plain on Gnangara Road in October 1989. On the way, I wanted to show my wife a pricklybark on the Bassendean sands. I found the trees — but where were all the *Dampiera* and *Hibbertia* and the other wild flowers that were once so common? Gone, smothered out by wild oats, burnt out by fire.

I wish I had had this book when I first came to Perth thirty years ago. If we had all read it, and learned from it, perhaps some of the big old jarrahs along the Yanchep Road would still be there, and still there for our children and our grandchildren.

George Seddon

George Seddon, a celebrated Australian academic, died in 2007. He was the author of books including *Swan River Landscapes*, *Sense of Place*, *Man and Landscape in Australia*, *Swan Song* and *The Old Country*; co-author of *A City and its Setting*.

---

[1] This foreword was written for the first edition of the book, 1990.
[2] John Curtin High School is now John Curtin College of the Arts, and the surrounds have been modified.

Contents

Part three Activities — 213

Appendices — 231

Maps and tables

Preface

About 1,500 plant species occur naturally in the Perth Metropolitan Region, yet most Perth residents hardly know any of them. Perth now spreads out in a vast area of suburbs, and most Perth residents are likelier to recognise a commonly cultivated exotic or eastern Australian plant than a local one. Local plants are, nonetheless, readily available to be discovered in Perth's many bushlands.

The aim of this book is to help readers get to know some of Perth's plant species. Its subject is a small group of 79 species: the trees and the tallest shrubs that occur naturally within the Metropolitan Region (Map 1, inside front cover). These are often the easiest species to spot, and the likeliest to have been retained on land developed for housing or agriculture. They are quite varied, including members of 14 different plant families. Between them they grew in almost all the available habitats. Wherever you live in the Perth Metropolitan Region, your natural environment would have included some of these.

Local plants are particularly rewarding species to get to know, since they are part of our natural environment. They evolved in close association with native animals and fungi, and are therefore vitally important in maintaining biodiversity.

Through learning to recognise even just one or two of Perth's trees or shrubs, we can start to notice where they occur, how well they are doing, how they are affected by fire, and so on. Before long, some of the other trees or shrubs with which they associate may become recognisable too. The bush may no longer seem strange and 'foreign', but meaningful and interesting. And this new familiarity may bring about another benefit: since our knowledge of Perth's plant species is incomplete, any information gathered by readers of this book may be useful to science.

This book has three main parts. The first, with chapters on the place of plants in our environment, will help readers appreciate plants and bushlands. The second — the main, central part of the book — provides an identification guide to Perth's trees and tall shrubs, and gives further information about each one. The third part will help you see how we can make the plants part of our lives.

More than one and a half million people now live in the Metropolitan Region — over two thirds of the entire population of Western Australia — and the number is still growing. With so many people, and with environmental changes such as global warming, the future survival of our natural flora is threatened. To keep our flora, we must be informed and caring custodians of our natural heritage. This book seeks to encourage that awareness.

Second edition

This book has been extensively revised. The scientific names of the plant, animal and fungi species treated or mentioned have been updated. Of the plant species discussed, 11 now have different scientific names. The genus *Dryandra* is now included in *Banksia*. In the genus *Eucalyptus*, two of the book's species now belong to a new genus, *Corymbia*; and two previously unnamed species have now been named. Also updated are the references to the numbers of known species in the various plant genera to which the plant species belong. For many genera this has increased, as new species are discovered or the taxonomy of groups of species becomes better known.

For many of the book's species, additional information has been provided on their associated animals, particularly insects, and in some cases their associated fungi. Advice on the occurrence of the plant species in the Metropolitan Region has been revised, since unfortunately some plant populations have disappeared as land continues to be developed. In discussing the human uses of the various species, more attention has been given to encouraging their use in cultivation.

Many of the chapters at the beginning and end of the book have been changed substantially. The chapter on the relationships between plants now reflects more recent ideas on how the angiosperms (flowering plants) are divided and on the evolutionary order of the plant families.

In the chapter previously called 'Fauna', now 'Associated life', insects and other invertebrates are given more prominence. Invertebrates are of enormous significance for their great diversity and their roles in the functioning of ecosystems; many are closely associated with plants. A section has been included on fungi, of which many species have beneficial relationships with plants. Like invertebrate animals, fungi are extraordinarily diverse, and have a profound influence on ecosystems. Also included are mistletoes, lichens and mosses.

The conservation chapter has been recast to give more attention to the threats faced by plants and ecosystems, which sadly have become much more apparent. Of special concern are global warming and the associated changes in climate. The chapter also refers to recent work towards conserving our plants and bushlands, such as the *Bush Forever* study and the research being undertaken by the Centre of Excellence for Climate Change and Woodland & Forest Health. Reference is also made to the conservation activities of community groups.

The chapter on cultivation has been expanded to give more emphasis to the various public lands where local trees and shrubs may be established — and to the useful purposes they can serve, in providing habitat corridors, for example, or helping to turn drains into living streams. The last chapter, 'Study and leisure', now refers to the use of the Internet for identifying plants, and to friends groups, nature-study groups and the Land for Wildlife scheme.

Acknowledgements

This book's first edition was initiated in 1983 by Stephen Hopper, now the Director of the Royal Botanic Gardens, Kew, who was then at the Western Australian Wildlife Research Centre. Susan Patrick, at that time working with Steve as a botanist and artist, began the botanical drawings. I became involved in planning the project, and took charge of preparing the text.

My work was in conjunction with three principal others. Steve had many ideas on the book's content. He also helped with botanical information and generally commented on drafts of the text. Peter McMillan, an Honorary Associate of the Western Australian Museum, provided much of the information on associated animals and accompanied me on several field trips. No-one helped me more than Jane Emberson, with whom I had frequent discussions about the text and indeed almost every aspect of the book.

Margaret Pieroni drew the identifying features (leaves, fruits, etc.) of 24 of the 79 plant species; Susan Patrick drew those of the other 55 species. Margaret did all the other drawings and painted the cover illustrations. The drawings of whole trees and shrubs, and most of the drawings in the early and late chapters of the book, were done from my photographs. The drawings of most of the insects and some of the other animals were from specimens or slides of Peter McMillan's; drawings of a number of birds and mammals were from materials held by the W.A. Gould League. The drawings of the identifying features of the trees and shrubs were from specimens taken by the artists or by me or from mounted specimens in the Western Australian Herbarium.

Other persons, then in the Department of Conservation and Land Management (now the Department of Environment and Conservation, or DEC), gave me encouragement or help, particularly Kevin Goss. Ray Bailey provided helpful editorial assistance in the final stages, and Robyn Mundy liaised with me closely in designing the book.

As well as the above, many others provided information and advice, particularly Ian Abbott, Allan Burbidge, Andrew Burbidge, Herbert Dermaz, Bob Dixon, Terry Houston, Penny Hussey, Roger Jaensch, Byron Lamont, Jonathon Majer, Bruce Maslin, Eric McCrum, Magnus Peterson, Joanna Seabrook, Phil Shedley, Jim Singleton, Peter Weston, Paul Wilson and Ken Youngson. Nancie Fienberg, Chris Hancock, Margaret Hansen, Jean Martin, Myee Powell and others helped in assembling information or with proof-reading.

Of the many scientific papers and other published works from which the first edition drew, a particularly valuable aid was *Flora of the Perth Region,* by Neville Marchant and others.

In revising the book for the second edition, no-one helped me more than the entomologist and naturalist Jan Taylor. Jan accompanied me on trips to examine 30 of the book's species for associated insects and other invertebrates, capturing and identifying for me many of the creatures encountered.

Barbara Rye provided much advice on taxonomy and referred me to many relevant publications. Barbara also advised me on current thinking on the relationships between plants, for the chapter that bears that name. Vanda Longman read the entire text and made many useful comments on botanical and other aspects. My main adviser on the text was Jane Emberson, whom I consulted frequently for help in my efforts to express facts and ideas clearly. Jane also helped me determine the best structure for the conservation chapter. Robyn Benken spent several sessions with me proof-reading the text, and Robyn Weir helped with some of the final checking.

In the chapter on associated life, the information on fungi is adapted from a text written for that purpose by Neale Bougher. Many of the mentions of fungi elsewhere in the book are derived from further information provided by Neale, who also gave me the ideas and most of the materials for the fungi illustrations in the book.

Peter White provided advice on wandoo, Tony Start on mistletoes, and Ray Cranfield on mosses, liverworts and lichens.

Mark Webb and staff at Kings Park and Botanic Garden advised on cultivation aspects of species in the book, as did Graham Harris and John Murray.

Of the drawings for the book's first edition, mentioned above, by Margaret Pieroni and Susan Patrick, all except the fruits of flooded gum have been used again for the present edition. Several new illustrations appear in this edition, all by Margaret Pieroni. These include all the cover paintings, based on those of the first edition, and similarly the drawing on the titlepage. Seven drawings of new subjects have been added to Parts One and Two, and the fruits of flooded gum have been redrawn from more typical specimens than those used originally. Lastly, Margaret has provided special versions of four illustrations to introduce the book's four main sections.

Many others helped with advice or information, including Ken Atkins, Paul Barber, Andrew Brown, Kate Brown, Jane Chambers, Pat Collins, Colin Crane, John Dunn, Christine Freegard, Stefan de Haan, Alison Hansen, Deborah Harding, Drew Haswell, Elaine Horne, Ric How, Penny Hussey, Bronwen Keighery, Greg Keighery, Tony Kirkby, David Knowles, Hans Lambers, Ross Lantzke, Bridgitte Long, Beng Siew Mahon, Jonathan Majer, Bruce Maslin, Peter Mawson, Trudy Paap, Grazyna Paczkowska, John Riley, Kevin Thiele, Matt Williams and Allan Wills.

My thanks go to all of those. None of them, however, is responsible for any errors I have made.

In the production of the revised book, I worked closely with Samille Mitchell and Tiffany Taylor, and Kaye Verboon in the early stages, who were most pleasant and helpful.

I was employed with DEC for much of the time I was revising this book. I thank Colin Ingram, Paul McCluskey, and especially Sharon Colliss and Peter Sharp, for their support, and for enabling me to spend some time each week outside my normal duties to devote to this task. Alex Errington's support, too, was much appreciated.

Robert Powell

*I dedicate this book to the memory of my mother,
Myee Powell (1912-2008), a naturalist who
encouraged my interest in trees.*

Part one
Introduction

'Beauty is in the eye of the beholder', runs the saying. The way we see trees and shrubs is conditioned by attitudes we learn in our society. Most books on horticulture are illustrated with pictures of spectacular displays of brightly coloured flowers, which we have been taught to recognise as beautiful. Most of nature's trees and shrubs, however, have more modest displays. Furthermore, books emphasise particular features of a tree or shrub, and largely ignore what it looks like as a whole. Where they do mention shape they praise regularity and compactness, whereas most natural trees and shrubs are irregular and diffuse.

With such preconceived ideas we see beauty only in a minority of species. This chapter explores other ways of looking at Perth's trees and tall shrubs. It aims at helping readers to see the beauty in every species.

Shape and character

Look at a tree as a whole and you will be aware of the space it occupies. It extends upwards and outwards in different directions. Walk round it and it changes shape and structure from every new angle.

Stand close to the tree and you will appreciate its three dimensions, particularly if the sun is high and parts of the tree are lit up. Stand further

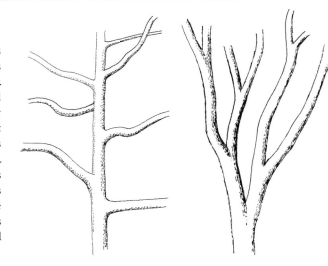

∧ *Fig. 2*
The shaft structure (left) and the splitting structure (right).

away and the tree looks more two-dimensional, particularly if the sun is low. If the sun is behind you, the tree looks heavy and solid, with thick, opaque foliage. Look at it against the light at sunrise or sunset, and the tree is a silhouette, delicate and detailed; the foliage is broken into a texture, and twigs normally hidden by foliage are revealed (see Fig. 1).

The same is true of shrubs and so too is what follows. For the sake of simplicity I shall refer mostly to trees.

Structure

The space a tree occupies depends on its shape, and its shape depends on its structure (see Fig. 2). The *shaft structure* consists of a main trunk with side-branches. In the *splitting structure* the trunk divides into two or more near-equal stems, which continue to divide fairly equally.

The shaft structure is more typical of trees, the splitting structure of shrubs, but there are many variations and combinations of the two. Often trees have the shaft structure as saplings — which helps them gain height rapidly — but develop the splitting structure with age (see Fig. 13).

∨ *Fig. 1*
The lacy effect of flooded gum in silhouette (only part of the crown is shown).

Different species also vary in the degree to which their member trees adhere to the structure typical of the species. At one extreme is what might be called *template growth*: all specimens develop the same structure. The introduced Norfolk Island pine is a good example of this. I shall call the other extreme *opportunistic growth*: each specimen grows according to its individual circumstances. Saltwater paperbark (p. 172) is largely *opportunistic*: it may have one trunk or several, and be upright or sprawling.

Pattern and detail

Different species of tree have characteristic patterns; for example, the foliage of bullich is arranged in tight clumps, whereas that of flooded gum is much more dispersed. Different sizes of leaf affect the texture of the foliage. Some patterns affect others; for example, terminal flower-spikes in banksias cause branching or bending of the stem (Figs 3 & 4), and heavy clusters of fruits on some eucalypts, particularly marri, often result in pendulous or wiggly branches (Fig. 5). Such patterns give the tree harmony and character. The individual variations between parts of the pattern — the precise shape of each clump of foliage, the curve of each branch — produce an abundance of detail to fascinate the eye. The tracery of twigs and branches both echoes the patterns of the live parts and adds a great deal of detail.

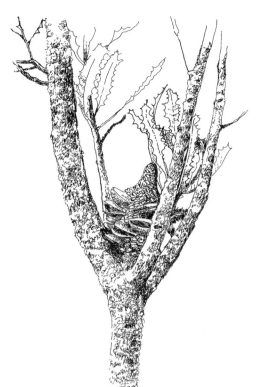

∧ *Fig. 3*
In this firewood banksia the flower-spike is terminal, and five new shoots have grown from beneath it.

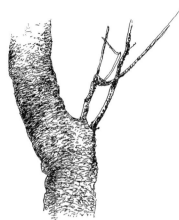

∧ *Fig. 4*
The same stems many years later will look something like this. The strongest one (left) has dominated and the others have died, leaving a wiggle in the branch. Such details, repeated many times, contribute to this banksia's pattern of meandering branches. (In saw-tooth banksia, however, the stems that fork round cones develop more equally, and two or three often persist. The result is a bushier habit — compare the drawings on pp. 72 and 74.)

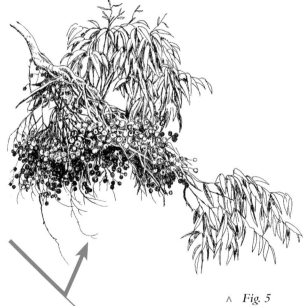

∧ *Fig. 5*
Jarrah branch weighed down by fruits. The strong new shoots along the branch will result in a bend, as shown by the arrows.

< *Fig. 6*
Fig. 6
*This picturesquely stunted chenille honey-myrtle
is growing in rocky limestone soil, which has not
allowed it to develop fully. Although mature, it is
only 1½ m tall.*

Effects of environment

With rare exceptions, no two human beings look
alike. The same is true of trees. The appearance
of trees, however, is affected by the environment
much more than that of humans. For example,
jarrah on the coastal plain is vastly different in size,
shape and structure from jarrah in the Darling
Range. Although the difference may be partly
genetic, the environment is the major cause.

General conditions

A tree will not grow to full size if the soil is
too shallow. Thus many trees growing in coastal
limestone, or in granite areas of the Darling Scarp,
are stunted (see Fig. 6).

Coastal trees often have a pronounced lean. Sea
winds deposit salt on the foliage, particularly
on the seaward side. This kills young shoots and
stunts growth on that side, causing a lean (Figs
7 & 8). Large trees can be affected up to 10 km
from the coast. If a number of upper branches
are killed by salt, a tree will often shoot from

dormant buds lower down to form additional
branches. Thus near the coast trees tend to be
lower and more branching.

A more general influence is climate. Even within
the Metropolitan Region there is enough
variation to have an effect. Trees grow larger in
the south of the region than in the north, where
rainfall is slightly less and temperatures and
evaporation slightly higher.

Other forms of life have an important influence
on trees and shrubs. Fungi in the inner wood
of old trees can cause branches to weaken and
break. Insects often alter the growth patterns of
trees. If leaf-eating insects eat a dominant shoot,
other shoots will take over. This will produce
either a fork or a slight change in the branch's
direction. Wood-boring insect larvae that
ringbark a branchlet have a more pronounced
effect. Eucalypts recover by means of dormant
buds (Fig. 9). Species without dormant buds, such
as wattles, divert their energy into other branches
rather than form new ones.

Insect attack is thought of as ugly, but is it?
Trees virtually devoid of insects in their foliage
or branches tend to be symmetrical and regular.
Those that support insects may well have basic

> *Fig. 7*
Fig. 7
*This moonah, near Parker
Point, Rottnest Island, is
exposed to very salty sea
winds. Its upper branches
have been killed, but its
lower branches have survived
to form a dense mass of
foliage that keeps out the
wind. Its windward side
(right), shorn by the salt, is
very smooth in outline.*

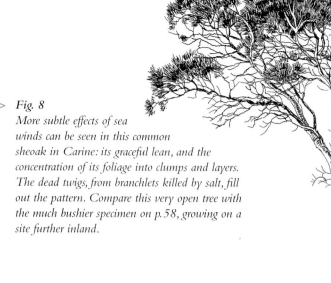

> *Fig. 8*
> *More subtle effects of sea*
> *winds can be seen in this common*
> *sheoak in Carine: its graceful lean, and the*
> *concentration of its foliage into clumps and layers.*
> *The dead twigs, from branchlets killed by salt, fill*
> *out the pattern. Compare this very open tree with*
> *the much bushier specimen on p.58, growing on a*
> *site further inland.*

symmetry, but will have subtle, yet pleasing, asymmetries and irregularities. Moreover, in a natural stand of trees, some specimens will be attacked by insects more than others, resulting in an increased variety of form and detail. Yet they will harmonise and present a pleasing unity.

As well as contributing to the beauty of trees, insect attack, in moderation, can benefit them: they have evolved to cope with it. Without insect attack a tree can be burdened by dense foliage or excessively large clusters of fruits.

Site conditions

The environment at each locality is often not uniform. A tree near the top of a coastal dune has drier soil and stronger salt winds to endure than a neighbour in a nearby swale.

Often the main influence on an individual tree is that exerted by its nearest neighbours (see, for example, Fig. 10). In a forest, competition for light causes trees to grow tall and straight. In a woodland, the dominant trees occur both singly and in irregular groupings, and therefore vary more in shape. Tree seedlings that germinate in the shade of an existing tree will grow out at an angle until they find light, then bend upwards. Many gracefully leaning trees are produced in this way.

> *Fig. 9*
> *The middle branch of this young tuart has twice*
> *been ringbarked by wood-boring insect larvae; the*
> *remaining stumps are clearly visible. Each time, the*
> *tree has recovered by shooting from further down*
> *the branch. The resulting bends contrast with the*
> *smooth flow of the branches on either side.*

> *Fig. 10*
> *Close pairs of trees have a special beauty. In this*
> *pair of wandoos, each is affected by its neighbour,*
> *most noticeably the left-hand tree, which leans*
> *to the left and sends out most of its branches on*
> *that side. Though individual in outline and detail,*
> *the two trees form a harmonious and visually*
> *satisfying pair.*

> *Fig. 11*
This bullich has recovered from a severe fire by shooting from the base and from its lignotuber, below ground. Originally a tree with a single stem (its remains are at the right), it is now a mallee, with many stems.

If a tree loses one of its larger near neighbours it will respond to the extra light and reduced competition. If it was originally forced to grow at an angle its main growth will now change to a vertical direction. New shoots are often put out along the trunk, and grow into strong new branches that eventually form most of the canopy.

Accidents of nature

Fire can have a dramatic effect on vegetation. In our hot, dry summers, fires can occur naturally, but have become more frequent, and sometimes more intense, since European settlement. One significant factor has been the introduction of exotic grasses.

Some species of tree or shrub are killed by fire. Of those species that survive fires, some are more resistant than others (see Figs 11 & 12). Even the most resistant can lose branchlets or whole branches. If fires are frequent and intense, trees many not be able to recover fully between fires. This is the cause of many of the stagheaded specimens seen in metropolitan bush areas.

Trees can also lose branches in strong winds or when other trees fall on them. The scars and irregularities add variety and detail.

> *Fig. 12*
Burnt candle banksia and common sheoak, Jandakot. The banksia is shooting near the ends of its branches; its crown will soon recover, and the tree will have changed little in shape or structure. The sheoak, however, is sprouting from the trunk and lower branches. Its crown has largely been destroyed and the regrown tree will be very different from the original.

Old trees and shrubs

Look at a young tree and an old one. The old one will probably hold your attention longer. Old trees are complex and individual. Their structure and patterns, and their many interesting irregularities, reveal something of their life-stories (see Fig. 13).

Some eucalypts can live several hundred years, and are an irreplaceable link with the past. Many of the large old trees we see today were alive before the European settlement of Western Australia. In our rapidly changing world, they offer a different perspective of time.

Local trees and shrubs

Local trees and shrubs — those that belong naturally to the site — have evolved in the local environment, and respond to it in meaningful ways. Jarrah's woody character and very moderate size on the coastal plain reflect the infertility of Perth's sandy soils. Tuart's elegant splitting habit, and its broad, rounded canopy and comparatively dense foliage, are a response to the salty winds near the coast. Because local trees and shrubs are used by many associated insects, they develop much irregularity and detail. These aspects of beauty are less characteristic of non-local trees and shrubs, which are in an environment alien to them, and which generally support fewer insects.

> *Fig. 13*
>
> *Old trees such as this marri (at Woodvale) offer a wealth of patterns and detail to fascinate the eye. Some patterns are typical of the species, for example the wiggly, downward-tending branches at the lower left. Others reflect the environment, for example the lean to the left and the flattish top, both caused by sea winds.*
>
> *The general structure of the tree reveals its history. In its youth it grew up straight, with a shaft structure. Having reached about half its present height, it split into several major branches. At the same stage it began to lean; by then it must have outgrown the surrounding vegetation and become exposed to sea winds.*

Fig. 14
Bush scene, Neerabup.
Tuart, parrotbush, chenille
honey-myrtle and balga
combine with smaller
plants in a harmonious
natural community.

Local plants in combination have a special beauty. In nature, plants that like the same conditions and get on well with one another occur together in a natural community (as in Fig. 14). This harmonious interaction makes their appearance harmonious too, supplementing the beauty of the individual members. There is no better example of a whole that is greater than the sum of its parts. Perth's plant communities are numerous, and the variation between them reflects subtle changes in the environment (see next chapter).

Our local trees and shrubs give us a sense of place. Jarrah and tuart, for example, occur naturally in no capital city other than Perth. Whereas jarrah is widespread in Perth, tuart provides a further

sense of place by being almost entirely restricted to a narrow coastal strip. Their sense of rightness in their situation is part of their beauty.

Present realities

Unfortunately, many of the remaining specimens of Perth's natural trees are no longer very natural in appearance, either because of human interference or because of changes to the environment. Specimens in many of Perth's parks have reduced detail to offer, because their dead branches and twigs have been cut off. The effect of changes to the environment, as the conservation chapter will explain, is most evident in bushlands, where many local trees are now in very poor health.

Many specimens of Perth's trees and shrubs have been planted in places outside their natural occurrence, which confuses our sense of place.

Nevertheless, there are still many fine specimens of Perth's trees and shrubs to find and admire.

Putting appreciation into practice

We can use nature as a model for parks and gardens. In planting such areas, species from quite different origins are often mixed for the sake of variety. The problem with this approach is that such species usually clash visually — and the whole is often unsatisfying. For example, many eastern Australian eucalypts have a strongly developed shaft structure, which looks out of place among the local eucalypts of Perth's coastal plain.

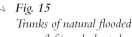 *Fig. 15*
Trunks of natural flooded
gums (left) and planted
river gums (right).
Naturally occurring trees
should be retained wherever
possible, for their aesthetic
as well as their biological
value. The flooded gums
are stout, mature trees,
beautifully varied in form,
and the natural grouping
has led to a variety of
interactions between them.
The river gums, by contrast,
are young and uniform,
and scarcely interact with
each other. The kinks in
several of them — all at
a similar height — are
caused by the stakes with
which they were planted.

In a natural remnant of vegetation there will always be both harmony and variety. Even in a stand of trees of the one species, the mixture of ages, the uneven spacing and the insect attack give considerable variation in form and detail; but whether there is one species or many, the plants are members of a natural community and will look well together.

We can retain more trees in our parks and gardens. Where we do plant, we can recreate the harmony of nature by using local species, by imitating nature's irregular groupings and by avoiding the tendency to space trees evenly. Better still, we can let trees and shrubs regenerate naturally and establish their own groupings.

In parks where non-local trees and shrubs are already established, it is still worth while planting groups of local species as reminders of Perth's natural setting.

Once we are aware of the structure and detail of trees and shrubs, we shall be less inclined to lop them, an act that destroys their natural structure. Where pruning is unavoidable, we can minimise its effect on their beauty (see p. 225).

If we appreciate the beauty of our natural trees and shrubs they will enrich our lives. That appreciation will also help us to create a more satisfying and harmonious environment in which to live.

↗ *Fig. 16*
This lopped limestone marlock displays features typical of lopped trees: the abrupt transition from thick branch to thin and from one branch to several; and, for slanting branches, a sudden change in direction (as at the left).

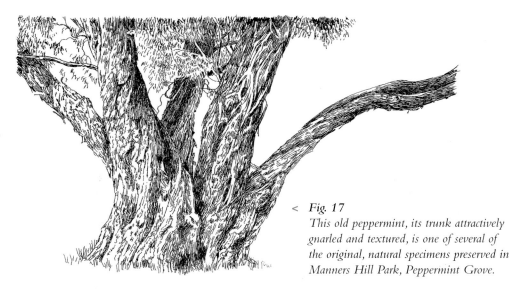

< *Fig. 17*
This old peppermint, its trunk attractively gnarled and textured, is one of several of the original, natural specimens preserved in Manners Hill Park, Peppermint Grove.

Plant communities

As you come to know the plant species in this book, you will discover that different ones are found in different habitats, such as near the coast, on the Darling Scarp, or near wetlands. Species needing the same conditions are often found together. A particular sort of habitat will therefore have a particular association of plants, or plant community. You can determine what plant community used to grow where you live, by noting your landform and soil and by observing any remnants of the original vegetation.

Plant communities are usually described according to the height and density of their tallest species. In the text that follows, forest refers to trees close enough together for their canopies to touch or overlap; if they are further apart they constitute a woodland. A low forest or woodland is one whose height is less than 10 m. Shrubby vegetation devoid of trees is a shrubland, sometimes called heath if it is less than 2 m tall, or scrub if more than 2 m.

The plant communities of the Perth Metropolitan Region come under three geographical divisions: the Darling Plateau, the Darling Scarp, and the Swan Coastal Plain.

Darling Plateau

The Darling Plateau can be broadly divided into the uplands, major valleys and minor valleys. The uplands are gently undulating, and the surface soil is gravelly. This is where the typical jarrah forest grows. Some marri is mixed with the jarrah, and bull banksia, common sheoak and the colourfully named snottygobbles grow as an understorey.

The major valleys (Map 2) are deep and broad. Their sides support marri, jarrah and sometimes wandoo, with yarri on the lower slopes and flooded gum and freshwater paperbark on the valley floor.

In these valleys, and less commonly elsewhere on the Darling Plateau, are outcrops of granite. On their shallow associated soils grow various communities of shrubs and herbs.

The minor valleys are those of tributary streams; the more prominent ones are shown on Map 2. Their sides support forest of jarrah, marri and yarri. Their swampy floors, sometimes narrow, sometimes broad, support vegetation that includes scrub of brook peppermint and other shrubs, and woodlands of modong and swamp banksia.

Darling Scarp

At the western edge of the Darling Plateau is the Darling Scarp, where varied conditions produce a rich and varied vegetation.

Erosion on the slopes of the scarp has exposed much granite and laterite. Shallow soils around these outcrops support communities of shrubs and herbs.

The Darling Scarp receives almost the highest rainfall in the Perth Metropolitan Region. Run-off from granite slopes provides moist sites for plant species more typical of high-rainfall areas further south. Where the soil is deep there are woodlands of marri, wandoo, flooded gum and jarrah.

Swan Coastal Plain

The vegetation of the Swan Coastal Plain is determined chiefly by the varied soils. These are described below, and Map 3 shows their distribution, with notes on their typical plant communities. Generally more than one plant community is given for each type of soil, reflecting different conditions at particular sites, such as depth of soil, and wetness or dryness. Some differences may be found between north and south or east and west; for example, tuart occurs far more commonly in the western half of the Karrakatta belt than the eastern half.

The map and descriptions will help you identify the soil of your site, and so either to identify its natural plant community or at least to narrow the range of possible plant communities to two or three.

Soil-types

At the foot of the Darling Scarp are areas of the Ridge Hill Shelf, formed from materials eroded from the scarp. The soils here, which are sandy to gravelly, are termed Forrestfield. The soils of the rest of the plain can be combined into three groups, according to their origin:

alluvial — carried down from the Darling Plateau or Darling Scarp by water;

aeolian — deposited on the coast by the ocean, then blown by the wind to form dunes;

estuarine — deposited round estuaries.

Map 2 – The Darling Plateau: river systems (as a guide to vegetation)

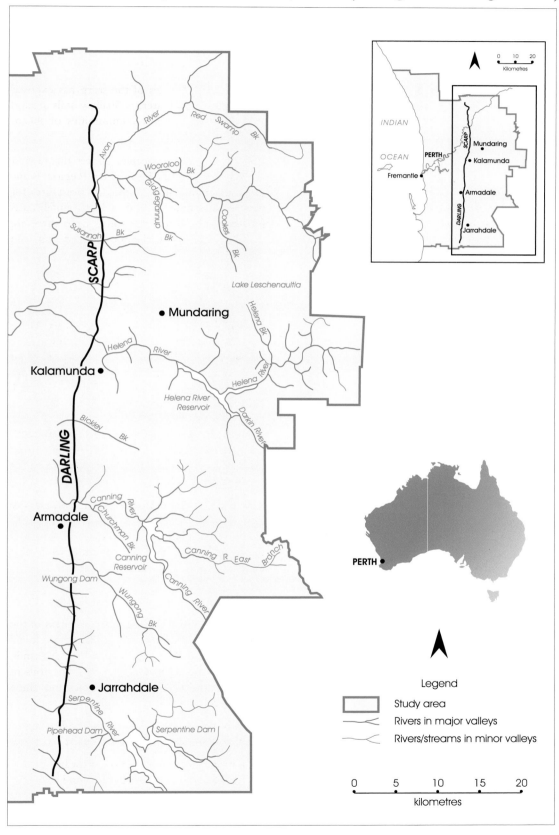

Legend

▭ Study area

Rivers in major valleys

Rivers/streams in minor valleys

0   5   10   15   20
kilometres

Map 3 – The Coastal Plain: soil-types and plant communities

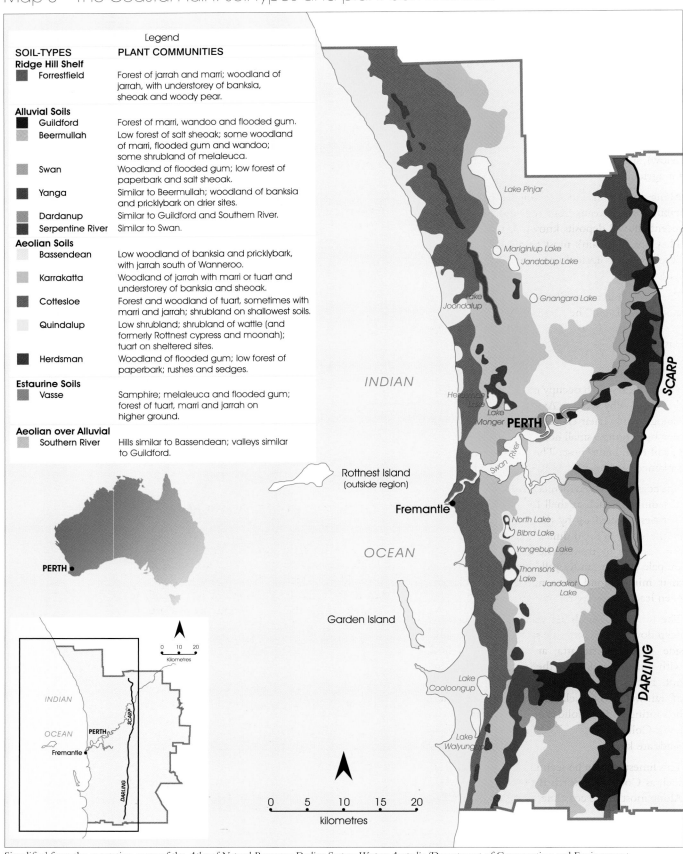

Legend

SOIL-TYPES	PLANT COMMUNITIES
Ridge Hill Shelf	
Forrestfield	Forest of jarrah and marri; woodland of jarrah, with understorey of banksia, sheoak and woody pear.
Alluvial Soils	
Guildford	Forest of marri, wandoo and flooded gum.
Beermullah	Low forest of salt sheoak; some woodland of marri, flooded gum and wandoo; some shrubland of melaleuca.
Swan	Woodland of flooded gum; low forest of paperbark and salt sheoak.
Yanga	Similar to Beermullah; woodland of banksia and pricklybark on drier sites.
Dardanup	Similar to Guildford and Southern River.
Serpentine River	Similar to Swan.
Aeolian Soils	
Bassendean	Low woodland of banksia and pricklybark, with jarrah south of Wanneroo.
Karrakatta	Woodland of jarrah with marri or tuart and understorey of banksia and sheoak.
Cottesloe	Forest and woodland of tuart, sometimes with marri and jarrah; shrubland on shallowest soils.
Quindalup	Low shrubland; shrubland of wattle (and formerly Rottnest cypress and moonah); tuart on sheltered sites.
Herdsman	Woodland of flooded gum; low forest of paperbark; rushes and sedges.
Estaurine Soils	
Vasse	Samphire; melaleuca and flooded gum; forest of tuart, marri and jarrah on higher ground.
Aeolian over Alluvial	
Southern River	Hills similar to Bassendean; valleys similar to Guildford.

Simplified from the vegetation maps of the *Atlas of Natural Resources: Darling System: Western Australia* (Department of Conservation and Environment [now Department of Environment and Conservation], 1980).

Alluvial soils

The Guildford and Beermullah soils, west of the Ridge Hill Shelf, were washed from the Darling Scarp and Plateau to form a flat landscape. Both of these comprise sand and loam over clay. The Beermullah soils are waterlogged in winter, when minor depressions such as wheel-ruts fill with water. The Guildford soils are quite fertile compared with the plain's aeolian soils (discussed below), and were among the first to be developed for agriculture.

Along the Swan and Canning rivers and their tributaries upstream from the Swan Estuary are recent alluvial deposits known as the Swan soils. They are the plain's most fertile soils and were developed for agriculture soon after European settlement.

The Yanga soils are similar to the Beermullah but sandier in places. The Dardanup and Serpentine River are similar to Guildford; the Serpentine River soils are less well drained.

Aeolian soils

These sands, which occupy much of the plain, are the reason why Western Australians are known as 'sandgropers'. Their characteristic colours can be seen by digging a small hole or by observing piles of soil round ants' nests. The surface soil is often darkened by humus or bleached by sunlight.

The coastal plain was formed by the accumulation of sediments, such as shell fragments and quartz particles, washed up by the ocean and piled up by the wind to form dunes. The oldest sands are the Bassendean, nearest the Darling Scarp. They are pale grey or faintly yellow, and very infertile: their minerals and plant nutrients have largely been leached out by rainwater.

The Karrakatta sands are yellow, with limestone deep down. The Cottesloe sands, on the western side of the Karrakatta, are brown to yellow, with limestone close to the surface or cropping out. The limestone is derived from the action of rainwater on shell fragments in the sand, depositing and consolidating the lime at a lower level. Collectively the Karrakatta and Cottesloe sands are known as Spearwood.

This limestone can be seen in places on the coast, such as Cottesloe, North Beach and Naval Base. Along most of the coastline, however, is the white sand familiar to beachgoers. These Quindalup sands have been washed up over the past few thousand years. They are limy and infertile. The landscape is hilly, for these young dunes are in the process of being formed, rather than gradually worn away like the Cottesloe, Karrakatta and Bassendean dunes.

Associated with lakes and swamps within the Bassendean, Karrakatta and Cottesloe belts are peaty soils known as Herdsman.

Estuarine soils

Estuarine deposits known as Vasse soils border parts of the Swan Estuary.

Soils in combination

The Southern River soils are aeolian over alluvial, probably the result of Bassendean sand being gradually blown eastward (by strong winds at times when the vegetation cover was temporarily destroyed in a fire). The hills have a large accumulation of Bassendean sand. The drainage-lines and valleys, however, contain little or no Bassendean sand, and are like Serpentine River or Guildford.

The Quindalup coastal sands are notoriously vulnerable to erosion. In some places, for example Trigg Bushland and Bold Park, Quindalup sand has been blown inland in the past to cover areas of Cottesloe and Karrakatta sand.

Our place in the natural community

Most of Perth is so modified that it bears little resemblance to its natural state. Nevertheless we can build up a picture of what our own locality used to look like, by working out its type of soil or landform and the plant community that used to grow there. If we live on the coastal plain we can consult the *Bush Forever* report[1] to find an example of that plant community near where we live. The website for the Perth Biodiversity Project, under Perth Region Plant Biodiversity Project, contains information on reference sites in the Bush Forever study, such as plant lists. We can thus get to know not only the trees and tall shrubs but also some of the great wealth of smaller plants that grew under them. Growing some of the species in our gardens (see 'Cultivation', pp. 214-25) will give us a living link with our natural environment.

---

[1] State of Western Australia. *Bush Forever: Keeping the Bush in the City: Volume 1, Policies, Principles and Practices; Volume 2, Directory of Bush Forever Sites*. Perth: Western Australian Planning Commission, 2000.

Jarrah and tuart are both eucalypts: they belong to the genus *Eucalyptus*. They have features in common that are not shared by members of other genera, such as petals and sepals fused together to form a bud-cap (Fig. 18).

The genera that contain the trees and tall shrubs of Perth are listed in Table 1. A brief account of each is given in Part Two.

Just as species can be grouped together in a genus because of shared features, genera can be grouped into families because of more basic features that they share. For instance, *Eucalyptus*, and other genera such as *Leptospermum* (the tea-trees) and *Melaleuca* (the paperbarks and honey-myrtles), all belong to the myrtle family (Myrtaceae). Members of this family all have oil-glands in their leaves; crush a leaf and you can smell the oil. The names of families and larger groupings in the table are according to those published in 2003 by the Linnean Society of London.

The cypresses and native pines (Cupressaceae) are the least related to the other plant families. They belong to the gymnosperms (conifers and their allies). 'Gymnosperm' is derived from the Greek *gymnos*, meaning 'naked', and *sperma*, meaning 'seed'. These plants house their seeds on modified leaves, arranged in cones. Most species are wind-pollinated. Gymnosperms form the pine forests of the cooler regions of the northern hemisphere, and many are important for their softwood timber. In Australia they are most prevalent in the eastern states, particularly Tasmania.

The rest of Perth's trees and tall shrubs are angiosperms (flowering plants). They used to be

∧ *Fig. 18*
Eucalypt bud, with cap being pushed off by uncurling stamens.

divided into the monocotyledons, or monocots, and the dicotyledons, or dicots. The monocots were all the plants with one seed-leaf, such as grasses and lilies, and the dicots all the plants with two seed-leaves, including most trees and shrubs. Genetic studies late last century, however, suggested that the ways in which the flowering plants had been grouped and ordered did not reflect their true evolutionary relationships. The flowering plants are now recognised as a larger number of groups. The monocots do form a true group, but nested within the other groups, rather than a sister group to all the dicots. The table names the groups — monocots, commelinids, eudicots, etc. — to which the different flowering plants in this book belong. These groups, and the plant families within them, are arranged in what is believed to be their order of evolution. Within each family, the genera are arranged in alphabetical order.

> *Fig. 19*
Three examples of pods, borne by all plants in the legume family.

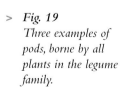

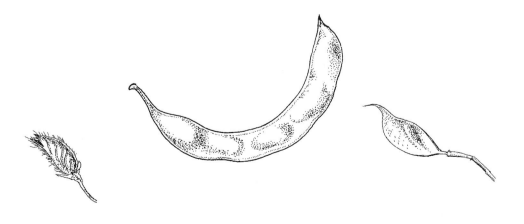

Table 1 – Trees and tall shrubs of Perth: families and genera

	Family	Genus	Number of species in this book
gymnosperms (conifers and their allies)	Cupressaceae (cypress family)	Actinostrobus	1 ⎤ 2
		Callitris	1 ⎦
monocots	Xanthorrhoeaceae (grasstree family)	Xanthorrhoea	1
commelinids	Dasypogonaceae	Kingia	1
eudicots	Proteaceae (banksia family)	Adenanthos	1 ⎤
		Banksia	8
		Conospermum	1
		Grevillea	2 ⎱ 18
		Hakea	3
		Persoonia	2
		Xylomelum	1 ⎦
core eudicots	Loranthaceae (mistletoe family)	Nuytsia	1
	Santalaceae (sandalwood family)	Exocarpos	1 ⎤ 2
		Santalum	1 ⎦
	Myrtaceae (myrtle family)	Agonis	1 ⎤
		Callistemon	1
		Calothamnus	1
		Corymbia	2
		Eucalyptus	14 ⎱ 30
		Kunzea	1
		Leptospermum	1
		Melaleuca	8
		Taxandria	1 ⎦
eurosids I	Fabaceae (legume family)	Acacia	4 ⎤
		Callistachys	1
		Gastrolobium	2
		Jacksonia	2
		Labichea	1 ⎱ 13
		Mirbelia	1
		Paraserianthes	1
		Viminaria	1 ⎦
	Casuarinaceae (sheoak family)	Allocasuarina	3 ⎤ 4
		Casuarina	1 ⎦
	Rhamnaceae (buckthorn family)	Spyridium	1
eurosids II	Gyrostemonaceae	Gyrostemon	1
	Sapindaceae (hop-bush family)	Dodonaea	3
euasterids I	Loganiaceae	Logania	1
euasterids II	Pittosporaceae	Pittosporum	1

angiosperms (flowering plants)

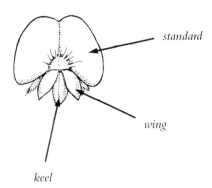

standard

wing

keel

∧ *Fig. 20*
A pea-flower, borne by plants in some genera in the legume family, such as Gastrolobium, Jacksonia *and* Mirbelia.

Since the monocots are nearly all soft plants such as grasses and herbs, the grasstree family (Xanthorrhoeaceae) is unusual in containing balga and other grasstrees with woody trunks. Outside Australia, the only woody monocots are the bamboos, palms and pandanuses.

The myrtle, banksia and legume families (Myrtaceae, Proteaceae and Fabaceae) provide the largest groups of Perth's trees and tall shrubs. The myrtle and banksia families occur in South America, South Africa, South-East Asia and Australasia, lending weight to the theory that Australia was once part of a huge southern continent. Between 100 and 200 million years ago it began to split up and drift apart to form the continents and islands of today. The myrtle and banksia families are thought to have begun their evolution during that time.

There are more than 5,500 species in the myrtle family, including a large number of important timber trees. About half the species occur in Australia, ranging from small shrubs to large trees.

The banksia family has more than 1,500 species, of which more than 1,000 occur in Australia. Many grow in very infertile soils. These have what are called proteoid roots, which form dense mats near the surface, and enable the plant to absorb nutrients more efficiently. Such roots are highly susceptible to the root-rot water-mould *Phytophthora cinnamomi*, and many banksias die very quickly from the disease it causes.

Western Australia's South-West region is particularly rich in species of both the myrtle and the banksia families, as are the rainforests of northern Queensland. The rainforests contain a number of primitive members of the banksia family, which provide information on how it evolved.

Unlike the myrtle and banksia families, the legume family is well distributed in both hemispheres. The wattles (genus *Acacia*) are particularly numerous in tropical and subtropical regions. The family also contains a number of basic food-plants, such as peas and beans, and important fodder plants. Plants in this family improve the soil's fertility: their roots, in association with bacteria, convert atmospheric nitrogen into organic nitrogen compounds, which are important plant nutrients.

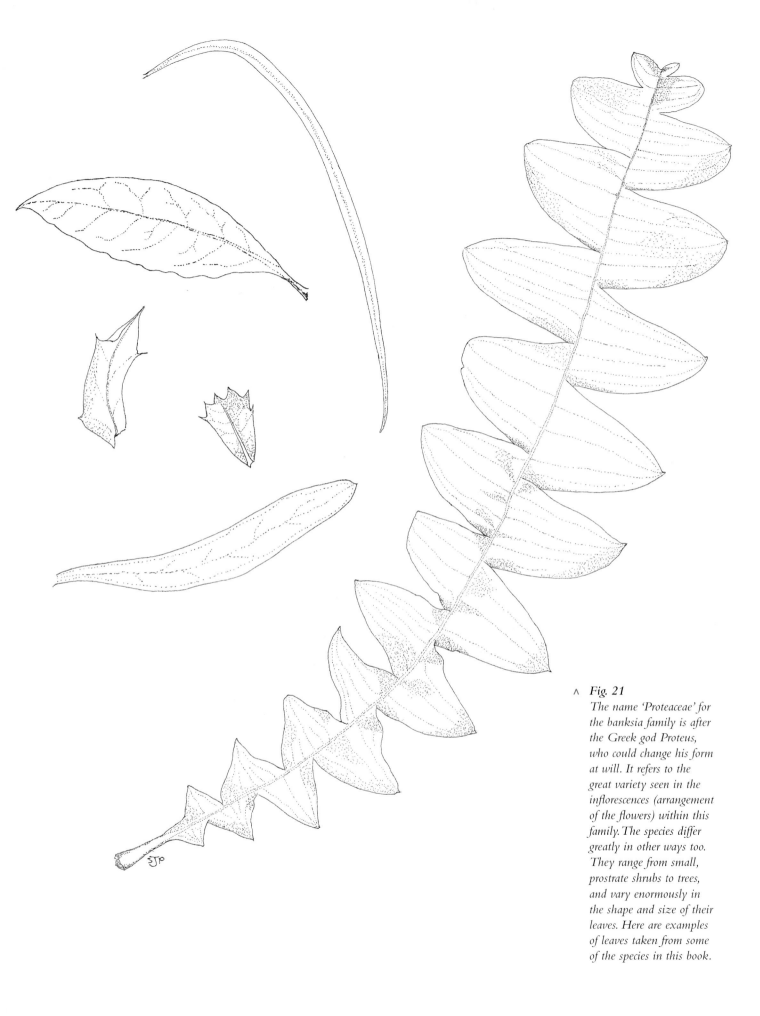

∧ *Fig. 21*
The name 'Proteaceae' for
the banksia family is after
the Greek god Proteus,
who could change his form
at will. It refers to the
great variety seen in the
inflorescences (arrangement
of the flowers) within this
family. The species differ
greatly in other ways too.
They range from small,
prostrate shrubs to trees,
and vary enormously in
the shape and size of their
leaves. Here are examples
of leaves taken from some
of the species in this book.

Plants do not live just by themselves, but in association with other life, including plants, animals and fungi (sometimes referred to as the "three 'f's: flora, fauna and fungi"). The trees and tall shrubs in this book are rich in associated life. This is partly because they are the largest of our plants, but also because they occur in Perth naturally: they are part of the natural associations of plants with other life in this region that have evolved over millions of years.

Perth's trees and tall shrubs may be found in bushlands, where they occur naturally. Many may also be found elsewhere as planted specimens, either where they used to occur naturally, or in places where they did not occur. As might be expected, it is in bushlands where they will have the most associated life, being part of a reasonably complete ecosystem. But even in cleared areas, planted trees and shrubs may still support quite a rich associated life, particularly on sites where they used to occur naturally.

This book gives examples of associated life for each of the 79 species of tree or tall shrub featured. While associated life has been well documented for a few tree species, for the rest very little is known, and a great deal remains to be learnt. One of the aims of this book is to stimulate interest in this subject, since an increased knowledge will contribute greatly to conservation.

Let us start with the animals, to which most of the references in this book are made.

Animals

To many of us, 'animals' are furry creatures, but these are just the mammals. Mammals are vertebrates (animals with backbones), which also include birds, reptiles and amphibians (frogs and toads). But for every vertebrate species there are probably a hundred or more invertebrates. The main invertebrates associated with trees and shrubs are the insects and spiders. Other invertebrates include springtails, scorpions, mites, centipedes, millipedes, snails and earthworms.

All animals depend on plants, directly or indirectly, for their food. Animals also need plants for shelter or nesting, or for hiding from predators.

Some plants, however, are of very little value to animals. That is true of many of the exotic trees and shrubs grown in Perth's parks and gardens, and of the many plants occurring in Perth as weeds. A few animal species have learnt to use

∧ *Fig. 23*
A jarrah leaf showing signs of the jarrah leaf-miner.

∨ *Fig. 24*
A beetle-pruned stem. The larva of a long-horned beetle has cut off this stem of green stinkwood neatly and tunnelled further down it.

∧ *Fig. 22*
The Australian painted lady.

some of these non-local plants. The larvae of a common butterfly, the Australian painted lady, for example, feed on the introduced capeweed, as well as on native daisies. On the other hand, many local plants — those species that occur or used to occur on the site naturally — are of enormous value to our native animals.

Some relations between local plants and animals are very specific. A particular insect may, for example, lay its eggs on plants of only a few closely related species, or in some cases just the one species.

Invertebrates: insects, etc.

Invertebrate animals may seem quite small and insignificant in the scheme of things. However, as mentioned above, they comprise probably over 99 per cent of terrestrial animal species. Moreover, many are present in teeming numbers, and the collective mass of invertebrates is surprisingly large. In his documentary series *Life in the Undergrowth*, the famous naturalist and presenter Sir David Attenborough states that "for every pound of people on Earth, there are 300 pounds of insects".

And far from being insignificant, invertebrates are the animals that enable life as we know it to exist. To quote Sir David Attenborough again:

> *"If we and the rest of the backboned animals were to disappear overnight, the rest of the world would get on pretty well. But if the invertebrates were to disappear the land's ecosystems would collapse".*

Our clean air, fresh water and productive soil, our food and many of our raw materials, depend on services provided by invertebrates.

Of the invertebrates, insects are especially significant. They are the largest group, comprising about four fifths of Perth's terrestrial invertebrate species. They are also the most diverse in their forms and ways of life. Insects have segmented

bodies (comprising a head, thorax and abdomen), and share a common ancestor with other segmented invertebrates, such as spiders, centipedes and millipedes. The spiders and their relatives, including scorpions, mites and ticks, comprise the second-largest group of these segmented terrestrial invertebrates. Spiders are very important as predators. Mites, many of them microscopic, are exceedingly common in the soil and leaf litter, and no doubt have an important influence on ecosystems.

In other parts of the world many insect species, particularly moths, butterflies, dragonflies and beetles, are greatly admired. In Western Australia there is a wealth of exciting things to be discovered about these fascinating creatures.

Take bees, for example. We all know the honeybee, an introduced insect, but few of us are aware of our many native bees. Most are much smaller, and nearly all are solitary nesters. They are important pollinators of native plants, and some plants have evolved designs to enable them to be pollinated by particular types of native bee.

Houseflies, blowflies, march flies and mosquitoes are members of a large and diverse order of insects named Diptera, meaning two-winged (from the Greek *di-* 'two-' and *pteron* 'wing'). The order also includes hoverflies, which feed at flowers and whose larvae eat aphids; and robber flies, which catch flying insects. Other groups are the bee-flies, soldier flies, craneflies and mydaid flies.

The several species of cockroach that live in our houses are nearly all introduced. Perth's native cockroaches are mostly very much smaller and much more appealing! By eating plant litter, they are important in breaking down this material into plant nutrients.

Although all insects are often loosely referred to as 'bugs', the true bugs are a group of insects with straw-like mouthparts adapted for piercing and sucking. They include such colourful or prominently marked species as the harlequin bug and the crusader bug. Most bugs are vegetarian, but assassin bugs capture other insects.

How important are our trees and shrubs to insects? In England it is known that 280 species of insect feed on oak, and 150 on hawthorn. In Western Australia it is only in recent years that we have begun to document the invertebrates associated with some of our trees — and their numbers are greater than anyone had ever imagined! For a single species of eucalypt growing in its natural environment in the Perth Metropolitan Region, there are typically between 600 and 1,000 different associated insects and spiders. The same is true in south-eastern Australia, demonstrating that the temperate forests of southern Australia are surprisingly rich in life. The foliage of trees such as jarrah and marri support over 400 invertebrate species, and the bark a further 200 to 300 species. Eucalypts that grow in more fertile soils, such as flooded gum, wandoo and tuart, support even more invertebrate species. In addition, there may be 200 or so invertebrate species living on the ground or in the topsoil under the eucalypt, particularly in the litter of leaves and fallen branches. These include silverfish, springtails, termites, crickets, beetles, native cockroaches, millipedes and slaters, which are important in breaking down the ground litter and helping return to the soil the chemicals essential for plant nutrition.

∨ *Fig. 26*
A native bee (twice life-size) in the family Megachilidae.

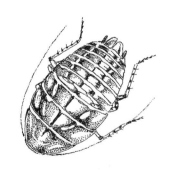

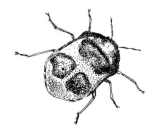

< *Fig. 27*
Most native cockroaches do not enter houses but live in the bush. Many species are brightly coloured or conspicuously patterned. This one (Polyzosteria sp.) has cream markings on the body and blue lower legs. It is one of the largest species (drawn at life-size).

< *Fig. 28*
Harlequin bug (twice life-size). This insect is brightly coloured, in orange, green and blue.

  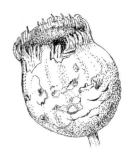

Fig. 29
The different marks made on marri fruits by the ringneck parrot (left), the red-capped parrot (centre) and Baudin's black-cockatoo (right).

Most of these foliage, bark or ground insects are not easy to see, since they hide away or are masters of camouflage. But we can find some of the marks they leave. A blister with an oval hole in its middle is caused by the larva of a leaf-miner, a small moth. Scallops of various shapes and sizes are made by different insects, as are galls (swellings) on leaves or stems. Sap flowing from a trunk, branch or stem is usually caused by the wood-boring larvae of a moth or beetle.

Birds

Trees and shrubs are vitally important to birds. Foliage shelters them from the elements and from predators. Many birds roost, rest, nest and feed in trees and shrubs.

Most bird species will roost (sleep) or shelter in a wide range of plant species, as long as they provide cover, although some have marked preferences. The nankeen night-heron prefers trees with a dense canopy. It roosts in paperbarks and the dense clumps of foliage of other trees, including introduced pines. Several species of owl roost in dense clumps of foliage or in hollows in trees.

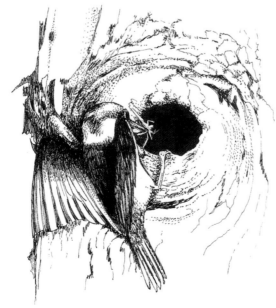

Fig. 30
A sacred kingfisher returning to its nest, a hollow in a flooded gum.

Many birds rest in trees and shrubs for short periods. Dead branches are used as vantage points by birds that catch insects in the air, such as the bee-eater and the Australian hobby. They are also used by swallows and tree martins for resting in groups; in cities they have taken to using power lines as well.

Bird species vary greatly in where they choose to nest. Parrots and some smaller species, such as the tree martin and the striated pardalote, use hollows in trees, provided by mature and old eucalypts; these birds can no longer nest in bush where such trees have been felled. Some bird species, such as the sittella, nest in vertical forks in branches. The scarlet robin often nests thus in a grasstree, and the white-breasted robin in a paperbark. Others, such as pigeons and the black-faced cuckoo-shrike, prefer forks in horizontal branches. Still other species suspend their nests in the outer foliage of plants, often in a young eucalypt. Many of the species that nest in the foliage or branches of trees often choose as their nest site a clump of mistletoe.

Because of their different growth habits, different species of tree and tall shrub provide nest-sites for different species of bird. The usefulness to nesting birds of a eucalypt or other large tree depends on its age. Old trees are particularly valuable for their hollows, and many cannot be replaced in a human lifetime.

Most bush birds obtain their food from trees and shrubs, either directly or indirectly. Honeyeaters and lorikeets drink nectar from the flowers of eucalypts, banksias and other plants. Pigeons eat seeds on the ground, and Carnaby's black-cockatoo extracts seeds from the fruits of marri, banksias and hakeas. The emu eats the fleshy fruits of quandong. Honeyeaters eat the gum exuded by marri and other plant species.

But trees and shrubs are even more important as an indirect source of food. Insects are attracted to the flowers of eucalypts, banksias and other plants, where they are caught by honeyeaters and other birds. Insect larvae are taken from

the foliage of eucalypts such as flooded gum by pardalotes, thornbills and other small birds. Sittellas extract insects from the bark of rough-barked eucalypts and other trees. Of particular importance, therefore, in providing food for birds, are plant species that support numerous insects. These include the wattle species in this book, and many of the eucalypt species.

Since European settlement, habitats have been greatly altered, and all bird species have been affected in some way. A few species, such as the silver gull, have become more abundant. The supply of food for this scavenging bird has been greatly increased by rubbish-dumping. The welcome swallow has taken advantage of urbanisation by nesting in buildings. The clearing of land has helped some species that need open country. The magpie, raven (often called a crow) and white-faced heron have increased in numbers; and other species that did not originally occur on the coastal plain round Perth have become established here. Some, such as the galah, black-shouldered kite, crested pigeon and straw-necked and white ibises, have done so by expanding their range. Others, such as the kookaburra and the rainbow lorikeet, have been deliberately or accidentally introduced here.

The overall effect of European settlement, however, has been negative. A number of species have disappeared from the coastal plain near Perth, including the long-billed corella, brush bronzewing and white-breasted robin. Others, such as the black bittern and barking owl, are on the verge of disappearing. Many further species have declined seriously in numbers: waterbirds such as the freckled duck and the shoveler; bush birds such as the scarlet and yellow robins, red-winged fairy-wren, rufous treecreeper and yellow-plumed honeyeater; and birds of prey such as the whistling kite and the brown falcon.

Some of the birds that have declined or become extinct in this region are associated with wetlands. In the Perth area many wetlands have been filled or drained. Most of those remaining have lost all

or much of their fringing vegetation of thickets and paperbark forest, which are essential to many birds for shelter or nesting. On the coastal plain, many further bird species have declined as a result of the clearing of vegetation, for agriculture or housing. Up to the 1980s, the tuart, marri, wandoo and jarrah forests had suffered more clearing than the less timbered areas dominated by banksias, and it was the forest birds in particular that had declined. Now much of the banksia country has been cleared as well, and its associated birds are declining too.

To maintain a diversity of bird species in Perth's suburbs we must preserve the remaining stands of vegetation wherever possible, and provide further habitat by planting. The plant species in this book are very important for the conservation of Perth's birds.

Mammals

Native mammals have largely disappeared from the Perth area, as a result of the destruction of their bushland habitats, together with the introduction of predators such as foxes and cats. A few bat species — such as Gould's wattled bat, the chocolate wattled bat and the white-striped free-tailed bat — still survive in Perth. By day they roost under the bark of trees or in the hollows that old trees provide. Many of our other mammal species are nocturnal too; they are not often seen, but signs of them may be. Scratch-marks on the trunk of a tree may indicate possums.

Reptiles

Perth is remarkably rich in reptiles, with more than 70 species. Most lizards and snakes live on the ground, in the leaf litter or in the upper layers of the soil. Many skinks that live in the soil have reduced legs or none at all. Trees and shrubs are valuable in providing leaf litter, and some reptiles hunt their prey on them or use them for refuge. Apart from a few that are commonly seen, such as the bobtail and the fence skink, they retreat rapidly into cover or keep out of sight. Some, such as geckoes, are largely nocturnal.

< *Fig. 31*
The barking owl, a bird that is now rare in the Metropolitan Region (unlike the common boobook).

v *Fig. 32*
The western spiny-tailed gecko is one of the few geckoes that come out during the day (to raise their body temperature). It makes itself inconspicuous, however, by lying along a twig and remaining motionless, and by its grey colouring. This one is blending well with a cluster of the fruits of chenille honey-myrtle.

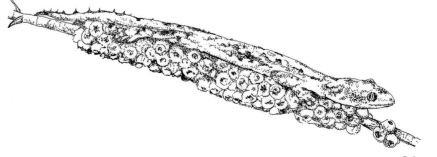

Plants

The 79 trees and tall shrubs in this book are the tallest species of Perth's rich flora of about 1,500 native species of vascular plant. Of these, a few are medium to large shrubs — but the vast majority are small shrubs or perennial or annual herbs. Most of the smaller species are loosely associated with the species in this book, by liking the same soils or moisture and thus occurring in the same places, or by needing the shade cast by the larger plants. Some orchids thrive in the litter that accumulates under rock sheoak or common sheoak. Some plants, however, associate with the trees and shrubs more directly, by growing on them. These include the mistletoes, and some non-vascular plants, the mosses and liverworts.

Mistletoes

Mistletoes are appealing plants, with their profusion of bright flowers, foliage or fruits. They are hemiparasites (half-parasites): they use their own leaves to carry out photosynthesis, but extract water and minerals from other plants.

Five mistletoe species in the family Loranthaceae grow on the trees and shrubs in this book: stalked mistletoe, wireleaf mistletoe, slender-leaved mistletoe, sheoak mistletoe and moonah mistletoe. In the Perth region, stalked mistletoe grows on eucalypts, particularly wandoo, marri and tuart. Wireleaf mistletoe grows on certain wattles, such as coojong and some cultivated species from eastern Australia. Sheoak mistletoe and slender-leaved mistletoe grow on salt sheoak; and moonah mistletoe, as its name implies, grows on moonah.

Mistletoes are of great ecological value. Many honeyeaters visit their flowers to drink their copious nectar. Some bird species eat mistletoe berries, the mistletoebird almost exclusively. The mistletoebird is the main agent in spreading the mistletoe. The berry's seed is excreted, but being sticky tends to stick to the bird. To free itself of it, the bird wipes its rear end on the branch of the host tree, thus 'planting' the seed where it may grow.

Mistletoes are of further importance to birds as nest sites. With their rigid structure of branching stems and their dense foliage, mistletoes provide places where nests can be built relatively easily and where they are well hidden from predators. The dense foliage also regulates the temperature and increases the humidity within the nest. Consequently many birds, in many bird families, often nest in mistletoe.

Mistletoes are valuable also for insects. In the Perth region three butterfly species breed on them: the brightly coloured spotted jezebel and the brilliant, metallic-blue satin azure and silky azure. Other insects include the mistletoe moth, strikingly marked in black and white, and the mistletoebird-dropping weevil, which avoids predators by resembling the mistletoebird's droppings.

One further mistletoe species in the family Loranthaceae, Christmas tree, is described in this book (pp. 190-1). It is most unusual in growing in the ground, as a tree, and in having dry, winged fruits.

Mosses and liverworts

Mosses are small, soft plants that grow together in clumps or mats. They occur in damp places, on various surfaces, such as the soil, rocks or the bark of trees or shrubs. On trees they grow usually on the trunk or lower branches, and prefer old, decaying rough bark. Smooth-barked eucalypts, whose bark is regularly shed, rarely support mosses, whereas eucalypts with rough bark at their base often do. Cracks or furrows in the bark provide moisture and protection, and crevices where branches join trunks trap moisture and collect dust, a source of organic and inorganic

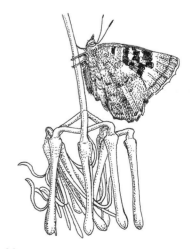

∧ *Fig. 33*
Female satin azure on an inflorescence of wireleaf mistletoe (life-size), with most of the flowers still in bud.

< Fig. 34
Ghost fungus, growing at the base of a banksia.

nutrients. Trees and shrubs may also assist the growth of mosses on the ground underneath by providing shade. Many of the mosses that are able to survive in Perth exist in a desiccated state during the hot, dry summer. After rain, however, they take only a few hours to become green and active again.

Several species of mite are found in moss mats, from which they may derive their food, as well as using them for shelter. Various insect larvae and several species of ant can be found in association with moss, but may be using it only for shelter.

Liverworts depend on water even more than do mosses. Some species grow on bark, including several that may be found in the southern Perth area. Most of these are tiny and well camouflaged.

Fungi

Many people are surprised to learn that fungi are not plants, but have their own kingdom, which in the tree of life lies closer to animals than to plants. Also surprising is that there are many more fungi than plants. In Western Australia there are perhaps 140,000 species of fungi, about ten times the number of vascular plant species. We do not know much about our fungi, and can only guess as to how many thousands of species occur in the Perth region. There is much still to be learnt about how our fungi species are defined, where they occur, if they are common or rare, and what roles they play in bushlands. In the past, most biological surveys have not included fungi. Since 2004, however, the Perth Urban Bushland Fungi project has undertaken fungi surveys in many of Perth's bushlands, revealing that different vegetation types in the region harbour different fungi.

The most familiar fungi to most people are mushrooms and toadstools. These, along with other forms such as puffballs, corals and truffles, are the spore-bearing fruiting bodies of the so called larger fungi or macrofungi. The vast majority of our fungi species, however, are entirely microscopic.

The macrofungi's fruiting bodies, seen in Perth mostly in autumn or winter, display a multitude of intriguing colours and forms. Some, such as the ghost fungus, which can be seen in Perth on eucalypts, glow in the dark. Some are long-lasting. The fruiting bodies of the scarlet bracket fungus, often seen on stumps, comprise an abundance of tough, orange brackets that retain their colour for many months, eventually becoming bleached but persisting for many more months. Some other bracket-like fungi on living trees, often referred to as 'conks', produce hard, woody fruiting bodies that can extend themselves by adding extra layers over a period of many years. Other fruiting bodies are extremely short-lived. Those of fungi known as 'ink-caps' digest themselves, becoming black and inky, sometimes within a matter of hours.

Fungi live in many different places. As mentioned above, some live on trees or stumps. Others live on rotting wood, in leaf litter or in the soil. Mushrooms and toadstools can occur out in the open, whereas other fungi hide below the litter. Some may favour certain situations: for example, along roadsides, or in other disturbed sites; amid moss; on particular types of wood; or near a particular type of plant. Although some bushland fungi are highly visible, it takes a trained eye to see most, since many are well camouflaged, or barely emerge from the soil or leaf litter.

The vegetative part, or main 'body', of a fungus is its network of microscopic threads, called a mycelium. Unlike their fruiting bodies, which are usually short-lived, fungal mycelia are often long-lived and are active all year round. They capture nutrients using enzymes (proteins that cause chemical reactions) to degrade tough materials such as the cellulose and lignin in wood and leaf litter.

∧ *Fig. 35*
Black-cockatoo pecking at a white punk, a large bracket fungus.

Fungi promote the health of plants and bushlands. Like the invertebrate animals, fungi are major recyclers of nutrients. Fungal networks spread all through the soil, litter and wood, and ferry nutrients about. They release nutrients in forms that are readily available to plants and other living things. They also bind soil particles, helping to resist erosion.

Many fungi attach themselves to plants, often forming with them a mutually beneficial relationship, called a symbiosis, or mycorrhiza (from the Greek *mukēs* 'fungus' and *rhiza* 'root'). These mycorrhizal fungi act like an extra root system for plants, exploring the soil, retrieving nutrients and delivering them to the plants in forms available for uptake. In return the plants supply sugars to the fungi. Such fungi are particularly beneficial in helping plants thrive in areas with poor soil, low in nutrients, such as much of Perth. Here they partner many of Perth's trees and shrubs, including wattles, sheoaks, eucalypts, pea-plants and honey-myrtles, as well as many smaller plants, such as grasses and orchids. Banksias and other plants in the family Proteaceae, however, have developed non-fungal ways of coping with poor soils, by having proteoid roots (see p. 16). Networks of mycorrhizal fungi may also link together different types of plant. Eucalypts, for example, which cannot fix nitrogen, may be linked to nitrogen-fixing plants such as wattles.

Native mycorrhizal fungi have co-evolved with native plants and are different from the fungi associated with introduced trees. Local foresters in the early 20th century were disappointed at their attempts to establish pine plantations in Western Australia: the pines grew pale and stunted. Mycorrhizal fungi were then introduced from pine plantations overseas, enabling a prosperous plantation industry to be founded.

Fungi also have links with many animals. The fruiting bodies and mycelia are rich sources of carbon and nutrients, and are used as food or habitat by myriads of small insects, as well as microbes such as bacteria and protozoa. The hundreds of springtails that may erupt from a picked mushroom are an example of the many invertebrates that may use fungi, which also include flies, slugs, beetles and millipedes (including the Portuguese millipedes that are now abundant in many parts of Perth).

Some larger animals too depend on fungi for food. Truffles — fungi that produce their fruiting bodies below the ground — emit odours that attract bandicoots and woylies, which dig up the truffles and eat them. The fungal spores are deposited in the animals' dung, and thereby effectively dispersed — and can then germinate to form mycorrhizal partnerships with plants near by. Hence truffles are part of a three-way, mutually beneficial interaction with animals and plants. Several dozen species of truffle have so far been found in Perth. In the absence of fungus-eating mammals in many of Perth's bushlands, the truffles may need to rely on invertebrates to disperse their spores.

Some fungi cause diseases, but even they are of enormous benefit in healthy ecosystems. The woody galls common on coojong and other Perth wattles, caused by the gall rust-fungus, are inhabited by many animals, such as moths and weevils. Some fungi eat the wood of living or dead trees. That creates hollows, used by many birds for nesting, as well as producing a supply of fallen wood, whose decay will release nutrients for recycling. The Australian honey fungus, *Armillaria luteobubalina*, can kill trees and shrubs by attacking their roots. It is considered to be a native fungus, perhaps long present in the Perth region. In healthy ecosystems it will have performed a valuable role, creating gaps in the vegetation where younger trees or coloniser shrubs can grow, thus promoting a healthier and more diverse ecosystem.

In disturbed ecosystems, which are now the norm in Perth, disease fungi can become too prevalent and cause problems. This has occurred with the honey fungus from time to time, owing to the disturbances associated with urban development. Outbreaks of the fungus have occurred in areas where tuart trees have been felled and large stumps left in place, or where the roots of trees have been damaged. Human activities have unbalanced some aspects of the environment.

On the other hand, some introduced disease fungi can be put to work for us. An introduced rust-fungus is now being used in Perth's bushlands to help combat infestations of the introduced bridal creeper.

One introduced organism commonly called a fungus is in fact quite unrelated to fungi. This is the very destructive root-rot organism *Phytophthora cinnamomi*, which kills many native plants, by causing a disease commonly known as 'phytophthora dieback'. Although like a fungus in some respects, it is a water-mould, less related to fungi than are animals or plants.

Efforts towards knowing and understanding our fungi must continue. To maintain or improve the conservation value of our bushlands, the interactions between plants, animals and fungi need to be managed. The clearing of vegetation greatly reduces the fungal diversity. In projects to re-establish original vegetation in cleared areas, thought should be given to monitoring and, if necessary, assisting the return of native fungi, in order that the interactions may be restored.

Lichens

Some fungi combine with a partner, such as an alga, and the result is a lichen. This is a good example of a symbiosis, the living together of two organisms for the benefit of both. The alga provides the fungus with food, which it makes by photosynthesis; and the fungus provides water for the alga, and helps it obtain minerals.

Lichens encompass many different colours and forms. Some have a leafy appearance, whereas others form a crust. The crust lichens, which are more resistant to harsher conditions, are probably the commoner in Perth. Like mosses, lichens grow on many different surfaces. They are able to survive in drier places than mosses, and are thus more widespread. They take some time to become established — so those that grow on bark do so only if it is not shed too frequently.

Lichens are eaten by a few animals that are able to digest them. Some can do so with the aid of bacteria or protozoa in their guts, including the larvae of many different moths.

Although lichens can grow in harsh environments, most are nonetheless sensitive to human pollutants. They are therefore widely used to indicate the quality of the air or the health of an ecosystem.

< *Fig. 36*
A quenda eating truffles.

In a world highly dominated and modified by our own species, how will Perth's trees and tall shrubs fare in the future? Let us consider first the main threats to their survival and then what is being done to address those threats.

Threats

Some of the threats to Perth's trees and shrubs are global, affecting the entire planet, such as global warming. Others are local, such as competition from weeds at a particular site, or regional, such as a disease causing the decline of a particular tree species.

Australia is more vulnerable to environmental problems than many other parts of the world. Much of the country is arid or semi-arid, and such landscapes are fragile. Moreover, Australia is an island, albeit a very large one. It has until recently been largely isolated from influences from elsewhere. Since European settlement, many exotic animals, plants, fungi and other organisms have been introduced, to which our native plants, animals and fungi are not accustomed.

Many of the threats discussed below relate to bushlands, where most of Perth's trees and tall shrubs still occur. Some, however, such as diseases, may also affect specimens cultivated in parks or gardens.

> *Fig. 37*
> *Introduced lupins are common weeds in many of Perth's bushlands. Pearl lupin, illustrated, is not considered naturalised, but is similar in appearance to four lupin species that are.*

Clearing, fragmentation

More than two thirds of the Swan Coastal Plain within the Perth Metropolitan Region has been cleared, most of the uncleared land being in the region's northern extremities. What natural vegetation remains elsewhere is very fragmented. Many bushlands on the plain are like islands — small areas of habitat isolated from other bushlands by large stretches of developed urban or rural land.

In small bushlands, many species of plant, animal and fungus disappear sooner or later, either as a result of disturbance (such as fire), or because their populations cannot sustain themselves. Small populations of plants or animals can die out as a result of inbreeding. Moreover, a small bushland often cannot support a balanced and diverse ecosystem. It may be lacking the pollinators or partner fungi on which particular plants depend.

If the bushland is isolated, many of the plants, animals and fungi that die out will not be able to re-establish themselves. A few highly mobile animals may be able to do so by travelling in from other places. Plants, however, may re-establish themselves only if there are other specimens close enough to the bushland for their seed to disperse into it.

Over time, many animals move from one region or locality to another as conditions change. This is now happening at an unprecedented rate as a result of global warming and the accompanying changes in climate (see 'Climate change', p. 28). To some extent, plants and fungi move too. Although of course the individual plants cannot move, plant species can move over the generations, as their seeds are dispersed by the wind, birds or other animals. Many plant species do not disperse their seeds very far, but may still be able to move from, say, a drier to a moister site within the immediate locality. Little is known about the movement of Perth's fungi, but the spores of some may be borne some distance by the wind.

Many small, isolated bushlands do not allow their plants to move, since in the urban or rural surrounds they will have nowhere to move to. Moreover, additional plant species will not be able to move in to replace them.

Weeds

The weeds referred to here are bushland weeds, non-local (usually exotic) plants that have become established there. Some weed species have been introduced accidentally; many others are cultivated species. They vary from herbs, such as grasses and bulbous plants, to trees. Whereas most of the smaller weeds are from countries overseas, many of the trees are cultivated species from other parts of Australia. Most weeds are highly opportunistic, able quickly to take advantage of any disturbance to the environment. And since most are largely free of the plant-eaters of their place of origin, they are healthy, robust and vigorous, and produce an abundance of seed. Many are naturally aggressive. They thus compete very strongly with our local trees and shrubs. Where introduced grasses or other small weeds grow thickly, they often prevent seedlings of our local species from establishing themselves. The result is that, unless weeds are managed, they progressively replace our local flora.

Because very few Perth people are skilled observers of our local trees and shrubs, many of the weeds from other parts of Australia go unnoticed, their differences from our local species not being recognised. River gum and swamp oak, which few people distinguish from Perth's flooded gum or salt sheoak respectively, are spreading, and threaten to take over from or hybridise with their related local species.

Fire

Although fire is part of the ecology of Perth's vegetation, it can seriously damage our bushlands if too frequent or too hot. Many fires are started by people, some accidentally, others willfully. Fires can therefore be frequent in bushlands on the coastal plain, where so many people live.

Some trees, such as saw-tooth banksia, Rottnest cypress and salt sheoak, are killed by fire. If fires are too frequent to allow their seedlings to mature and produce seed, they will die out. For other species, such as summer-scented wattle and many mallees and shrubs, fire kills all their above-ground parts, but they survive by resprouting from their rootstocks. Like seedlings, the regrowth needs several years to mature and produce seeds. Other trees, such as the paperbarks and many of the larger banksias and eucalypts, have bark that resists fire — but they can nonetheless be badly damaged in a hot fire, taking at least several years to make a good recovery.

Fire affects the bushland's animals too, which comprise a great many insects and other invertebrates, as well as reptiles, birds and other vertebrates. Many animals that survive the fire itself may die if their food or cover has temporarily been destroyed. If all or nearly all the bushland is burnt, many of its animal species may thus die out. Once the bushland recovers, some of the more mobile animal species may recolonise it, but the less mobile species will not, unless they occur in other bushland very close by. These may include useful pollinators, or seed-dispersers, on which some of the bushland plants may depend.

Many fungi live in the top 10 centimetres of the soil, and are readily killed by a fire's heat. Like animals, they may disappear from a bushland that is totally burnt, to the detriment of the plant species they partner.

Exotic animals and fungi

Many exotic animals have become established in Western Australia, including foxes, cats, rabbits and pigs, as well as doves, pigeons and other birds, and many different insects and other invertebrates. Grazing animals such as the rabbit can affect the natural regeneration of Perth's trees and shrubs by eating many of their seedlings. By disturbing the soil, pigs can directly kill many native plants, and also encourage weeds and spread disease (see below). Less is known about the effects of exotic invertebrates, but many no doubt have a major influence too.

There are also many introduced species of fungi. These predominate where land has been cleared or disturbed, and continue to do so on sites revegetated with local plants. Introduced fungi can affect local trees and shrubs by displacing beneficial native fungi associated with their roots, and also by associating with weeds, boosting their vigour and competitiveness.

Diseases

Many Perth people will have heard of 'dieback'. In its general sense, 'dieback' is the dying back of plants, starting at the shoots and progressively working its way down the branches. There can be many causes, including frequent fires or heavy, repeated attack by insects. In Western Australia 'dieback' is also used to refer to the effect of a particular introduced organism that attacks plants' roots, *Phytophthora cinnamomi*. The *Phytophthora* is often incorrectly called the 'dieback fungus' — incorrectly because, as noted in the previous chapter, it is a water-mould, quite unrelated to

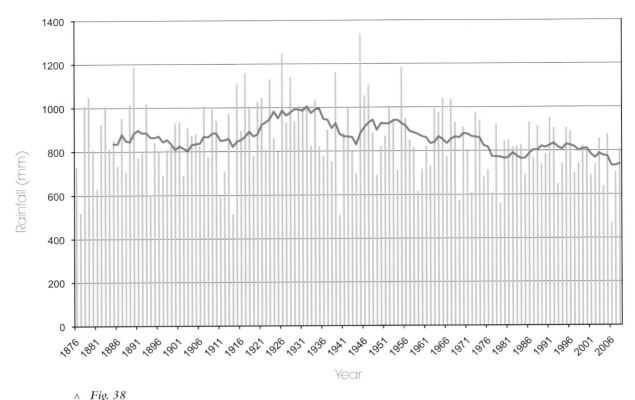

^ Fig. 38

Perth's annual rainfall, from when records first began to 2008.[1] The wiggly line is the 10-year moving average — which, for a given year, is the average of the amounts for that year and the previous nine years. It shows the rainfall's general trend.

Periods of higher and lower rainfall can be seen. In the 1920s and '30s, for example, it was generally higher than that recorded for the years up to 1920. Since the mid 1970s, however, there has been a progressive decrease in rainfall, a trend expected to continue. The amount recorded in 2006 was lower than for any previous year.

fungi. The 'dieback' is derived from the water-mould's effect on jarrah in the Darling Range, where the tree progressively dies back over a number of years. The name 'phytophthora dieback' is preferred for this disease, to distinguish it from 'dieback' in the general sense. It should be noted, however, that most plant species susceptible to the water-mould do not die back gradually but succumb quickly and die quite suddenly. They include most banksia species and many other plants, in various plant families. Many infestations of the water-mould occur in the Perth area, where it particularly affects the jarrah forest in the Darling Plateau, and the banksia woodlands on the more inland parts of the coastal plain. The water-mould is readily spread by the movement of infected soil, on vehicles, or walkers' boots.

In addition to *Phytophthora cinnamomi* are several more species of *Phytophthora*, some of which kill various susceptible plants.

Another pathogen affecting the roots of plants is a native species, the honey fungus, discussed in the previous chapter. Its effects are most obvious where ecosystems have been disturbed.

Many further species of fungi, some native, some introduced, attack aerial parts of susceptible trees or shrubs. These are known as canker fungi, since they produce wounds on the stems or branches, called cankers. Some betray their presence by disturbed bark and bleeding resin; others are hidden under the outer bark, and not very obvious. Small or large branches may die, and sometimes the whole tree. Many banksias and some eucalypts, such as marri, may be affected. Trees are normally badly affected only if they are already under stress from drought or some other factor, reducing their resistance.

Climate change

The world's climates are now changing as a result of global warming, the continuing rise in the temperature of the air and oceans, believed to be caused by an increase in gases such as carbon dioxide.

Between 1910 and 2008, Australia became almost 1°C warmer, with most of the warming occurring after 1950. By 2030, Australia is expected to become 1°C warmer than it was in 1990. One or two degrees may not seem much warmer, but it does significantly increase evaporation, making conditions drier for plants.

The warmer global temperatures influence the circulation of the air and oceans, resulting in changes in rainfall, some parts of the world receiving more and others less. Perth, and most of the region between Geraldton and Esperance, has become drier. Much of the region's rain is provided by passing cold fronts, in the cooler months of the year. Since 1975 there have been fewer cold fronts, and those that have come have generally brought less rain. Further decreases in rainfall are expected in the future.

The higher temperatures and lower rainfall combine to make Perth's climate much more arid. This can be seen in the drying out of many of Perth's lakes and swamps. Many permanent lakes have now become seasonal swamps, and areas that used to flood no longer do so. Many of these lakes and swamps are an expression of the water-table, which in many places has dropped significantly. The drop has been not only from the drying climate, however, but often also from the increased extraction of ground water for water supply, horticulture or industry, as the human population increases.

What will happen to Perth's vegetation? To gauge the effect of both the increasing temperatures and decreasing rainfall, we can examine the vegetation of places on the coast to the north, such as Jurien Bay and Geraldton, where the temperatures are higher and rainfall lower. The vegetation of Jurien Bay and Geraldton is predominantly shrubby. What trees do occur are stunted, and largely restricted to the more fertile soils, or moist sites along rivers. We can therefore expect the trees in Perth's bushlands to die out. Moist, fertile sites may be places where we can re-establish them in the future.

There is also likely to be an invasion of plant species from elsewhere. Already animal species, both here and in many other parts of the world, are changing their distributions markedly. To give just one example, the bridled tern historically occurred no further south than the Houtman Abrolhos Islands, 370 kilometres north of Perth, but now occurs on islands off Perth and further south. The same is happening for some fungi species. For plants, movements on such a large scale will be confined to those species whose seeds are transported far, by birds or other animals, or by the wind. Many of the plant species that invade will be weeds, which tend to be very efficient dispersers of their seeds. Many native plant species will at best be able to move only short distances, such as from an upland to a moister valley. In largely cleared landscapes, many species will not have that opportunity, and die out.

Many of Perth's trees and shrubs are already feeling the stress of the drying climate, making them more vulnerable to disease and less able to cope with supporting their associated insects. Wood-boring beetle larvae often target trees under stress, resulting in their further decline or death. Climate change may cause plants further stress by affecting the health and function of the fungi associated with their roots. Indeed, useful partner fungi may die out, as climate change alters the composition of the fungi in the soil.

Interaction of factors

The factors discussed above do not operate independently but interact, and thus enhance one another. Whereas one factor can be damaging enough, the interaction of factors can be particularly devastating.

A good example is weeds, fire and climate change. Weeds encourage fire, since many weeds are grassy species that dry out over the summer and are easily ignited. Where grassy weeds grow in abundance they also increase a fire's intensity, and the damage it does to the native vegetation. And fire encourages weeds, which quickly colonise the open ground it leaves. Climate change too encourages weeds, the plants that most readily adapt to or benefit from changed conditions. And the higher temperatures resulting from climate change promote more frequent and hotter fires.

Fire also interacts with disease. Trees damaged by fire are often more susceptible to disease. And trees suffering from disease can be much more damaged by fire, often being killed, or recovering only by shooting from their rootstocks.

In a healthy, diverse ecosystem, pests and diseases are controlled and ecological processes largely guaranteed. When an ecosystem is upset, by factors such as the above, things can easily go awry. The health of plants can suffer, as can the processes by which they are pollinated or their seeds dispersed.

Perth's trees and tall shrubs: observed changes

How are Perth's trees and tall shrubs coping with the above threats? All have become less common since European settlement, because of large-scale clearing. Some appear to be doing well at present, others much less so. In our rapidly changing world, it is difficult to predict how the different species will fare in the future. We can, however, consider those that give cause for concern at present. These are in two categories: those that are presently uncommon; and those that are presently common but are, at least in some places, in decline.

The uncommon species

Twenty-four of Perth's trees and tall shrubs, listed in Table 2, are uncommon in the Perth Metropolitan Region.

Table 2 – Trees and tall shrubs uncommon in the Perth Metropolitan Region

Common name	Botanical name
white-stemmed wattle	Acacia xanthina
swamp cypress	Actinostrobus pyramidalis
dune sheoak	Allocasuarina lehmanniana
wonnich	Callistachys lanceolata
toobada	Callistemon phoeniceus
Rottnest cypress	Callitris preissii
lesser bloodwood	Corymbia haematoxylon
coast hop-bush	Dodonaea aptera
Perth hop-bush	D. hackettiana
sticky hop-bush	D. viscosa
powderbark	Eucalyptus accedens
Yanchep mallee	E. argutifolia
limestone marlock	E. decipiens
Fremantle mallee	E. foecunda
salmon white gum	E. lane-poolei
bullich	E. megacarpa
rock mallee	E. petrensis
heart-leaf poison	Gastrolobium bilobum
corkybark	Gyrostemon ramulosus
white spray	Logania vaginalis
moonah	Melaleuca lanceolata
gorada	M. lateriflora
coast pittosporum	Pittosporum ligustrifolium
woody pear	Xylomelum occidentale

Many species are uncommon because they have specific habitat preferences. Limestone ridges, near the coast, are quite a restricted habitat. Their species were never especially common, and have become less so as these ridges have been cleared for housing or mined for limestone. Eight of the species in the table — white-stemmed wattle, coast hop-bush, Yanchep mallee, limestone marlock, Fremantle mallee, rock mallee, white spray and coast pittosporum — grow in this habitat. Although most of them are widespread outside the region, Yanchep mallee and rock mallee are uncommon in general. Yanchep mallee is declared as 'rare flora' under State legislation, and is also listed as 'vulnerable' under the Commonwealth's Environmental Protection and Biodiversity Conservation Act. Coast pittosporum is common on Rottnest and Garden islands but uncommon anywhere on the mainland.

Some sorts of habitat were once common but are now largely cleared, such as the alluvial soils on the eastern side of the coastal plain, where the land began to be developed for agriculture soon after European settlement. Three species in the table — swamp cypress, salmon white gum and gorada — are largely confined to these soils.

In the above habitats, it is not only their associated trees and tall shrubs that will be uncommon: many of the habitat's smaller plant species will be uncommon too, as will many of its animals. The same is probably true of fungi, since some species are known to favour particular soils or habitats. We need to make a special effort to preserve these habitats.

For nine species in the table — wonnich, toobada, lesser bloodwood, powderbark, bullich, heart-leaf poison, corkybark, gorada and woody pear — the Perth area is at or near the edge of their distributions. Toobada, powderbark, corkybark and gorada are more typical of drier areas, to the north or east, whereas wonnich, lesser bloodwood, bullich, heart-leaf poison and woody pear occur chiefly in wetter areas, to the south. Plants growing near the extremes of their distributions are of scientific interest, and also may be important to their species for its conservation. Specimens near the northern extreme are likely to be the best adapted to drier conditions, which may be important for the survival of the species as the climate becomes more arid.

Dune sheoak, Rottnest cypress and moonah have suffered not only from clearing but also from

^ *Fig. 39*
Wetlands on the eastern side of the coastal plain, whose soil-type is clay or (as in this example) sand over clay, support a rich and interesting flora. It is important to conserve those few that remain in their natural state.

changes in the ecology. These species are killed by fire, which since European settlement has become more frequent in their environment.

Common species in decline

The common species in decline in the Perth area include jarrah and some of the large banksias. Many jarrah trees have either died completely or have died off above ground, surviving by shooting from their lignotubers. Many banksia trees have died, either abruptly or slowly. Species such as bull banksia, holly-leaf banksia, candle banksia and firewood banksia have, in many of Perth's bushlands, been progressively dying out for some decades, at a much faster rate than they are replacing themselves by natural regeneration. Since the 1990s many common sheoaks too have died or died back.

Another species in decline is marri, but in this case more generally, throughout much of its range. Three other Perth eucalypts are having problems more outside the Perth area than within. Wandoo has been in decline particularly in much of the western Wheatbelt. Many specimens have died back significantly since the late 1980s, in some areas most of them subsequently recovering but in others continuing to decline. In a large area south of Mandurah, enormous numbers of tuart trees have died or severely declined since the late 1990s. Flooded gum is in poor health

in many areas developed for agriculture, but is generally faring much better in more vegetated areas.

What are the causes of these various declines? A major factor for the banksias is drops in the water-table. Perth's large banksia species have both lateral roots, which run near the soil's surface, and deep roots. The lateral roots supply most of the banksia's moisture needs during winter and spring, when the surface soil is moist. In summer and autumn, however, when the surface soil is dry, the banksia gets most of its moisture from its deep roots, in the moist soil just above the water-table. If the water-table drops too far in summer, as the result of a drought, or the extraction of groundwater, the banksia may die from a lack of moisture.

In the declines of the eucalypts, particular insects or fungi are involved. They are unlikely, however, to be the primary cause. Trees generally succumb to insects or fungi because they are under stress, from factors such as climate change or fire, discussed above.

We should note that there are not only declines but recoveries too. In Perth's older coastal suburbs, many tuart trees that had died back severely in the 1950s, 1960s and 1970s from heavy use by a beetle, the tuart longicorn, have since made quite spectacular recoveries.

< *Fig. 40*
Telegraph sedge, one of many species of small plant found in conservation reserves and other bush areas.

> Fig. 41
One of Perth's nature
reserves.

What is being done?

What is being done to address the problems discussed above? An important measure has been the creation of conservation reserves. There is also an increasing emphasis on managing the reserves to offset the threats discussed above. Valuable research is being carried out on the ecology and propagation of many of Perth's plant species, and the reasons why some are in decline.

Conservation reserves

For many years areas have been set aside as reserves to conserve our plants and animals. Early examples are Kings Park and John Forrest National Park.

Conservation reserves are important in containing not only Perth's trees and tall shrubs but also the many smaller plant species that make up our flora. They also support a great diversity of animals and fungi.

Most of the more significant conservation reserves, including the various national parks, conservation parks and nature reserves, are managed by the Department of Environment and Conservation (DEC), on behalf of the Conservation Commission of Western Australia.

The number of such reserves in the Perth Metropolitan Region has been growing. In 2008 there were 14 national parks and about 50 nature reserves. Most of the national parks are in the Darling Range, where over 10 per cent of the land within the region is in conservation reserves.

Kings Park and Bold Park, in the heart of the city, are managed by the Botanic Gardens and Parks Authority. There are also several hundred bushlands in the region under the control of local governments, with a total area of over 4,000 hectares. Examples are Star Swamp Bushland Reserve, in the City of Stirling, Wireless Hill Park, in the City of Melville, and Bungendore Park, in the City of Armadale.

Since the late 1990s, a number of open spaces of regional significance for conservation, recreation and their landscapes have been designated as regional parks. Examples are Yellagonga, Beeliar, Canning River and Woodman Point regional parks. They are managed by various agencies and owners of incorporated private lands, under the co-ordination of DEC.

In addition to conservation reserves and regional parks, many private properties contain bushlands managed for conservation, including over 260 in the Perth Metropolitan Region registered under the Land for Wildlife Scheme (see p. 229); there are also a number with conservation covenants.

Adequacy of reserves: studies

Ideally, conservation reserves should collectively conserve viable populations of all the plants, animals and fungi within the region concerned.

In the 1970s a study was carried out to try to meet that aim, at least for the plants and animals. The State was divided into 12 'systems', and a body called the Conservation Through Reserves Committee reported to the Environmental Protection Authority on areas to be set aside as reserves for conservation. Perth was included in System Six, an area of the Swan Coastal Plain and Darling Plateau extending from the Moore River to south of Bunbury.

Further important studies have been undertaken since then, making use of a greatly increasing knowledge of Perth's ecosystems. These include *Bush Forever*[2] and the *Forest Management Plan 2004–2013*[3], which recommend areas to be managed for conservation. *Bush Forever* is a detailed review of regionally significant bushlands on the Swan Coastal Plain within the region. *The Forest Management Plan* examines the future of lands managed by DEC in the State's forested south-west corner, including the Perth Metropolitan Region, with a focus on State forest and timber reserves. As a result of those studies, many valuable bushlands have been set aside as conservation reserves.

Links

Because of the effects of the fragmentation of bushlands, mentioned above, it is vitally important to have links between them wherever possible, to facilitate the movement of animals, plants and fungi. These can be 'corridors': unbroken strips of suitable vegetation that join bushlands together. Or they can be 'stepping-stones': areas of bushland or other good habitat scattered between larger bushlands, and helping to bridge the gap between them. Since in practice most corridors are quite narrow, comprising vegetated roadsides or river foreshores, it is best to have corridors and stepping-stones in combination.

Bush Forever defines the most important links between bushlands on the coastal plain within the

Perth Metropolitan Region. It draws information from an earlier report to the Ministry for Planning[4] that proposes that Perth should have a system of 'greenways' — links intended for both ecological purposes and also, where possible, recreational use. Unvegetated stretches within them are to be planted with plant species local to the site.

Management

To offset the threats mentioned above, bushlands need to be appropriately managed. DEC manages its bushlands in accordance with management plans it prepares, and increasingly local governments are doing likewise.

The management work done by the staff of those bodies is often with the assistance of community groups, many of which have formed for particular bushlands. Since they usually call themselves the 'friends' of the bushland concerned, they are generally known as 'friends' groups. Examples are the Friends of Shenton Bushland, and the Friends of Lightning Swamp Bushland. They aim to protect the bushland and raise the public's awareness of it. They usually work to control such threats as weeds, fire and diseases, to increase the bushland's health, and encourage the local plants' natural regeneration.

Planting is done chiefly on degraded edges of the bushland, to establish a better barrier against weeds, and to improve the appearance of the areas most seen by the public. By holding planting days they involve the wider community in their work.

Other groups, such as Cottesloe Coastcare and CRREPA (Canning River Residents' Environment Protection Association), take an interest in a wider area, where their activities usually involve revegetation with local plants.

As well as groups that look after particular bushlands, there are also community groups that focus on conserving particular plants or animals. Examples are the Wandoo Recovery Group and the Friends of the Western Swamp Tortoise.

Through its Urban Nature program, DEC provides technical advice to bodies and people, including community volunteers, involved in managing sites identified in the *Bush Forever* report.

The Perth Biodiversity Project

Initiated in 1999, the Perth Biodiversity Project aims to foster the protection and management of bushlands in the Perth Metropolitan Region. It is

∧ *Fig. 42*
Balgas and tuarts preserved in gardens in a Perth suburb. Such vegetation helps provide 'stepping stones' between bushlands.

encouraging local governments to produce 'local biodiversity plans', which are to give attention to maintaining or improving the condition of bushlands and enhancing the links between them. Techniques are to be used to promote the natural regeneration of disturbed bushlands. Revegetation is to be encouraged in areas near by, by using natural regeneration where possible, or otherwise by the planting of local trees and shrubs.

The trees and shrubs planted in the past on public lands have largely been non-local, including eastern Australian eucalypts and various exotic species. Such species will no doubt continue to be widely used. There has nonetheless been an increased appreciation in recent years of the value of local species, which the Perth Biodiversity Project will further encourage.

The project also directs its attention at the community, to help community groups and members of the public undertake some of the work involved in looking after bushlands or undertaking revegetation.

Research

In addition to the above studies to identify areas for conservation reserves, much other valuable research — by organisations such as the Botanic Gardens and Parks Authority, DEC and tertiary institutions — is being undertaken that pertains to the management of these areas. This is helping to determine such things as the best ways to propagate many Perth plants or encourage their regeneration, or to control weeds and pest animals.

Of particular relevance to Perth's trees and tall shrubs is the Centre of Excellence for Climate Change and Woodland and Forest Health. It is based at Murdoch University and involves a collaboration between tertiary institutions, government bodies (particularly DEC) and various industries and environmental groups. It is researching the declines of various tree species and working on methods and policies for rescuing woodlands and forests.

Environmental Education

In Perth's urban environment, where few of the local trees or shrubs have been retained, and most of the planted species are non-locals, many people have little experience of their local vegetation. Many will have heard of tuart or jarrah through the media, but very few can recognise those or any other local trees.

Organisations such as DEC and Greening Australia (W.A.) have programs to help schoolchildren and others learn about their natural environment. DEC has a number of 'EcoEducation' programs, for students, teachers and the community. They include one called Bush Rangers, under which students in secondary schools, usually together with parents and other members of the community, undertake conservation projects for the community's benefit. Greening Australia's 'Grow Us a Home' program introduces students to the soils, plant communities and some of the plants and animals of Perth's coastal plain and Darling Range; and its 'Stepping Stones' program encourages schools, urban communities and local governments to preserve local plants and animals.

Conclusion

Perth's trees and tall shrubs are important species to conserve. Because they support so many different animals and fungi, they are vitally important in maintaining our ecosystems. They also inform us about our natural environment and the changes it is undergoing.

In Perth, much is being done that will help these plants survive, at least in the immediate future. Significant measures include the creation of conservation reserves, and actions to manage them and create links between them. Valuable research is being undertaken on species in decline.

Some of the trees and tall shrubs not doing well in bushlands are benefiting from the work done by friends groups and some local governments in establishing them elsewhere. This could be extended, with the idea of increasing the representation of local species in Perth's urban environment. The 'Cultivation' chapter in this book (pp. 214-25) draws attention to the many sorts of place in which these plants can be established, including private gardens.

The public plays a very significant role in conservation in Perth. It is therefore important to maintain and augment programs that help people become more aware of their natural environment. Schools should be encouraged to plant some of their local trees and shrubs in their grounds, not only to encourage familiarity with, and pride in, our natural species, but also as a resource for study.

A particular concern for the future of Perth's trees and tall shrubs is climate change. Efforts to minimise the effects of this global phenomenon need to be addressed by action and co-operation throughout the world. It is necessary to adapt to climate change, by anticipating as well as possible what changes it will cause, and taking action to minimise the effect of those changes. Maintaining our biodiversity needs to be considered as part of that action.

Perth's trees and shrubs may be helped to survive in a drying climate by giving them supplementary water. That water can be obtained by harvesting it. Rainwater that runs off from streets or factory roofs can be channelled and collected to irrigate a local park. House roofs can be used in the same way for private gardens. Harvesting water may not be possible on a scale suitable for bushlands, but may help the survival of street trees, or trees and shrubs in small suburban parks.

Another way to help Perth's trees and shrubs is to pay attention to the moister, more fertile places, such as river valleys and the surrounds of lakes and swamps, as sites for nature conservation. Here the effects of a drying climate are less felt. Such land, of course, tends also to be the most suitable for agriculture, and much of it is cleared and privately owned. It may be possible, through financial or other incentives, to encourage the owners to establish local trees and shrubs on parts of their land. We need not only to survive ourselves, but also to make sure our natural home survives with us.

[1] Source: Bureau of Meteorology.
[2] State of Western Australia. *Bush Forever: Keeping the Bush in the City: Volume 1, Policies, Principles and Practices; Volume 2, Directory of Bush Forever Sites.* Perth: Western Australian Planning Commission, 2000.
[3] Conservation Commission of Western Australia. *Forest Management Plan 2004-2013.* Perth, Western Australia, 2004.
[4] Tingay, Alan, and Associates. *A Strategic Plan for Perth's Greenways: Final Report.* Perth, Western Australia, 1998.

Part two
The trees and tall shrubs

The trees and tall shrubs

The individual plant species included here as Perth's trees and tall shrubs are those that:
(a) occur naturally in the area defined as the Perth Metropolitan Region (see Map 1, inside front cover); and
(b) commonly grow to three metres or more in undisturbed conditions.

They are arranged in alphabetical order by botanical (scientific) name.

The size to which plants grow depends not only on the species but also on the site. Some sites are moister than others, or have deeper or more fertile soil, enabling plants to grow larger. Another factor affecting the size of plants is fire. Many of Perth's trees and shrubs are either killed by fire or burnt to the ground. The resultant seedlings or regrowth from the ground will attain the plant's full size only if there is enough time to do so before the next fire. In (b), above, 'undisturbed conditions' refers particularly to an adequate time between fires for the species to attain its full size.

Plant species that only occasionally grow to three metres have been excluded. So have species that commonly grow to more than three metres outside the Metropolitan Region, but not where they occur naturally within it. The Perth form of Geraldton wax, for example, is smaller than forms from further north, on which the cultivated forms are based. Climbing plants, of which some species climb to heights of more than three metres, have been excluded because they are not trees or shrubs.

A few species that commonly grow to three metres or more have been excluded on the grounds that their natural occurrence in the region is extremely limited and that they are much more typically found outside it.

How to identify species

To find some of the plant species in this book, visit a bushland. Perth's parks and gardens contain mostly cultivated trees and shrubs, usually species not native to Perth but to other parts of the State, Australia, or the world. If you are interested in a particular species, the text on it will provide spots where it can be found, or at least give a general idea of where to look.

To identify a species in the book, compare its features with the drawings of the various species. You can, of course, narrow down the choice considerably if you can recognise the genus. If the plant looks like a wattle (*Acacia*), banksia (*Banksia*), sheoak (*Allocasuarina* or *Casuarina*) or eucalypt (*Eucalyptus* or *Corymbia*), go straight to the species in that genus and see whether the plant fits any of them.

For each species in the book there is a drawing of the whole tree or shrub and drawings of its botanical features. The latter are approximately life-size, except where indicated. When you have found drawings that appear to match the features of the plant, check against 'Distinctive features' in the text. Where there are two or more very similar species, a means of clearly identifying the species in question is provided.

The drawings of the whole tree or shrub are of less value for identifying a species, since the individual specimens of most vary greatly. Jarrah, for example, is tall on the Darling Plateau, but is stout and spreading and of only medium size on the coastal plain. Grey stinkwood is an erect shrub or small tree in most places in the Metropolitan Region, but is much lower and sprawling round Rockingham.

The drawings are more to show the character of a healthy, mature plant (wonnich, of which only saplings could be found in the Perth area, is an exception). I hope that they will inspire readers' appreciation of the character and beauty of each species. Today, such well developed specimens tend to be quite uncommon. Many of the old jarrahs round Perth, for example, were cut for timber, and most of the specimens we now see are the subsequent regrowth. Moreover, as noted above, many of Perth's trees and shrubs do not attain their mature size as a result of too frequent fires.

Getting to know a species

Plants of interest become recognisable. Rather than having to inspect the plant closely to examine its leaves, flowers or fruits, we can learn to recognise the species instantly, at a distance — just as we recognise many exotic species, or a person we have met. We can learn more quickly by deliberately observing the species at a distance and noting its colours, textures and shapes.

Recognising a plant species with ease is the first step towards getting to know it. We can discover where it occurs, how well it is faring, whether it is being cultivated. We can note the seasons when it puts on its new growth, or produces

∧ *Fig. 43*
Young shoot of bull banksia, seen here against mature leaves. One of the pleasures of getting to know a plant is finding out what its new growth looks like and when it is produced.

its flowers or fruits, and can perhaps also observe some of the insects, birds or fungi that use it.

Just as getting to know a person is rewarding, so too with plant species. Moreover, with the knowledge you will acquire, you can play an important role in protecting these species and their environment.

Common names

The names of Perth's trees and tall shrubs should be part of our everyday language. A common name has thus been given for every species; where no suitable name is established, one is suggested. Where a species has two or more common names, the most suitable one has been adopted, and the reasons given for the choice. In the index, both common and scientific names are given in most cases. Birds are listed only under their common names, as these are well established.

Since the Aboriginal people had a great familiarity with the indigenous plants, their names can be very appropriate common names. They are already used for a number of Perth's trees and tall shrubs: jarrah, marri, tuart, wandoo, bullich, yarri, moonah, quandong and pingle.

The original sources for most of the Aboriginal names used in this book can be found in the report by Abbott (1983).[1] The following names, however, were taken from other sources. 'Mangite', an alternative to 'bull banksia' as a common name for *Banksia grandis*, is taken from a paper by Sara Meagher[2] on Aboriginal foods in south-west Western Australia, and refers to the flowers of this banksia and the nectar obtained from them. 'Moonah', for *Melaleuca lanceolata*, is from a book on Australian roadsides by Edna Walling[2], and 'modong', for *M. preissiana*, is from a vocabulary of Western Australian Aboriginal words by George Fletcher Moore[2]. From this last source come three further names for melaleuca species in this book. 'Gorada', meaning 'little' or 'short', is used for *M. lateriflora*, a paperbark species much smaller than Perth's better-known paperbarks. 'Banbar', meaning 'round' or 'cylindrical', is used for *M. teretifolia*, referring to the leaves, which are round in cross-section. 'Mohan', meaning 'dark-coloured', describes the dull, dark general appearance of *M. viminea*.

As might be expected, the pronunciation of most Aboriginal names is now quite different from the original. In south-western Australia, Aboriginal languages were poorly recorded by the European settlers, and only some of the original names of Perth's trees and tall shrubs survive. Different tribes often had different names, and different recorders varied the spelling. Where there are two or more names for one species, only one has been listed, for the sake of simplicity. Of the alternative spellings, I have chosen one that suggests a sound similar to the original, but that is easily intelligible to today's Australians. In some cases the spelling has been changed to provide a name that is easily pronounced, in a way not too dissimilar to the original pronunciation.

The common names for birds are those used in Christidis (2008)[3], except that a few have been shortened where no ambiguity exists, for example 'Pacific black duck' to 'black duck'. A few of the insect names are my own suggestions.

Some important genera

The 79 plant species in this book belong to 38 different genera. The major ones are discussed below; the rest are introduced briefly where they first appear in the sequence of individual species.

Genus *Acacia*: wattles

Acacia is the largest and most successful plant genus in Australia, where about 960 of the world's 1,500 or more species grow. Of the Australian species — commonly known as wattles — well over half occur in Western Australia. Wattles can be found in every part of the continent, from the coast to the dry interior, where they dominate a vast area known as the mulga.

The 'leaves' of most wattles are really flattened leaf-stalks, known as phyllodes, that function as leaves. This feature probably helps many wattles survive in arid conditions or salty coastal environments. In the moister parts of Western Australia — the South-West and the Kimberley — many species do have true leaves, such as Perth's common prickly moses. All wattle seedlings have leaves, the transition to phyllodes beginning soon after the first leaves develop (Fig. 44).

All wattles have flowers grouped into globular or cylindrical heads, and pods for fruits. Most species have seeds with nutritious, edible stalks; these are eaten by animals, which disperse the seeds.

Those with red, orange or yellow seed-stalks retain their seeds when the pods open, displaying the colourful seed-stalks to attract birds, which have good colour vision. The birds swallow the seeds with the stalks but digest only the stalks and excrete the seeds.

The other wattles have white or off-white seed-stalks. In these species the seeds are shed, and are carried away by ants. The stalks are eaten but the seeds remain stored in the ants' nests. They germinate if disturbance of the soil brings them to the surface, or after the heat of an intense fire causes their hard coats to crack.

Most wattles are killed by fire but regenerate readily afterwards. They are usually good colonisers of disturbed land, where the young plants grow vigorously.

As mentioned on page 16, wattles and other plants in the legume family are important in maintaining or increasing the soil's fertility. Being nutritious plants, wattles support many different insects, and are thus biologically valuable.

Wattles throughout Australia were often used by the Aboriginal people as food. They roasted and ate the seeds, ate the gum and drank the sap. Bardi grubs, the larvae of swift-moths, were extracted from the stems. The wood was used to make many of their implements.

Many wattle species are cultivated. In arid regions they are important for timber and shelter.

Genus *Banksia*

There are 173 species in the genus *Banksia*, which include the 93 species that were previously in the genus *Dryandra*.

Banksias are indeed very Australian plants. Every species occurs in Australia, and only one extends beyond its shores, to New Guinea and nearby islands. Western Australia is particularly rich in banksias, with 156 species.

The 'flower' of holly-leaf banksia, or any species previously in the genus *Dryandra*, is, in fact, a head of flowers, grouped tightly together, attached to the end of the stem. Most of the larger

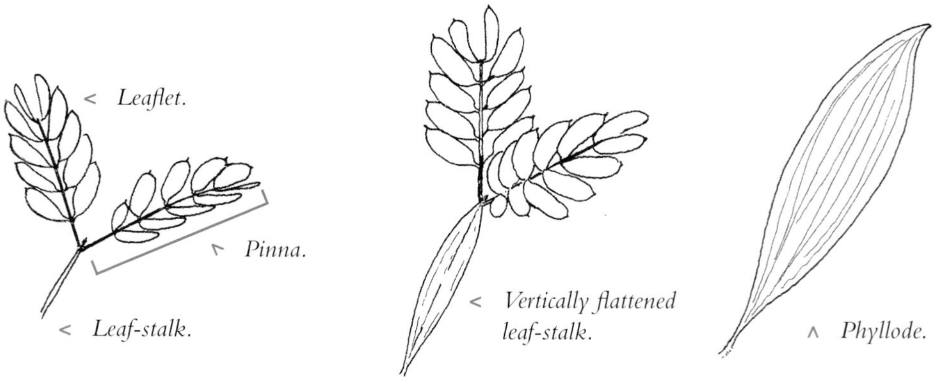

> *Fig. 44*
> *The leaves of wattle seedlings (left) comprise a stalk and two pinnae. Mature wattles of most species, however, have phyllodes (right); as their seedlings develop, an intermediate stage (centre) is often seen.*

< *Leaflet.*

ʌ *Pinna.*

< *Leaf-stalk.*

< *Vertically flattened leaf-stalk.*

ʌ *Phyllode.*

banksias, however, are particularly distinctive when in flower, their 'flower' being a flower-spike: a dense cluster of several hundred flowers arranged spirally around the end of a stem. If the flowers on the spike are of a different colour from the unopened buds (as in firewood banksia), the spikes are two-coloured while the buds progressively open. In some species, the buds at the bottom open first; in others, those at the top.

The flower-spikes are important feeding-sites for nectarivorous animals, of which many are pollinating agents, especially honey-eating birds, and such mammals as brush-tailed possums, honey possums, pygmy possums and various bats. The robust spikes are rigid enough for birds and small mammals to cling to while feeding at them. Cockatoos often break off the spikes to extract insects from the base; this is why one often finds numerous flower-spikes lying on the ground.

Banksias are an important component of Perth's vegetation. Bull banksia is the main understorey tree in the jarrah forest of the Darling Plateau. It is on the coastal plain, however, that banksias are particularly prominent, with several common species. Their specialised roots (see p. 16) have made them very successful in the infertile yellow and pale grey sands that occupy much of this region. Sadly, nowadays, they are dying out in many places, unable to cope with rapidly falling water-tables, or introduced pathogens.

The fallen wood and logs of banksias are habitat for many fungi. A conspicuous example is the golden wood fungus, which in Perth fruits more abundantly on banksia wood than any other type. The fungus *Campanella gregaria* seems to favour the inside surface of banksia bark that is just beginning to separate from a fallen log. It produces clusters of many (sometimes hundreds) of small shell-like fruiting bodies.

The Aboriginal people of south-western Australia were fond of sucking the flower-spikes to drink the sweet nectar. They also ate grubs extracted from the trees.

Today many banksia species are cultivated. They are grown in parks and gardens, and on wildflower farms, where their flower-spikes are cut for sale. Since Perth's species were formerly so common on the coastal plain, their cultivation on public lands and in private gardens should be encouraged.

Genera *Casuarina* and *Allocasuarina*: sheoaks

Sheoaks are easily recognised by their distinctive foliage. Sheoak 'needles' are slender green branchlets that function as leaves. Inspect one of these and you will see that it has a number of segments. Under a magnifying glass the true leaves, tiny teeth encircling the branchlet at each joint, can be seen. The shed branchlets carpet the ground beneath the tree, providing a good habitat for orchids.

The early English settlers, to whom the wood resembled that of their native oaks, invented the name 'sheoak'. The botanical name *Casuarina* is from the Malay *casuari*, meaning 'cassowary', an emu-like bird, and refers to the resemblance of drooping sheoak branches to the bird's feathers.

Most of the world's 95 species of sheoak (family Casuarinaceae) occur in Australia, the rest in Indonesia, south-east Asia or islands of the Pacific. There are four different genera, of which two are found in Western Australia: the closely related *Casuarina* and *Allocasuarina*. They differ in the colour and longevity of their nuts, and in features of their cones and branchlets.

In Australia sheoaks occur over most of the continent in a wide range of habitats, but are most typical of harsh environments. They favour the coast, dry regions, and sites with shallow or waterlogged soils. One of the most impressive species, the desert oak, grows in arid central Australia as a tree of up to 12 metres or more.

Sheoaks have tiny separate male and female flowers. The male flowers are borne at the ends of branchlets, and the female flowers on short branchlets of their own. In most species an individual tree normally bears only male or female flowers, so we can speak of male and female trees. The male flowers are brown and are borne in profusion, giving the foliage a rusty colour. Sheoaks are wind-pollinated. The fertilised female flowers develop cones bearing winged nuts (usually called 'seeds').

A number of sheoak species are cultivated, some simply for their beauty, others for their ability to grow close to the ocean or in other harsh environments. In the past, some species were cut for timber. Like wattles and pea-plants, sheoaks can fix nitrogen in the soil, and improve its fertility.

Genera *Eucalyptus*, *Corymbia* and *Angophora*: eucalypts, gumtrees, gums

Eucalypts, commonly called gumtrees or just gums, are Australia's best-known trees. 'Gum' refers particularly to species with smooth bark.

There are more than 900 species of eucalypt, comprising over 800 species in the genus *Eucalyptus*, about 115 in the genus *Corymbia* and 15 in the genus *Angophora*. Nearly all of them occur in Australia. A few Australian species extend to New Guinea or to some of the islands of Indonesia or the Philippines, and a few are confined to those regions.

Nearly all the Perth species are in the genus *Eucalyptus*. There are no angophoras and only two corymbias, marri and lesser bloodwood. The latter species reflects the general name of 'bloodwoods' for many of the corymbias.

In Australia, eucalypts do not grow in regions with a rainfall of less than 250 mm, except in special habitats, such as watercourses, and are thus absent from the greater part of the continent. In this respect they are far less typically Australian than, say, the wattles.

Eucalypt leaves are distinctive in their shape and the way they are held on the tree. As an adaptation to conserve water, they hang down; their surfaces are thus exposed to the sun more in the early morning and the late afternoon than in the middle of the day. Seedlings, however, need more light, since they are overshadowed by mature trees and shrubs. Thus the seedlings of most eucalypts have rounder, broader leaves, held flat.

Eucalypt flowers too are distinctive. The petals of some species, and the petals and sepals of others, unite to form a cap, sometimes called an operculum (this feature is absent in the angophoras). As the stamens mature they push off the operculum, and the flower opens. The name *Eucalyptus* means 'well covered', and refers to this feature.

Eucalypts are Australia's largest trees and have great economic importance. Many provide hardwood timber of outstanding quality; for example, jarrah. Others, such as wandoo and marri, are important honey producers. The bark of several Wheatbelt eucalypts, particularly brown mallet, yields a valuable tannin. Many eucalypts are cultivated in Australia, and many are widely planted abroad for timber, shelter or ornament.

Eucalypts also have great biological value. They dominate the vegetation wherever they occur, and contribute most of the habitat for wildlife. Their foliage, bark and shed branches provide cover. Mature specimens of many species develop hollows, which are used by a wide variety of animals for shelter. The flowers of nearly all species are important to animals that eat pollen or nectar. Especially noteworthy is that eucalypts are rich in associated insects, which play important roles in the functioning of ecosystems, not least as food for many other animal species.

The Aboriginal people made medicines from the oil from eucalypt leaves, and sometimes eucalypt seeds. The bark and wood were used for a variety of artefacts and implements. Water was collected from the roots of some species, and grubs extracted from the trunks and eaten.

Although Perth has a rich flora, it is poor in eucalypts, with only 16 species occurring naturally in the Perth Metropolitan Region. A comparable area in the Goldfields would contain a much higher number. There are probably several reasons why Perth has so few eucalypt species. The coastal plain is geologically recent, and eucalypts have probably not had time to evolve many new species. (Smaller plant species, most of which are shorter-lived, go through their generations more quickly, and can thus evolve more quickly.) The Darling Plateau is largely dominated by two very successful eucalypts, jarrah and marri, which are well adapted to its environment. Both the coastal plain and the Darling Plateau are subdued landscapes. In eastern Australia, where there are more eucalypts, the landscape is more mountainous, creating a greater diversity of environments.

In Perth's suburban landscapes, most of the eucalypts we see are cultivated specimens, of species mainly from eastern Australia. Many of Perth's own species are useful in cultivation, and their use for this purpose should be encouraged.

Genus *Melaleuca*: paperbarks and honey-myrtles

Species of melaleuca vary from small shrubs to large trees. A number of the trees are known as paperbarks. These are mostly wetland species, and one or more can be found in or by most Australian wetlands. The shrubby species of melaleuca are generally known as honey-myrtles, since many produce abundant nectar. Melaleucas are also sometimes called tea-trees — but this name is more commonly used for another genus in the same family, *Leptospermum*; an example is the widely cultivated Victorian tea-tree.

Melaleucas occur in Malaysia, Indonesia and New Caledonia, but are predominantly Australian: about 215 of the world's 220 or so species occur in Australia. Western Australia has a good share, with 193 species. They grow in a wide range of habitats, and cover almost the entire State, with a high concentration of species in the South-West.

Melaleucas are important to animals in producing an abundance of nectar. Stands of paperbark or other wetland melaleucas provide good refuges and breeding-sites for waterbirds and other animals.

The Aboriginal people of northern Australia used the bark of cadjeput, a paperbark, as a sheath for hunting-tools, as tinder for starting fires, and as an insulating material. Paperbarks in other parts of Australia are likely to have been similarly used.

Many melaleuca species thrive in cultivation, being adaptable and readily grown. A number have become popular garden plants.

< *Fig. 45*
The bark of a paperbark.

---

[1] Ian Abbott, *Aboriginal Names for Plant Species in South-Western Australia* (Technical Paper No. 5), Forests Department of W.A. (now DEC), Perth, 1983.
[2] see 'Works consulted'.
[3] Christidis, Les, and Walter Boles. *Systematics and Taxonomy of Australian Birds*. Collingwood, Victoria, 2008.

Red-eyed wattle

Acacia cyclops

Red-eyed wattle, a common species of our coast, is easily recognised by its conspicuous seed-pods, which remain on the plant for a long time.

In late spring to early summer, when the pods first open, the shiny black seeds, encircled by thick, orange-red stalks, resemble bloodshot eyes. The botanical name refers to this feature too: the Cyclops were a race of one-eyed giants in Greek mythology.

Most wattles flower in one great display, but red-eyed wattle produces a few flower heads at a time over a long period, from early spring to late summer. The pods, however, which result from the fertilised flowers, all mature at the same time.

Growth habit and environment

Near the ocean, red-eyed wattle is subject to salt spray, sandblast and being buried by sand or having sand swept away from its roots. Its growth habit (see illustration) helps it survive. Its dense, domed shape protects much of the foliage from salt and sandblast. It also shades the soil and protects it from erosion.

Red-eyed wattle can be found also in the shelter and shade of the tuart forest. Here it has no need for the domed shape, and grows sparser and more upright, up to 7 m.

Associated life

Red-eyed wattle is one of the most important large shrubs that grow in the harsh environment near the ocean, in the swale behind the primary dune. Ants, spiders, lizards and other small creatures shelter from the hot sun under its dense foliage.

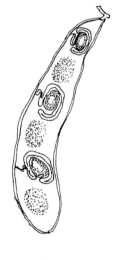

∧ *Inside of pod, showing seeds and their encircling stalks.*

Like other large wattles, it is rich in associated insects. Various insects eat the phyllodes or the stems. The larva of the ant-longicorn burrows into the twigs, working its way down into larger stems as it grows; the adult beetle is often found on the phyllodes. The large larvae of wood moths tunnel in the main stems, pupating near the base of the plant. Other insects, such as native bees, nest in the abandoned holes.

The larvae of a tiny butterfly, the two-spotted line-blue, feed on the flower buds, flowers and young pods. Red-eyed wattle is especially valuable to this butterfly, since it continues to produce flowers through the summer, when few other wattles are flowering.

The seeds or seed-stalks are eaten by weevils and other beetles, as well as a species of jewel bug that is spectacularly marked to camouflage with its surroundings. It is glossy black with orange-red patches, including a red circle on its abdomen, resembling the wattle seeds and their surrounding stalks.

In addition to the many insects that feed on the wattle itself, further species feed on rust-fungi that grow on it, such as one that often forms conspicuous globular galls on the wattle's smaller stems.

Ringneck parrots attack the young, green pods and eat the soft, immature seeds. These and other birds, such as silvereyes and red wattlebirds, feast on the seed-stalks when the pods open.

Seed dispersal

This species is a splendid example of a wattle that uses birds to disperse its seeds (see p. 40). In wide-open pods, the seeds, with their bright surrounding stalks, are well displayed. Because

the birds often roost or nest in large trees such as tuarts, many of red-eyed wattle's seeds are deposited in the birds' droppings underneath the trees, where many specimens of the wattle may be found growing. Emu droppings may be found packed with the seeds of this wattle.

Any seeds with stalks not completely digested are gathered by ants to store in their nests. Here they germinate after an intense fire, or if disturbance of the soil brings them to the surface.

Occurrence and distribution

Red-eyed wattle is widely distributed along the coast, from Jurien Bay to the south coast and east into South Australia. In Perth it is common near the coast, in sand or on limestone. It also favours the maritime environment round the Swan Estuary, as far inland as Salter Point.

Human uses

Red-eyed wattle is used to help stabilise coastal sands. In South Africa, where it was introduced for this purpose, it regenerated prolifically and became a serious pest.

It is a most desirable species to include in revegetation projects in the coastal strip. It contributes enormously to biodiversity in providing food or shelter for a great many different insects, which in turn support lizards, birds and bats.

Collection

Probably collected by botanists on the Nicolas Baudin expedition to Nova Hollandia in 1801-03.

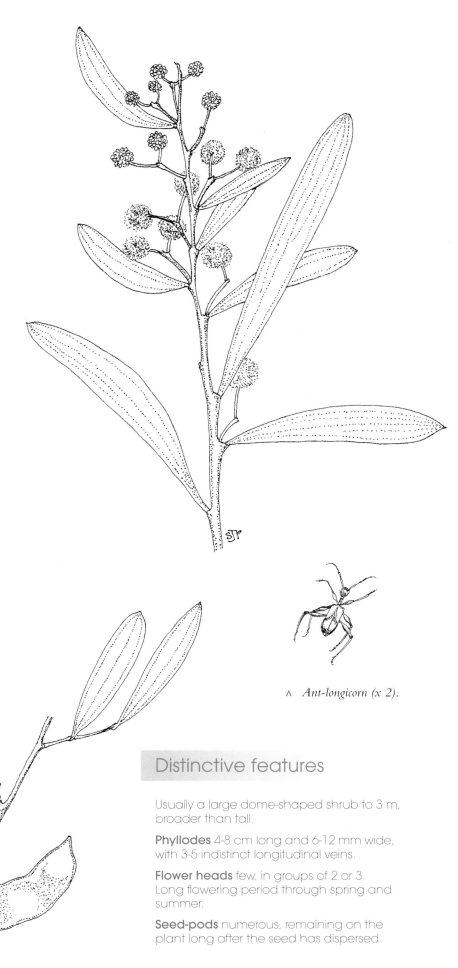

∧   *Ant-longicorn (x 2).*

Distinctive features

Usually a large dome-shaped shrub to 3 m, broader than tall.

Phyllodes 4-8 cm long and 6-12 mm wide, with 3-5 indistinct longitudinal veins.

Flower heads few, in groups of 2 or 3. Long flowering period through spring and summer.

Seed-pods numerous, remaining on the plant long after the seed has dispersed.

Summer-scented wattle

Acacia rostellifera

This large coastal wattle rarely reproduces from seed. New plants grow as suckers from a network of underground stems. Nourished by the parent plant, suckers are more capable than seedlings of surviving in coastal conditions. The underground stems run near the surface and help stabilise the soil, and the plants develop into a mutually protective thicket.

Thickets of summer-scented wattle often cover whole hillsides. They regenerate readily, quickly covering any tracks that are not frequently maintained. The plants send out spreading branches on the edge of the thicket, forming a dense dome of foliage that helps to deflect salt winds. The thickets have a pleasant scent, most noticeable in summer, which seems to come out of the ground, since the soil underneath the plants gives off this scent when disturbed.

The suckering method of reproduction is used also by some other coastal Australian wattles, including the smaller Perth species rigid wattle (*A. cochlearis*). Suckering is even more highly developed in coastal spinifexes, the toughest plants of the primary dunes, which are significant in controlling coastal erosion.

Effects of fire

Summer-scented wattle's suckering habit also helps it withstand today's frequent burning. Fire kills the stems, but the plants resprout vigorously. As a result, summer-scented wattle has survived in many areas where trees such as Rottnest cypress (p. 84) and moonah (p. 176) have died out.

Fire does, however, affect the size of summer-scented wattle. It is Perth's tallest wattle and can grow to 10 m or more on sheltered sites, but only if there is sufficient time between fires. It is now usually a bushy shrub of 2–3 m, even less in places where fires are frequent.

Occurrence and distribution

Summer-scented wattle is found near the coast, both in sand and on limestone, and on a number of offshore islands, including Rottnest, Garden, Carnac and Penguin. It sometimes occurs in saline areas away from the coast, such as near Bullsbrook.

It is widely distributed, occurring from Kalbarri to Australind, and on the south coast as far east as Israelite Bay.

Associated life

Thickets of summer-scented wattle provide valuable habitat in the coastal dunes. Many insects eat the phyllodes or gather pollen from the flowers. Birds and reptiles find shelter and hunt insects in the thickets.

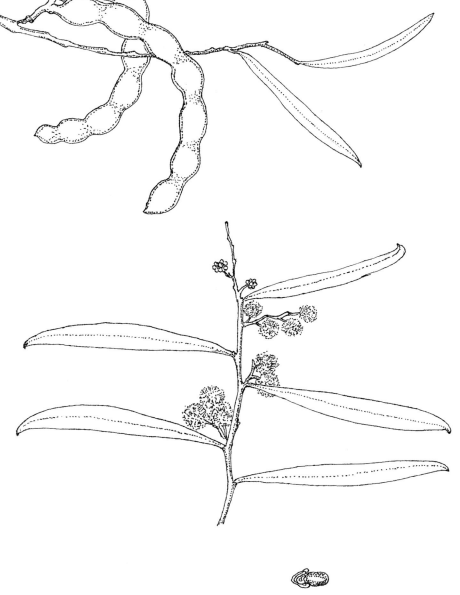

^ Seed.

Caterpillars of the bag moth spin silken bags in the foliage. By day they rest or moult inside the bag, and by night eat the phyllodes. If they defoliate one plant, they descend to the ground and move off in a procession, head to tail, to find another. They come to the ground also to pupate. Another caterpillar causes the stems near the ends of the shoots to swell into galls. Whereas on the mainland birds break open many of the galls to eat the caterpillars, on Rottnest Island the galls are left in place and are very numerous. The larvae of ghost moths feed on the roots, as do the large larvae of a weevil. The adult weevil, which feeds on the foliage, has a 'snout' like a pig, and pinkish colouring, and is known as 'wattle pig'. On Rottnest fossilised pupal cells of this weevil may be seen.

Summer-scented wattle protects itself from leaf-eating insects by means of nectaries — glands that produce a sugary fluid — located at the bases of its phyllodes. The nectaries attract ants, which attack and reduce the numbers of other insects. The fluid is produced in greatest quantity by the soft, new phyllodes, which are most susceptible to insect attack. The introduced rainbow lorikeet visits these nectaries to feed on their nectar.

On Garden Island, summer-scented wattle is the prime habitat for mammals such as the tammar. The same used to be true for the quokka on Rottnest Island. Since the 1920s the quokka population on Rottnest has exploded, and the animal has eliminated most of the wattle stands by overgrazing. In plantations fenced to exclude quokkas it is now reappearing. It does not need to be replanted: it simply regrows from its underground stems.

Collection and naming

Collected in 1839, probably from coastal dunes near Perth, by James Drummond, a botanist and naturalist, and the superintendent of agricultural operations in Western Australia. Specific name, from the Latin *rostellum* 'small beak' and *ferre* 'to bear', refers to the beaked tip of the phyllode.

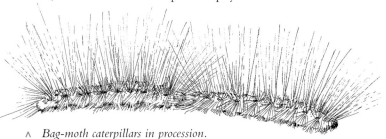

^ *Bag-moth caterpillars in procession.*

Coojong, golden-wreath wattle

Acacia saligna

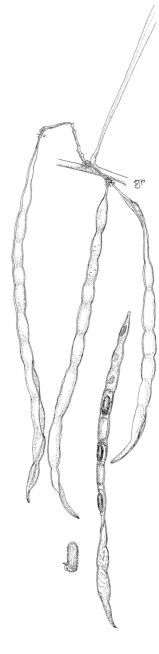

No Perth tree survives better in the city than coojong. It is common along the freeway, and is seen in parks and gardens, even on demolition sites in the inner city. In late winter and early spring it catches attention with its masses of yellow flowers.

It is surprising that it has no well established common name. 'Orange wattle', a name sometimes used, suggests the wrong colour. 'Golden-wreath wattle' is more appropriate, but could also apply to other wattles. 'Coojong', an Aboriginal name, is more specific.

Coojong is a coloniser, popping up where the soil has been disturbed. Unlike many native species, it is actually encouraged by disturbance, which helps its hard-coated, long-lived seeds to germinate, and reduces competition from other native vegetation. Coojong is extremely vigorous, often growing over a metre a year when young.

Coojong is now abundant in many metropolitan bushlands. This was not always so. It used to be plentiful only near wetlands, with isolated specimens elsewhere. Its abundance now in a dryland environment is a sign that the bushland has been disturbed.

Ecological notes

Ants disperse the seeds of coojong by storing them in their nests to eat the seed-stalks. Disturbance of the soil often brings the seeds to the surface and allows them to germinate.

Like summer-scented wattle, coojong protects itself from leaf-eating insects by means of nectaries at the bases of its phyllodes, the ants attracted by the nectaries attacking and reducing the numbers of other insects.

Coojong is a variable species. Some forms of it can resprout from the ground after fire. Other forms are killed, including the one common in Perth.

Like many plants that grow extremely quickly, coojong is short-lived. In Perth it often survives less than 12 years, its life being shortened by wood-boring insects and the gall rust-fungus (see 'Associated life'). During its short life it can nonetheless produce an enormous number of seeds, to perpetuate the species. In countries overseas, where coojong's associated insects and fungi are largely absent, coojong lives 17 or 18 years.

∧ *Seed-pods (x ⅔) and seed (x 1).*

Associated life

The four species of large wattle in this book are all important for supporting a diverse and abundant insect life, coojong especially so. Coojong is known to support some 40 species of bug and 55 of beetle, as well as at least 36 different moths and butterflies.★

Bugs have their mouthparts fused into a straw-like tube, through which they suck juices from plants. A conspicuous species commonly found on coojong is the crusader bug, so named for the cross-shaped pattern on its abdomen.

Different beetle species eat the foliage, the flower buds, the seeds, the pods or the wood. The larva of a jewel beetle tunnels into a stem, then makes a straight cut through it so clean that, when the top part of the branchlet dies and falls, the stem looks as though it has been pruned by secateurs. Birds and reptiles use coojong for food (insects), shelter and nesting.

The butterflies that breed on coojong include the wattle blue, two-spotted line-blue, varied hairstreak and fiery jewel. The moths include the old lady, a large brown species with beautiful blue eyespots on the forewings, which often seeks refuge in buildings. Even larger are the wood moths, whose larvae tunnel in the main stems and pupate in the trunk.

The holes left by the beetle and moth larvae are used by native bees and spiders for nesting. The larger holes provide refuges for fence skinks. Marbled geckoes use old, decaying coojongs for foraging or shelter.

Large globular swellings commonly seen along coojong's stems are those of the gall rust-fungus, which in turn supports moths and weevils.

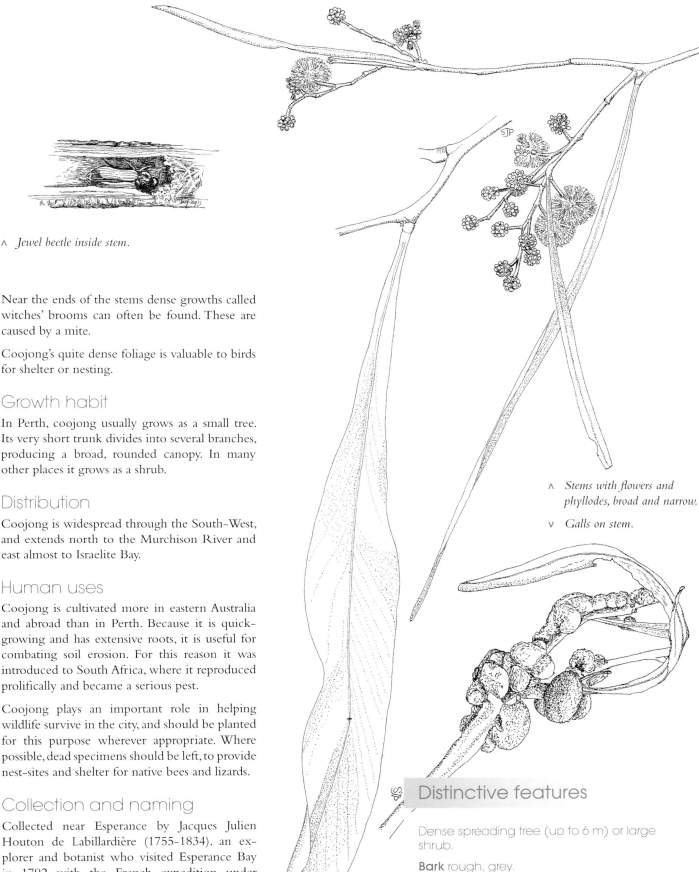

^ *Jewel beetle inside stem.*

Near the ends of the stems dense growths called witches' brooms can often be found. These are caused by a mite.

Coojong's quite dense foliage is valuable to birds for shelter or nesting.

Growth habit

In Perth, coojong usually grows as a small tree. Its very short trunk divides into several branches, producing a broad, rounded canopy. In many other places it grows as a shrub.

Distribution

Coojong is widespread through the South-West, and extends north to the Murchison River and east almost to Israelite Bay.

Human uses

Coojong is cultivated more in eastern Australia and abroad than in Perth. Because it is quick-growing and has extensive roots, it is useful for combating soil erosion. For this reason it was introduced to South Africa, where it reproduced prolifically and became a serious pest.

Coojong plays an important role in helping wildlife survive in the city, and should be planted for this purpose wherever appropriate. Where possible, dead specimens should be left, to provide nest-sites and shelter for native bees and lizards.

Collection and naming

Collected near Esperance by Jacques Julien Houton de Labillardière (1755-1834), an ex-plorer and botanist who visited Esperance Bay in 1792 with the French expedition under d'Entrecasteaux. Specific name from the Latin *salignus* 'willow wood'. The phyllodes and small branches droop like those of a willow, particularly when the plant is flowering profusely.

★ Fox, J.E.D., 1995: see 'Works consulted'.

^ *Stems with flowers and phyllodes, broad and narrow.*

v *Galls on stem.*

Distinctive features

Dense spreading tree (up to 6 m) or large shrub.

Bark rough, grey.

Phyllodes large, 8-25 cm long with conspicuous midrib; most hang downwards.

Flowers in early spring or late winter. Flower heads in groups of up to 10.

White-stemmed wattle

Acacia xanthina

This fresh-looking shrub is, like red-eyed wattle and summer-scented wattle, a coastal species. Its occurrence in the Perth area, however, is more restricted: it does not grow south of Fremantle, and is found only on limestone.

Occurrence and distribution

White-stemmed wattle extends from Fremantle to Geraldton and is also found near Shark Bay.

In the Metropolitan Region it is found mostly on limestone slopes bordering the lower Swan River; for example, below the Esplanade (Peppermint Grove) and on Cantonment Hill (Fremantle). A good population is found in Bold Park, on the northern and north-eastern sides of Reabold Hill, extending to the limestone ridge north of Oceanic Drive. There are few other occurrences between Mullaloo and Fremantle, in spite of the numerous (although more minor) limestone hills in the area.

Appearance

White-stemmed wattle is similar in size and shape to red-eyed wattle, but its branches meander more. As specimens in the open reach maturity, their upper branches bend downwards. They often cascade right to the ground and grow out or up again.

This species can be distinguished at a distance from red-eyed and summer-scented wattle by colour. The phyllodes are a fresh bluish-green, sometimes yellowish, and the branchlets are greenish-white. This combination of colours gives the foliage a brighter look.

Ecological notes

White-stemmed wattle is closely related to summer-scented wattle. Both species reproduce strongly, forming thickets, although white-stemmed wattle reproduces by seed, not by suckering. As the seed-stalks are drab, it is likely that ants, rather than birds, disperse the seeds.

White-stemmed wattle is killed by fire and, in some areas, has been greatly reduced by frequent burning. It has possibly been eliminated from some limestone hills by this means. On Cantonment Hill, the absence of fire in recent years has allowed this species to flourish, greatly suppressing weed growth.

Associated life

Sticky ants (*Crematogaster* sp.) and other insects harvest secretions from nectaries at the base of the phyllodes. In spring, native bees are attracted to the pollen-laden flowers.

A spiny *Catasarchus* weevil, restricted to Western Australia, feeds on the phyllodes. Other beetle species found on the plant include three species of jewel beetle (*Agrilus australasiae*, *Cisseis* sp. and *Melobasis terminata*) and two species of small grey long-horned beetle.

In summer, parasitic wasps can be seen examining the foliage for moth larvae. One such larva, the wattle caterpillar, protects itself by resembling a preying mantis.

Thickets of white-stemmed wattle provide shelter and good nest-sites for birds.

Collection and naming

Collected by James Drummond near Perth in 1839. Specific name, from the Greek *xanthos* 'yellow', refers to the colour of the flowers.

∧ *A jewel beetle (Cisseis sp.) (x 3).*

< *Pod and seed.*

Large dome-shaped shrub of 2-4 m; often much broader than tall. Branchlets white or greenish-white.

Phyllodes fresh bluish-green, 6-11 cm long and 1-2 cm wide, with 2 pale longitudinal veins and pale margins.

Flowers in spring or late winter. Flower heads usually in groups of 6-9, but sometimes up to 15.

Swamp cypress

At the first sight of swamp cypress, many West Australians would believe this conifer to be an introduced plant. In shape and colouring, it is similar to cultivated conifers such as the pencil pine. Like other cypresses, it has tiny, scale-like leaves, which completely cover the stem.

There are only three species in the genus *Actinostrobus*, and all are confined to south-western Australia.

∧ *Brown honeyeater.*

Growth habit

Although swamp cypress is woody and grows to 4 m, it is better described as a shrub than as a tree, since it branches at or near the ground, and carries its foliage almost to the ground.

Associated life

Neither swamp cypress nor Rottnest cypress (p. 84) appears to support many insects, but they are nonetheless of value to other animals. The

brown honeyeater and other small birds shelter and nest in the dense foliage and network of stiff branchlets. Carnaby's black-cockatoo eats the seeds.

Few insects apart from booklice are found in the foliage. Dead sections of the shrub appear to be caused by the wood-boring larvae of beetles or moths; a sign of their activities is sawdust at the base of the dead branches. An inspection of older dead branches where the bark has been shed reveals small emergence holes and larger tunnelling marks, suggesting the presence of at least two species of borer.

Ecological notes

A characteristic of many woody fruits is that drying causes them to open and release their seeds. This is true of the cones of swamp cypress, as one can witness by picking a cone and leaving it in a dry place for a few days. Seeds are released from cones on the plant if the branch, or the whole plant, dies. In a bushfire, swamp cypress is killed, and a great many seeds are released all at once.

The subsequent regeneration can be prolific, as was observed when an isolated specimen on Jeegarnyeejip Island, in the Murray Delta, was killed by fire in the mid 1970s. The following winter there were about 800 seedlings per square metre within a couple of metres of the original specimen, and about 150 per square metre 10 metres away. Although only a few of them survived the intense competition between them, four years later there were still about 10 per square metre within two metres and about three per square metre 10 metres away. At that stage, they were about half a metre tall and beginning to set seed.

∧ *Seeds (enlarged).*

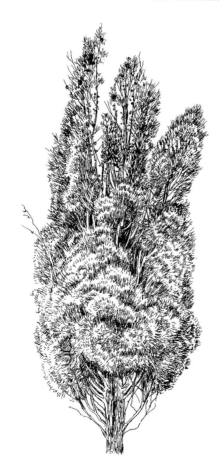

Occurrence and distribution

Swamp cypress ranges from Wongan Hills to Tambellup, and east to Meckering and Ravensthorpe. In the Perth area, it is found on swampy clay–based soils on the eastern side of the coastal plain; for example, in Kenwick and north of Bullsbrook. At Mt Henry, most unusually, it occurs on the lower slopes of a limestone hill. One or two specimens are also found near by, at Salter Point.

Collection and naming

Collected from the Perth and Wellington areas by Johann August Ludwig Preiss, who came to Fremantle in 1838 and remained in Western Australia until early 1842, collecting more than 2,000 plant species. Specific name, from the Latin *pyramis* 'pyramid', refers to the shape of the shrub.

≪ *Female inflorescences.*

< *Male inflorescences.*

∧ *Cones.*

Shrub to 4 m, characteristically a cypress. Narrowly flame-shaped.

Foliage dense, dark green; leaves tiny and scale-like.

Cones egg-shaped, 1½–3 cm long, with 6 valves of equal value.

Distinguished from Rottnest cypress (p. 84) by its occurrence in swamps on the eastern side of the coastal plain, its narrow shape and its smaller cones with equal valves.

Woollybush

Adenanthos
cygnorum

Woollybush is easily recognised by its grey-green or grey-blue colour, round shape and woolly appearance. From a distance, the closely packed, overlapping leaves look like woolly clothing, and, at closer range, the cover of hairs on the stems is like wool.

Woollybush does not have conspicuous flowers, which is unusual for a member of the banksia family (Proteaceae, see pp. 15-17). Unlike the banksias, on which hundreds of flowers are grouped together in brightly coloured spikes, woollybush carries single flowers. Moreover, they are quite dull, and hidden among the dense foliage.

The genus *Adenanthos* is largely confined to southern Western Australia, where 30 of the 32 species occur.

Occurrence

Woollybush is almost entirely restricted in the Perth area to the grey Bassendean sands, towards the eastern side of the coastal plain. Here woollybush is abundant, particularly along road verges. Like the stinkwoods and some of the wattles, woollybush seedlings readily establish themselves on exposed sites. In such open places, woollybush grows as a broad, globular shrub, usually less than 3 m.

In undisturbed conditions, woollybush is a common undershrub of the banksia woodlands of the Bassendean soils. In this environment it grows taller, up to 4 m or more, and is less spreading.

Ecological notes

Like some wattles, woollybush has nectaries. They are located on the tips of many of its leaves, and attract useful insects such as ants and wasps. The female wasp locates moth larvae in tunnels in the branches, inserts its ovipositor into a larva and lays its eggs, and the wasp larvae eat out the moth larva.

Most of the 17 known ant species attracted to the nectaries remove the fruits, which collect in the cups of the leaves along the stems. They take them to their nests, up to 8 m away, and store them to eat the flesh. The seeds germinate if disturbance of the soil brings them to the surface.

This direct transportation of seeds from the shrub to below the ground is a great help to woollybush. The few seeds that fall to the ground are liable to be eaten by seed-eating birds or rodents.

∧ *Ant collecting fruit from cup of leaves.*

Other associated life

The flowers are copious producers of nectar, and attract the western spinebill and the singing, brown, tawny-crowned and New Holland honeyeaters. Honeyeaters and other small birds use the dense bushes for cover or nesting.

Nowadays in the Metropolitan Region, the introduced laughing dove would be the main bird to eat woollybush's seeds. They would formerly have been eaten by native bronzewing pigeons, parrots and quails, as well as by native rodents.

Forms of woollybush

The common form of woollybush grows on sandy soils north to Kalbarri and inland to near Kulin. There is also a prostrate form (subspecies *chamaephyton*), which grows mostly on lateritic soils; in the Metropolitan Region it occurs at Mundaring and Chidlow, and outside the region at Muchea and Collie.

Collection and naming

Collected near Perth by J.A.L. Preiss in 1839 and by James Drummond in the mid 1800s. Specific name, from the Latin *cygnus* 'swan', refers to the Swan River.

 ≪ *Leaf without nectaries.*

 < *Leaf with nectaries.*

 < *Bud.*

Distinctive features

Shrub, usually 1½-4 m tall, often globular in shape, and grey-green in colour. Densely clothed in overlapping leaves that divide into several linear segments. Branches, stems and leaves hairy.

Flowers solitary or in small groups at the ends of the branchlets, produced over much of the year.

Peppermint, wonnil

Agonis flexuosa

Most Perth people know peppermint as a street tree, often pruned to resemble a large mop.

It occurs naturally in parts of Swanbourne and City Beach, and along the Swan Estuary downstream from Freshwater Bay. The suburb of Peppermint Grove is named after this tree, and some of the original peppermints still survive in Manners Hill Park, at the southern end of The Esplanade. These picturesque old trees are in varying stages of decay. Many have impressively thick, gnarled trunks (see p. 9).

Peppermint's main distribution is from Mandurah to Bremer Bay. The Perth population is a northern outlier.

Peppermint derives its name from the odour of the leaves when torn or crushed. The genus *Agonis* belongs to the myrtle family, whose members all have oil glands in their leaves. All four species in the genus are confined to near-coastal areas of south-western Australia.

Associated life

Mature and old trees provide hollows used by bird species (such as pardalotes and ringneck parrots) and possums for nesting. Until the early 1940s, brushtail possums could be regularly seen in some of the large peppermints in Peppermint Grove. They still remain but now live in the roofs of houses.

∧ *Brushtail possum.*

South of Perth, particularly round Busselton, peppermint is the chief habitat of a threatened species of possum, the western ringtail.

Two species of jewel beetle burrow into the stems of peppermint as larvae, and emerge to feed in the flowers. One of these — Roe's jewel beetle — was discovered before 1836, and was one of the first insects to be described in Western Australia. The larvae of the large and beautifully coloured green ghost moth tunnel in peppermint's stems. They pupate in the ground, sticking out of which the pupae may be seen — or the empty pupal cases, after the adult moths emerge, in February to May. The nymphs of a cicada, the red bandit, live in the ground under peppermint trees, and the adults drink sap from branches in the tree's canopy.

Also associated with peppermint is the aphid *Anomalaphis comperei*, one of the very few native Australian aphids, and the first to be found in Western Australia.

Often growing out of old peppermint trees are ghost fungi, which are luminous.

Appearance

Unlopped specimens of peppermint have a lovely form, with heavy, spreading branches and weeping foliage. The broad canopy is pleasantly shady, and the trunks become thick and gnarled with age. Some fine natural specimens are found at Blackwell Reach and west of Lake Claremont.

Although it normally grows as a tree, peppermint may sprout from its rootstock after a hot fire, and produce a many-stemmed shrub. It is seen in this form in City Beach.

Collection and naming

Collected from the west coast of Australia. The specific name *flexuosa* means 'full of bends', and refers to the zig-zag course of the stems, which change direction at each leaf-node.

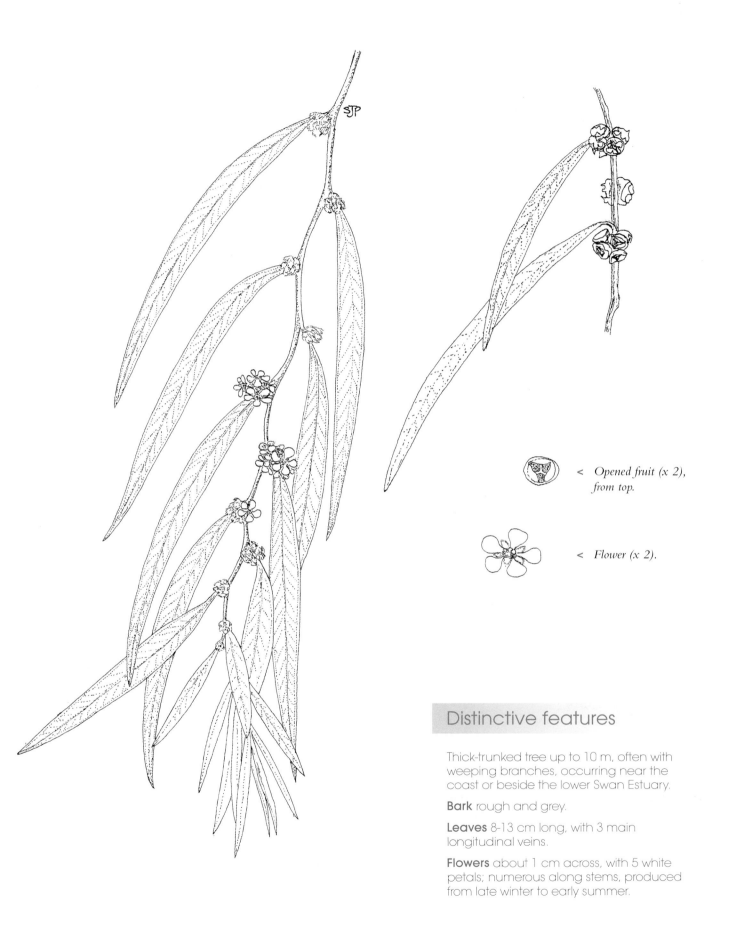

< *Opened fruit (x 2), from top.*

< *Flower (x 2).*

Distinctive features

Thick-trunked tree up to 10 m, often with weeping branches, occurring near the coast or beside the lower Swan Estuary.

Bark rough and grey.

Leaves 8-13 cm long, with 3 main longitudinal veins.

Flowers about 1 cm across, with 5 white petals; numerous along stems, produced from late winter to early summer.

Common sheoak, condil

Allocasuarina fraseriana

∧ *Tube of sap-sucking bug projecting from stem (x 2).*

Visitors to Kings Park during late winter or early spring will notice the rich brown hue taken on by male common sheoaks at this time. The tiny but numerous male flowers produce this colour. Their extra weight often causes the foliage to droop.

This species is the most widespread sheoak of the lower South-West. In the Metropolitan Region, it occurs in almost all the dryland soil-types. In the Darling Range, it is a common understorey tree of up to 15 m. On the coastal plain it is a slightly smaller tree, and grows on most of the better-drained soils, often in association with banksias. On the plain north of Perth it is less abundant and soon peters out, unlike the more drought-resistant banksias.

Beauty

Common sheoak is a modest tree: it does not boast showy features such as large leaves, bright flowers or a strongly patterned bark. But it does have a beautiful form, often with a graceful splitting structure (see p. 2), and an abundance of detail in its branches and twigs. And its foliage has a lovely soft effect.

It has thicker branches than rock sheoak or salt sheoak, and larger concentrations of foliage. It is also less regular in form: each tree has a pronounced individual character.

Common sheoak is less resistant to salt in the air than salt sheoak or dune sheoak. Where it grows within a few kilometres of the coast, the effect of sea winds adds further variety to its form. A lean away from the south-west and a more open habit often result, with the foliage concentrated into horizontal layers (see p. 5). Dead twigs killed by the salt are neatly patterned in straight and curving segments, providing an elegant decoration.

Associated life

Common sheoak harbours a great variety of insects, including three species of jewel beetle. Long-horned beetles burrow into the larger stems. Some of the associated insects are well concealed. A weevil species, for example, that eats the foliage is shaped and coloured to match the 'needles' (cladodes), as are the looper caterpillars of a moth.

A species of sap-sucking bug lives in the twigs, invisible except for its protruding tube (illustrated), which is fine, white and hair-like. This tube exudes a honey-dew, which collects on the branchlets, and falls to the ground to form damp, sticky areas. Ants and wasps eat this honey-dew, both in the tree and on the ground. The twig-mound ant, for example, uses this source of food when few banksias are in flower (see p. 68). A black smut-fungus often develops on the honey-dew, and is eaten by small native cockroaches. These, along with crickets, also eat the needles.

∧ *Nut (x 2).*

∧ *Stem with scale-leaves (x 8).*

On some specimens of common sheoak, distorted hanging branches, called 'witches' brooms', are found. These malformations are thought to be a response to the sap-sucking bugs mentioned above.

Ringneck parrots eat the seeds, which they pluck from the cones.

Common sheoak provides good shade, used by butterflies such as the marbled xenica and western brown for shelter on hot days.

Human uses

The timber was used by early European settlers for roof shingles. Later it was in high demand for the construction of kegs and casks. With its broad rays, the timber is prized for its beauty, and today is used for decorative turning or carving. It is not readily available for commercial use.

As a tree, however, common sheoak is poorly appreciated and rarely cultivated. It is unpopular with residents as a street tree because its shed cladodes get into vents in cars and stick to clothing. It should, however, be considered for planting in parks and median strips. Not only does it have a beautiful form but is also a typical tree of Perth's sandy soils, a reminder of Perth's original vegetation.

Ecological notes

Common sheoak is not as resistant to fire as candle banksia or firewood banksia, two species with which it usually associates. Mature specimens usually survive fire, but often die back to a large degree, resprouting from near the base.

In Kings Park, common sheoak has increased in numbers since the early part of last century, replacing candle banksia and firewood banksia, which have been gradually dying out. It was badly affected, however, by the droughts in 2006 and 2007, when many specimens died or declined.

Collection and naming

Collected by J.A.L. Preiss in 1840 at Perth and Wuljenup. Specific name after the botanist Charles Fraser.

∧ *Male flower-spikes (x ⅔).*

∨ *Female flower-spike.*

Distinctive features

Tree 8-15 m tall. Widespread on the coastal plain and in the jarrah forest.

Bark grey-brown, flaky; paler brown beneath.

Nodes on branchlets ½-1½ cm apart; 6-8 scale-leaves at each node.

Cones globular or egg-shaped, 1½-3½ cm x 1½-3 cm, reddish-brown in colour, becoming grey with age.

Nuts ('seeds') 8-11 mm long; body dark brown with white flecks; wing transparent, colourless.

∧ *Cones (x ⅔).*

Rock sheoak, sighing sheoak

∧ *The jewel beetle* Cisseis stigmata.

Listen to the wind in the foliage of rock sheoak, and you will hear the sound that gives rise to the name sighing sheoak. It is usually, however, called 'rock sheoak', because it often grows near granite rocks.

It is chiefly a tree of the Wheatbelt, extending west to the edge of the jarrah forest. It also occurs, however, in a few places in the Darling Scarp; for example, on a high rocky hill along the road into Serpentine National Park.

Associated life

As with common sheoak, abundant insect life uses this tree. The 'needles' (cladodes) are an important food for insects, including at least seven species of jewel beetle. Three live entirely on rock sheoak; their larvae burrow into the stems. The cladodes are also a favoured food for locusts, which when present in plagues often strip the trees bare. Birds such as the willie wagtail and the black-faced cuckoo-shrike nest in this tree, and ringneck parrots eat the seeds.

Various spider-orchids often grow in abundance in the litter that accumulates under the stands of trees.

Appearance

Rock sheoak is a delicate, graceful tree of 6-9 m. Its foliage is light and dispersed, revealing most of the tree's slender twigs and (in the case of females) cones. In winter and spring, flowering males have a richly coloured foliage, which becomes more opaque.

Young trees split repeatedly into slender branches, fanning out to give a rounded outline. They sometimes divide right at ground level, but usually have a bole of some metres. The tree's character changes with age. Older specimens lose many of their branches, becoming much more open. They have a simpler, bolder pattern, accentuated by their thicker trunk and branches. The bark (somewhat tessellated in young trees) becomes coarse and shaggy.

Ecological notes

Unlike common sheoak, rock sheoak is killed by fire. It is a good coloniser, and has grown up in many places along roadsides in the western Wheatbelt. Along back roads it is especially abundant, often forming thickets that inhibit the growth of weeds.

Collection and naming

Collected by J.A.L. Preiss in 1840 on Mt Brown, near York. Specific name after the Austrian traveller and naturalist Baron von Huegel.

< *Stem with scale-leaves (x 6).*

< *Nut (x 2).*

v *Stem with cone and female flower-spikes (x ⅔).*

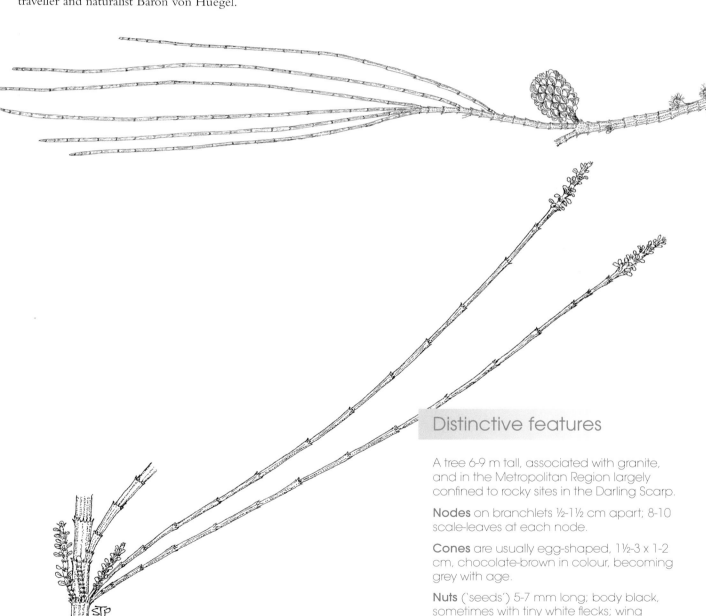

∧ *Male flower-spikes.*

Distinctive features

A tree 6-9 m tall, associated with granite, and in the Metropolitan Region largely confined to rocky sites in the Darling Scarp.

Nodes on branchlets ½-1½ cm apart; 8-10 scale-leaves at each node.

Cones are usually egg-shaped, 1½-3 x 1-2 cm, chocolate-brown in colour, becoming grey with age.

Nuts ('seeds') 5-7 mm long; body black, sometimes with tiny white flecks; wing transparent, and usually pale pink to yellow.

Dune sheoak

Allocasuarina lehmanniana

Like many sheoaks, dune sheoak tolerates harsh conditions. The soil it grows in is dry, limy and infertile, and the air salty. It prefers the tops and the sunny, northern slopes of coastal dunes, although it does not grow as close to the ocean as Rottnest cypress, moonah or the coastal wattles.

Distribution

Dune sheoak has a wide distribution, extending from Shark Bay to Israelite Bay, east of Esperance, but avoiding the extreme south-west corner. It occurs mostly near the coast but further inland in a few places, notably in the Albany district.

Perth localities

An extensive stand of dune sheoak survives in Trigg Bushland, on the dune slopes south of Karrinyup Road, east of Marmion Avenue; and a few specimens may be found in Bold Park. Further north, dune sheoak used to be common in dunes now occupied by the western part of Joondalup Golf Course, Connolly.

Since dune sheoak is killed by fire, repeated fires may have eliminated it or reduced its occurrence in some bushlands. Occasional specimens seen in some areas may be remnants of larger populations.

Appearance

Dune sheoak is a neat, upright shrub, 3–5 m tall, with side-branches that curve upwards. Like other coastal species (such as summer-scented wattle) it usually grows in mutually protecting thickets.

The male and female flowers are usually borne on separate plants but, as in most species of sheoak, are sometimes seen on the same plant. One such individual is illustrated, with both male flower-spikes and a cone (from a fertilised female flower-spike).

Associated life

Stands of dune sheoak provide valuable cover and food for insectivorous birds in Perth's coastal suburbs. In Trigg Bushland, birds using dune sheoak for cover include the rufous whistler, silvereye, white-browed scrubwren, variegated fairy-wren and white-winged fairy-wren. The

∧ *Nut (x 2).*

last two species are now uncommon in Perth. The inland thornbill, western gerygone, grey fantail and black-faced cuckoo-shrike feed on insects in the sheoak stands. Further bird species that use dune sheoak include generalised feeders common in Perth, such as the brown honeyeater, singing honeyeater and red wattlebird.

Potential for cultivation

Dune sheoak's dense foliage and its adaptation to coastal conditions make it a useful windbreak in coastal areas. It is surprising that dune sheoak is not grown nearly as much as Rottnest cypress, another species of the coastal dunes (see p. 84). Like the cypress, dune sheoak is readily grown from seed. Moreover, for planting where space is limited, dune sheoak has the advantage of small size, and a compact, upright habit.

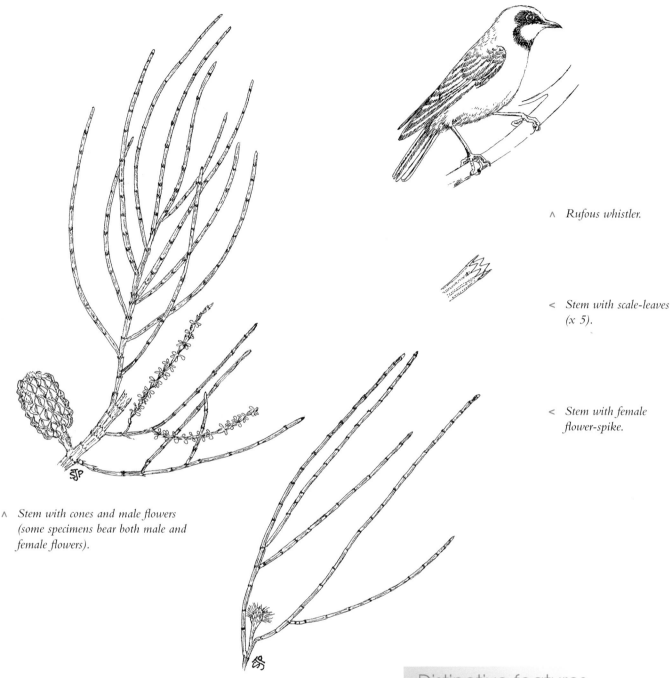

∧ *Rufous whistler.*

< *Stem with scale-leaves (x 5).*

< *Stem with female flower-spike.*

∧ *Stem with cones and male flowers (some specimens bear both male and female flowers).*

Collection and naming

Collected by J.A.L. Preiss in 1840 at Quangen, near Wongamine, east of Toodyay. Specific name after J.G.C. Lehmann, a professor of botany at Hamburg, and an editor of *Plantae Preissianae*, a major early work on the flora of Western Australia.

Distinctive features

Compact shrub up to 5 m growing in the coastal dunes.

Nodes on branchlets 3-8 mm apart; 6-8 scale-leaves at each node.

Cones usually cylindrical, 1½-3 x 1-1½ cm, grey in colour.

Nuts ('seeds') 4-7 mm long; body dark brown; wing transparent, slightly yellow-brown.

Candle banksia, biara

Banksia attenuata

Candle banksia produces slender, bright yellow flower-spikes for nearly half the year: from mid spring to early autumn. In spring and early summer the new, pinkish-grey shoots provide additional colour.

This and firewood banksia are the two commonest tree-banksias on the well drained sandy soils of the coastal plain.

Associated life

Birdlife is most plentiful in late spring and early summer, when candle banksia is in full bloom. Honeyeaters drink the flower-spikes' nectar, and they and other birds such as robins, willie wagtails and black-faced cuckoo-shrikes pluck insects off the spikes. Bee-eaters, summer migrants to Perth, will focus on a single candle banksia, catching feral honeybees in the air as they approach or leave the tree. The birds often return to a favourite perch, where they remove the stings by banging them on the branch. As many as 150 stings have been found on a single perch. Another bird to benefit greatly from candle banksia is Carnaby's black-cockatoo, which eats both the seeds and weevil larvae in the cones.

In Bold Park the rough bark of candle banksia provides habitat for the fence skink.

Moth larvae burrow into the axis of candle banksia's flower-spike, and the larvae of both moths and weevils burrow into the cones to eat the seeds.

Ecological notes

Candle banksia's bark resists fire. Mature trees are rarely killed by fire, and resprout strongly near the ends of the branches afterwards. Young saplings are often burnt to the ground but resprout from their rootstock.

Common name

This banksia is also known as 'coast banksia' or 'slender banksia'. 'Coast banksia' is inappropriate, since the species has a wide distribution that extends well inland, into the Wheatbelt. 'Slender banksia' refers only to the flower-spikes. The tree itself is spreading, and the knobbly branches of mature trees are anything but slender. The name 'candle banksia' refers to the slender yellow flower-spikes.

Human uses

The Aboriginal people sucked the nectar from the flower-spikes. They also made a sweet drink by lining a hole in the ground with paperbark, placing the spikes in the hole with some water, and leaving them to soak.

Candle banksia is the most useful of the Perth banksias to beekeepers, although the honey is not of high quality.

∧ *New Holland honeyeater.*

Distribution

Candle banksia has a wide range in south-western Australia, from the Murchison River to Bremer Bay.

Collection and naming

Collected by Robert Brown in 1801 or 1802 at King George Sound, Albany. Brown was the naturalist aboard the *Investigator*, in which Matthew Flinders explored the Australian coast. The ship arrived in King George Sound in December 1801, and for the next three and a half years Brown did extensive botanical work, collecting about 3,400 specimens. Specific name, from the Latin *attenuatus* 'narrowed', refers to the leaves, which narrow towards the base.

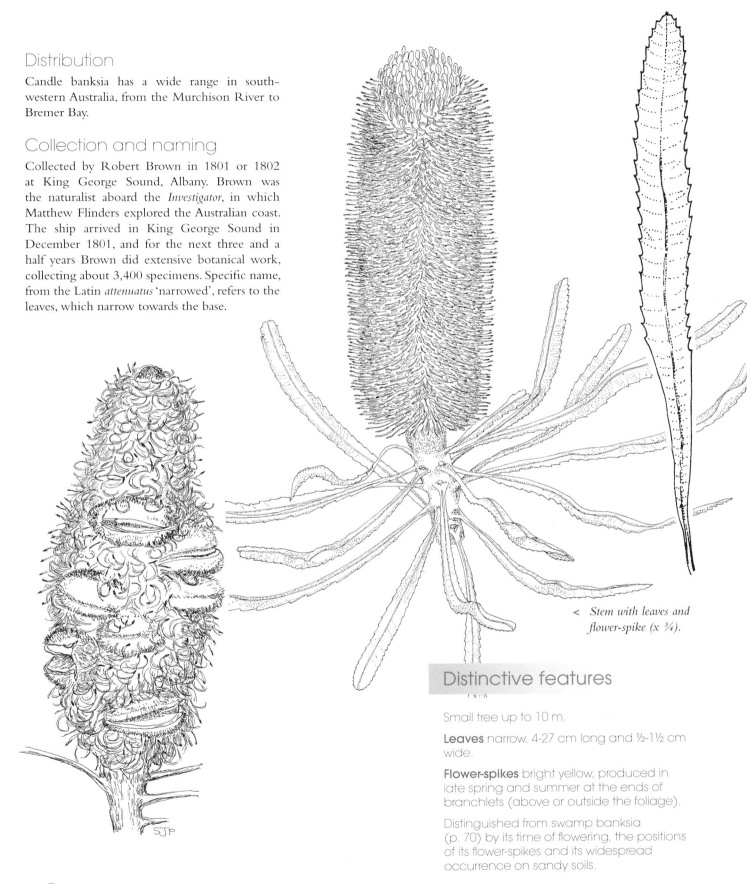

< *Stem with leaves and flower-spike (x ¾).*

∧ *Cone.*

Distinctive features

Small tree up to 10 m.

Leaves narrow, 4-27 cm long and ½-1½ cm wide.

Flower-spikes bright yellow, produced in late spring and summer at the ends of branchlets (above or outside the foliage).

Distinguished from swamp banksia (p. 70) by its time of flowering, the positions of its flower-spikes and its widespread occurrence on sandy soils.

Bull banksia, mangite

Banksia grandis

∧   *Seeds (x ⅔).*

Unlike Perth's other tree-banksias, bull banksia is most abundant in the jarrah forest. It is the only large banksia typical of the lateritic country of the Darling Plateau.

It also grows in nearly all soils on the coastal plain, but is much less common there. It favours heavily timbered country, such as the tuart forests of the Cottesloe soils and the marri forests of the Guildford soils.

Appearance

Bull banksia holds its large, bold leaves in clumps. In the forest, it is sparse and open, but specimens in full sun are spreading and densely foliaged. The trees themselves are bold, with few branches. Thick stems are needed to support the large leaves, and the trees lack fine detail.

Ecological notes

Bull banksia can live for 100 to 150 years. Mature specimens are fairly resistant to fire but can be killed if the fire is intense. Saplings can resprout from an underground rootstock.

Bull banksia protects its flowers and seeds from attack by insects. The flower-spike's woody axis is thick, and thus well able to withstand damage by burrowing moth larvae. The seed follicles barely protrude from the cone and so do not advertise their presence. They remain very small for a year or so, then develop rapidly and release the seed, minimising their availability to burrowing insects. The seeds are released in autumn and are carried, usually 5-10 m, by the wind.

Bull banksia thrives in the jarrah forest, where the seedlings germinate readily in the ground litter and have a high rate of survival. It grows in abundance even in heavily shaded virgin forest. Growth, however, is very slow in the forest environment. After 15 or 20 years, bull banksia will have grown only 1-1½ m. It grows much faster in the open.

Bull banksia succumbs very quickly to the introduced root-rot water-mould *Phytophthora cinnamomi*. The leaves turn yellow and the plant dies.

Associated life

Bull banksia is an important source of nectar in the jarrah forest. It flowers in spring and early summer, when insects are abundant. Other animals to benefit are the honey possum, and birds such as honeyeaters, wattlebirds and the silvereye.

The seeds are eaten by Carnaby's black–cockatoo, the red-capped parrot and moth larvae. Other moth larvae feed in the flower-spikes.

Human uses

The Aboriginal people used to suck the flower-spikes for their nectar. The nectar and pollen are now useful to beekeepers, particularly in bridging the gap between the flowering of parrotbush and jarrah.

∧ *Honey possum.*

Distribution

Bull banksia extends north to Jurien, inland to Katanning, and down to the south coast, where it grows as a shrub.

Collection and naming

Collected from a plant cultivated in Europe, probably raised from seed collected by Archibald Menzies in 1791 at King George Sound. Specific name, from the Latin *grandis* 'great', refers to the large leaves.

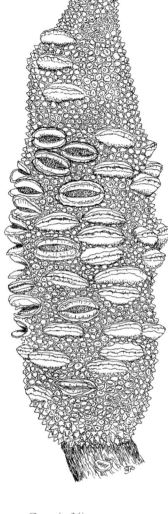

∧ *Cone (x ²/₃).*

< *Leaf (x ²/₃).*

Distinctive features

A tree up to 10 m.

Bark rough.

Leaves large and broad (10-45 x 3-11 cm), deeply divided into triangular segments.

Flower-spikes pale yellow, produced from mid spring to mid summer.

Cones cylindrical, large and broad, 10-40 x 7-9 cm.

Holly-leaf banksia

Banksia ilicifolia

This large banksia is unlike Perth's other large banksias, having its flowers arranged in heads, rather than long spikes; and with short, broad leaves, rather than long and usually slender. In both these respects holly-leaf banksia is rather like parrotbush.

Ecological notes

The flowers of holly-leaf banksia go through three colour-phases. They are initially yellow, then turn pink, then finally red. This enhances pollination. Although the pink and red flowers help to attract honey-eating birds (the main pollinators) from a distance, only the yellow flowers contain substantial amounts of nectar and pollen, and both insects and birds feed almost exclusively at these. These are also the flowers whose stigmas are receptive to pollination. Thus, by letting animals know which flowers to visit in order to feed without wasting time, the banksia also ensures that it is pollinated more efficiently.

It is important that the pollination of holly-leaf banksia should be efficient, for in several ways this species is at a disadvantage compared with the other Perth banksias with which it associates. It flowers throughout the year, and has to compete with other banksias that flower for a shorter time and therefore have more flowers out at once. Moreover, it has comparatively small clusters of flowers, and is one of the least abundant species, occurring as scattered individuals or in small groups.

The seeds of holly-leaf banksia develop more rapidly than those of many other banksias, taking less than three months. This is probably why the seeds are rarely destroyed by insects: there is apparently insufficient time for the insects to develop.

Holly-leaf banksia usually survives fire, unless it is intense. Like other Perth banksias, it produces its new leaves chiefly in summer.

Associated life

The western spinebill, the red and little wattlebirds and the brown and New Holland honeyeaters feed at the flowers. So do native bees, ants and beetles.

Because it flowers throughout the year, holly-leaf banksia is one of the most important sources of food for the twig-mound ant. The ants often build their distinctive nests near the bases of these trees. Different specimens of holly-leaf banksia have their flowering peaks at different times. When the nectar supply of one begins to dry up, the ant colony using that tree puts out scout ants to locate another tree with more nectar. When one is located, the colony builds a new mound near it.

Holly-leaf banksia's foliage supports more insect species than that of candle banksia or firewood banksia.

The larva of a moth burrows into the woody axis of the flower head. A different moth larva burrows into the stems.

Growth habit

Holly-leaf banksia is a similar size to Perth's other tree-banksias, growing to about 10 m. It is typically erect, its branches and branchlets tending upwards. The young stems produce a spiky outline.

Occurrence and distribution

Holly-leaf banksia extends from Mt Lesueur to the Cordinup River, east of Albany. It occurs mostly within 50 km of the coast, with scattered occurrences further inland.

∧ *Nest of twig-mound ant.*

In the Metropolitan Region, holly-leaf banksia seems to be confined to the coastal plain. It occurs widely in sandy soils, showing preference for low-lying areas.

Collection and naming

Collected by Robert Brown in 1801 or 1802 at King George Sound. Specific name, from the Latin *ilex* 'holly' and *folium* 'leaf', refers to the resemblance of its leaves to those of the European holly tree.

Distinctive features

Erect small tree with branches tending upwards.

Flowers grouped in a dome-shaped head, rather than a cylindrical spike. The cream and pink flowers become dull red with age. They are produced throughout the year, in greatest abundance between late winter and early summer.

Leaves 3-9 cm long, roughly elliptical in shape, usually having a slightly toothed edge, with several short spines.

Distinguished from parrotbush (p. 76) by its different habitat, larger size, less prickly leaves, the colour of its old flowers, and the woody base to its fruits.

Swamp banksia

Banksia littoralis

Wetlands, bordering rivers or lakes, or comprising just winter-wet depressions, often have more luxuriant vegetation than the surrounding country. It is therefore not surprising that swamp banksia, a wetland species, should have denser and brighter foliage than other Perth banksias. The leaves have green upper sides but the undersides are pure white. As gusts of wind pass through a swamp banksia its leaves will often turn over, and its foliage will appear to change colour from green to white.

The densely foliaged saplings have a shrubby appearance. They develop into widely spreading small trees with thick branches. Their trunks become thicker than those of the other Perth banksias, and they may possibly be longer-lived.

Associated life

Beetles from at least eight different families are associated with swamp banksia. The larva of the jewel beetle *Cyria vittigera* (illustrated) burrows into the trunk, and the adult feeds on the leaves. Weevil larvae enter the cones and eat the seeds.

Various moth larvae use the leaves, flower-spikes, cones or stems. The colourful larva of the banksia moth feeds on the leaves of this and other banksias. Much smaller moths cause galls on swamp banksia's leaf-buds.

Brown swellings on the midribs of leaves are caused by the larvae of a gall-wasp.

Swamp banksia flowers in winter, when it is an important source of nectar for honey-eating birds.

Occurrence and distribution

Swamp banksia is associated with most wetlands, both on the coastal plain and in the Darling Range. Around major wetlands there are often several distinct zones of vegetation. Swamp banksia often occurs in one of the middle zones.

It is widely distributed in the forested areas of the South-West. Along major rivers of the lower South-West, it is replaced by a close relative, the lovely river banksia (*Banksia seminuda*), a more upright tree that is one of Australia's largest banksias.

Cultivation

Swamp banksia is often planted in projects to restore degraded wetlands, and should be considered for planting elsewhere where there is a high water-table. It grows better in lawns than do most banksias, but fertiliser and excessive watering should be avoided.

Collection and naming

Collected by Robert Brown in 1801 or 1802. Specific name from the Latin *littoralis* 'of the seashore', as Brown discovered it growing near the shores of King George Sound.

∧ *The jewel beetle* Cyria vittigera.

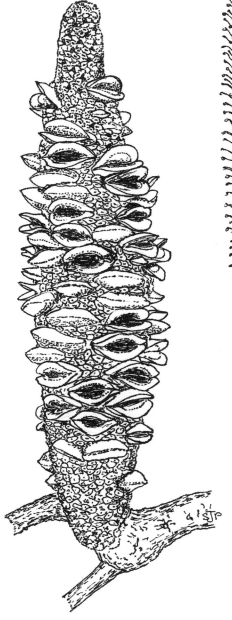

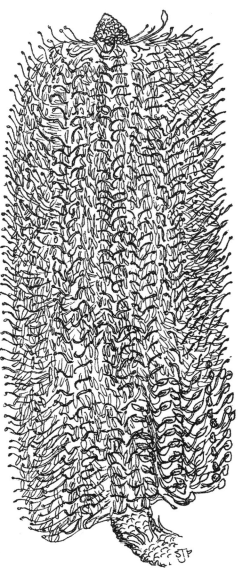

Distinctive features

A stout, spreading tree up to 10 m tall, growing in or by wetlands.

Leaves very narrow, 10-23 cm long and ½-1 cm wide; dark green above, white below.

Flower-spikes yellow, produced in autumn and winter and held within the foliage.

Distinguished from candle banksia (p. 64) by its winter flowering and its occurrence only on swampy ground.

Firewood banksia

Banksia menziesii

The richly coloured flower-spikes of this banksia change from silver-grey to rich pink to orange and pink as they develop. These colours contrast beautifully with the grey-green leaves.

Other characteristics of the larger banksias are clearly evident. Its many cones have prominent 'beaks', the leaves are toothed, the bark lumpy and the trees crooked and gnarled. It is surprising that a tree with so much character is seldom cultivated and has no more descriptive common name than 'firewood banksia'.

Associated life

Honey-eating birds such as the western spinebill, the red and little wattlebirds, and the singing, brown and New Holland honeyeaters drink the nectar of firewood banksia during its long period of flowering.

The cones are used by the burrowing larvae of two species of weevil, and the larva of a moth burrows in the flower-spikes. Another moth larva eats the tissue between a leaf's surfaces, producing scribble-marks.

Red patches on the growing leaves develop into brown pouch-like blisters, which can often be seen on some of the leaves. They are caused by a rust-fungus, whereas similar blisters on saw-tooth banksia are caused by a scale insect.

In Bold Park, over four years, more than 20 species of macrofungi have been observed fruiting on an individual log of firewood banksia. Different fungi appear in a succession as the log ages.

Association with candle banksia

Firewood banksia and candle banksia, the two commonest large banksias on Perth's coastal plain, are nearly always found together. One of the two is almost always in flower. Firewood banksia flowers over one half of the year (autumn to early spring) and candle banksia over the other. This timing possibly evolved so that the two species would not compete for pollinators.

Some animals depend on a supply of nectar the whole year round, and these two banksias almost ensure this. There are brief periods in autumn and spring (when one species is just starting to flower and the other is finishing) when only occasional flowers are produced — but at these times other plant species are providing flowers (saw-tooth banksia in autumn, and bull banksia, holly-leaf banksia and many shrub species in spring).

Distribution

Firewood banksia and candle banksia also have similar distributions north of Perth, extending to the Murchison River and east into pockets of sandy soils in the northern Wheatbelt. South of Perth, however, firewood banksia does not have the wide range of candle banksia, and extends only as far south as Pinjarra.

Collection and naming

Collected by Charles Fraser in 1827 near the Swan River. Fraser was the Superintendent of the Sydney Botanic Gardens. He went with James Stirling to the Swan River before the European settlement of what is now Perth. Specific name after Archibald Menzies, surgeon-naturalist on the *Discovery* expedition (1791-95) under George Vancouver, who discovered King George Sound in 1791.

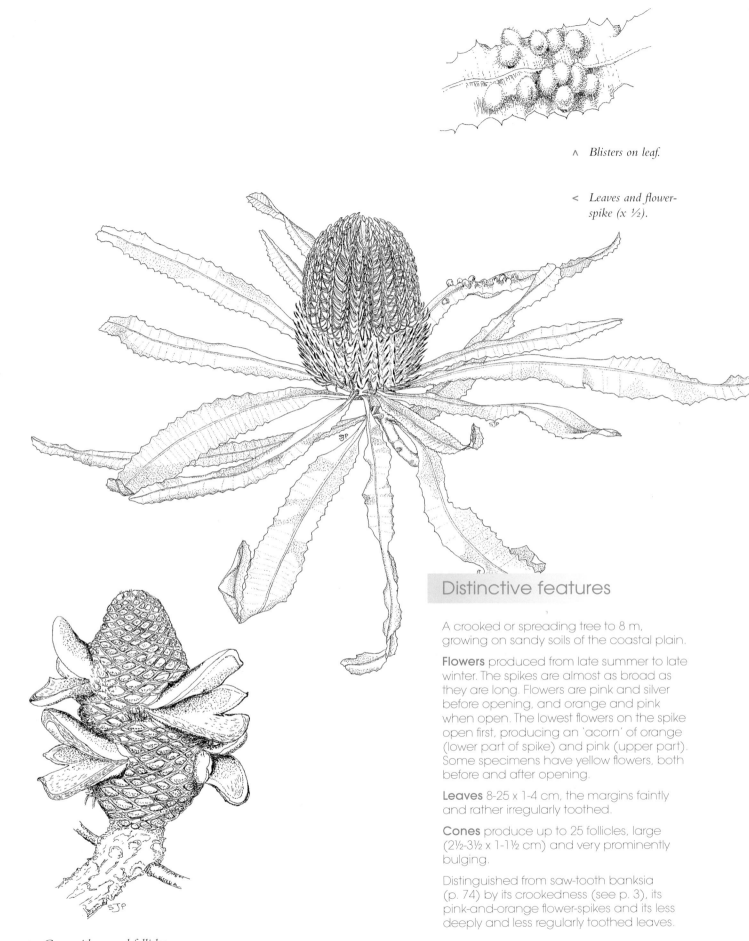

∧ *Blisters on leaf.*

< *Leaves and flower-
   spike (x ½).*

Distinctive features

A crooked or spreading tree to 8 m,
growing on sandy soils of the coastal plain.

Flowers produced from late summer to late
winter. The spikes are almost as broad as
they are long. Flowers are pink and silver
before opening, and orange and pink
when open. The lowest flowers on the spike
open first, producing an 'acorn' of orange
(lower part of spike) and pink (upper part).
Some specimens have yellow flowers, both
before and after opening.

Leaves 8-25 x 1-4 cm, the margins faintly
and rather irregularly toothed.

Cones produce up to 25 follicles, large
(2½-3½ x 1-1½ cm) and very prominently
bulging.

Distinguished from saw-tooth banksia
(p. 74) by its crookedness (see p. 3), its
pink-and-orange flower-spikes and its less
deeply and less regularly toothed leaves.

∧ *Cone with opened follicles.*

Saw-tooth banksia

Banksia prionotes

Of Perth's large banksias, this is perhaps the neatest, both in the outline of its leaves and in the shape of the whole tree.

The regularly saw-toothed leaf of this banksia is reflected not only in its common name, but also in its botanical name: *prionotes* means 'saw-like'. Many other banksias have serrated leaves, but few have such a well defined saw-tooth pattern. Saw-tooth banksia is also called 'orange banksia' or 'acorn banksia', but these names serve less well in distinguishing this species, since they describe equally well the flower-spikes of many other banksias.

The neat shape of saw-tooth banksia results from its habit of forking round its cones, and from the tendency of its branchlets to grow straight or curve smoothly upwards. Thus the tree is compact and erect. Straight or smoothly curving branches often imply rapid growth, and saw-tooth banksia is the fastest-growing of Perth's large banksias.

Associated life

In autumn, when in flower, saw-tooth banksia is a good source of nectar, and is visited by western spinebills and by New Holland, white-cheeked, brown and singing honeyeaters.

Holes seen in the follicles are likely to be made by the larva of a weevil. It burrows from one follicle to another, eating the seeds. It pupates in a follicle, and the adult eats a hole through which it emerges. The larvae are parasitised by a species of ichneumon wasp.

Numerous bits eaten out of the leaves show that the foliage supports many caterpillars or beetles. Small, neat orange blisters on the undersides of the leaves are made by a scale insect (whereas similar blisters on firewood banksia are made by a rust-fungus). Some leaves also show the signs of another scale insect: brown scales the size of pinheads, which put out a white powder.

Grey-brown coral-like growths on some of the smaller woody stems suggest a fungus.

Occurrence and distribution

Like most of Perth's other large banksias, saw-tooth banksia grows in sand, but unlike them shows a strong preference for yellow sand. Hence in the Perth area it is largely confined to the zone where tuart gives way to jarrah. Apart from Point Walter, it occurs only north of the Swan River.

Saw-tooth banksia is fairly widespread north of Perth, extending to Shark Bay, and occurring in scattered spots in the Wheatbelt.

Ecological notes

Saw-tooth banksia is Perth's only tree-banksia that is readily killed by fire. Not surprisingly, therefore, it is the best coloniser: its numerous seedlings establish themselves readily where the land has been disturbed. Hence it is often seen in thick growths along roadsides.

Whereas Perth's other large banksias are dying out in many bushlands, saw-tooth banksia appears to be maintaining a stable population in most; in some it is increasing.

Human uses

Since it grows faster than most other banksias and has an upright habit, saw-tooth banksia has been grown to some degree as a street tree. Like other banksias, however, it is sensitive to fertiliser and watering. It is better suited to median strips, where it should be watered in its first summer but not thereafter.

∧ *Western spinebill.*

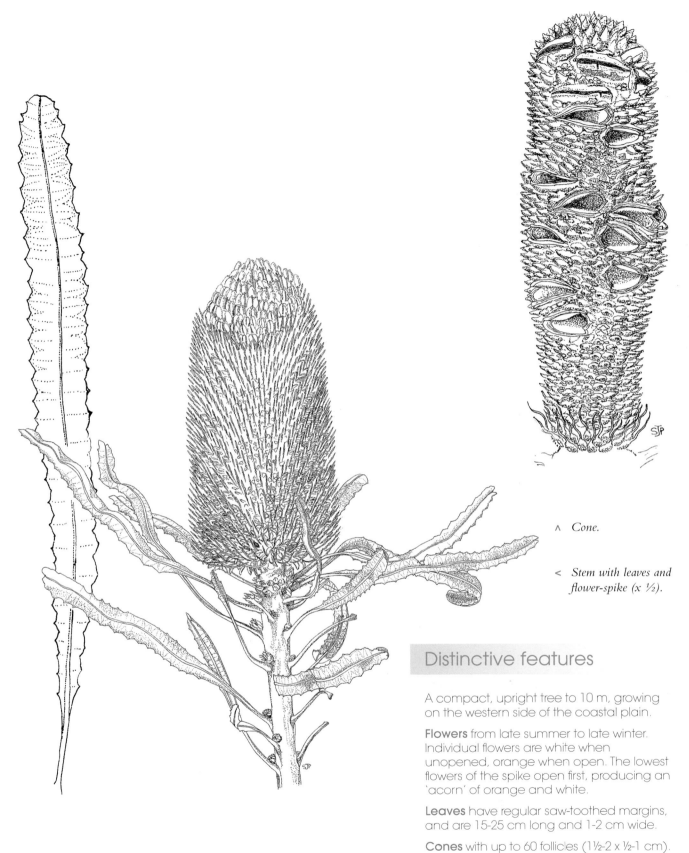

∧ Cone.

< Stem with leaves and
   flower-spike (x ½).

Distinctive features

A compact, upright tree to 10 m, growing on the western side of the coastal plain.

Flowers from late summer to late winter. Individual flowers are white when unopened, orange when open. The lowest flowers of the spike open first, producing an 'acorn' of orange and white.

Leaves have regular saw-toothed margins, and are 15-25 cm long and 1-2 cm wide.

Cones with up to 60 follicles (1½-2 x ½-1 cm).

Distinguished from firewood banksia (p. 72) by its compact habit with upwardly curving branches, its white-and-orange flower-spikes, and its distinctly saw-toothed leaves.

Collection and naming

Collected by James Drummond near the Swan River in the late 1830s. Specific name, from the Greek *prion* 'saw' and *otes* 'like', refers to the leaves.

Parrotbush, boojak

*Banksia sessilis
(formerly
Dryandra sessilis)*

Parrotbush is one of the State's chief honey producers. It provides a good flow of nectar over a long period (May to November) and also has valuable pollen for building up broods of bees.

Associated life

Parrotbush forms dense, prickly thickets that provide important cover and nesting-habitat for wildlife. Singing and brown honeyeaters commonly nest in parrotbush within the city. At Naval Base, quendas (bandicoots) make their nests in the shelter of parrotbush thickets. They pile up plant material and then make a shallow depression under it.

Parrotbush's flowers provide abundant pollen and nectar for insects and honey-eating birds. The seeds are eaten by ringneck parrots and black-cockatoos.

Occurrence and distribution

Parrotbush occurs in two belts in the Metropolitan Region. In the coastal limestone belt, parrotbush favours the ridges, where it often dominates the thick vegetation of these shallow soils. In the Darling Range it occurs on gravelly soils as an undershrub of the jarrah forest. It has a wide range in the South-West, extending north to Kalbarri and east to Bremer Bay.

Geographical forms

Parrotbush is a variable species. Four varieties are recognised, some of which are themselves variable.

In the Perth Metropolitan Region, the coastal and Darling Range forms are recognised as two different varieties. The leaves of the coastal specimens (var. *cygnorum*) are smaller, more fan-shaped and greener than those of the specimens in the Darling Range (var. *sessilis*).

Ecological notes

As its thickets suggest, parrotbush regenerates readily. A prolific flowerer, it produces many seeds. In the Darling Range it is a good coloniser of gravel-pits.

∧ *Mature specimen, coastal form.*

Parrotbush is killed by fire. The seedlings that germinate afterwards develop rapidly. They produce seed when only three or four years old, but only in small quantities; it takes several more years before they produce large quantities of seed. In many bushlands fires are too frequent, killing the plants before they have grown old enough to produce much seed, and therefore reducing parrotbush's abundance. On the coastal plain parrotbush used to occur on limestone ridges and extend some distance into the adjacent tuart or banksia country. It is now largely confined to the ridges.

Beekeepers prefer stands of parrotbush 8-16 years old, when they produce the most flowers. At about 16 years the plants tend to be more susceptible to insects and fungi. Their maximum age is not known but, on sites protected from fire, occasional specimens can be found with surprisingly thick trunks.

Collection and naming

Collected in 1791 from the west coast of Australia by A. Menzies, a naval surgeon who visited Western Australia in 1790-95. The specific name is Latin for 'fit for sitting on' and refers to the flower heads, which are nestled in the leaves.

< *Quenda.*

Individual plant species

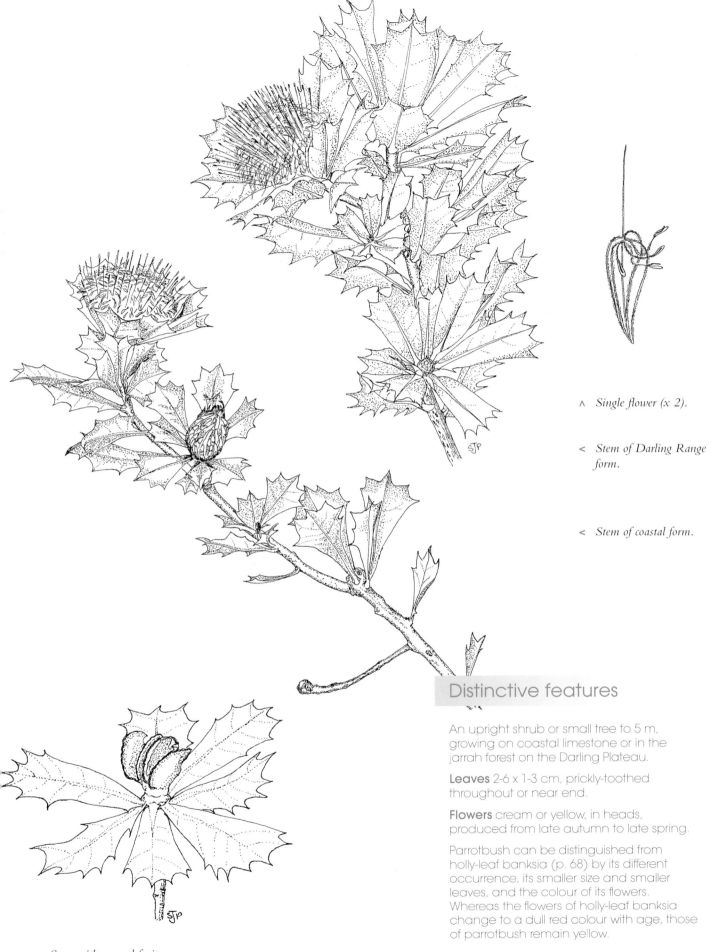

∧ *Single flower (x 2).*

< *Stem of Darling Range form.*

< *Stem of coastal form.*

Distinctive features

An upright shrub or small tree to 5 m, growing on coastal limestone or in the jarrah forest on the Darling Plateau.

Leaves 2-6 x 1-3 cm, prickly-toothed throughout or near end.

Flowers cream or yellow, in heads, produced from late autumn to late spring.

Parrotbush can be distinguished from holly-leaf banksia (p. 68) by its different occurrence, its smaller size and smaller leaves, and the colour of its flowers. Whereas the flowers of holly-leaf banksia change to a dull red colour with age, those of parrotbush remain yellow.

∧ *Stem with opened fruits.*

Pingle

*Banksia squarrosa
(formerly
Dryandra squarrosa)*

∧   *The brown beetle*
Copidita *sp. (x 2).*

Pingle ranges from New Norcia to the Whicher Range and Katanning. Its form is so variable that it was originally known as two species: *Dryandra squarrosa* and *D. carduacea.*

Growth habit

In the Metropolitan Region, pingle is an erect or sometimes spreading shrub, typically 3-4 m tall. Older specimens sometimes reach 6 m.

Pingle splits near the base into a number of branches that elongate without branching much more. For much of their length these branches are clothed in foliage. Unlike most trees and shrubs, which shed leaves that are two or three years old, pingle retains its old leaves for much of its life.

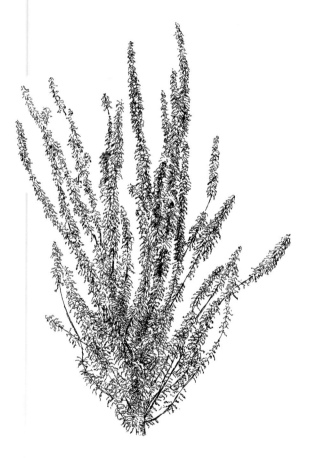

Ecological notes

Like parrotbush, pingle is killed by fire, and is a good coloniser of disturbed areas such as gravel-pits and road verges. In the Darling Range, both pingle and parrotbush grow in gravelly soil, so it is interesting that they do not often intermix; pure stands of one or the other are usually found.

Pingle begins flowering in winter, a little later than parrotbush, which sometimes starts in late autumn. Both flower in greatest abundance in early spring.

Human uses

Like parrotbush, pingle is a good producer of pollen and nectar. As a result of fire and land-clearing, pingle is less abundant now than in the past, and is now used less by beekeepers.

Associated life

Dense stands of pingle are valuable to birds for cover and nesting. The flowers are a good source of nectar and pollen for birds and insects. Large numbers of brown honeyeaters have been observed in pingle stands in spring.

Native flies and several species of beetle have been observed on the flowers. A moth larva shelters in dead leaves it ties together. It eats the leaf surfaces, leaving brown patches.

Occurrence in the Metropolitan Region

Scattered populations of pingle occur in the Darling Range, particularly in the eastern part of the region, from which it extends into the western Wheatbelt. It occurs in places along the Great Eastern Highway, for example Bakers Hill, and the Toodyay Road.

Collection and naming

Collected by W. Baxter in 1829 near King George Sound. Specific name, from the Latin *squarrosus* 'spreading at right angles', probably refers to the wide angle of the leaves on the stem.

∧ *Stem with flowers.*

< *Stem with fruits.*

Distinctive features

An upright or spreading shrub about 3 m tall, occurring sporadically in heavy soils mostly to the east and north of the Metropolitan Region.

Leaves 3-12 x 1-2 cm, deeply lobed.

Flowers pale yellow, in heads, produced from mid winter to late spring.

Wonnich, native willow

∧ *The jewel beetle*
Melobasis *sp.*

The soft look of this robust plant suggests that wonnich is adapted for fertile, moist environments rather than harsh, dry ones. It is indeed found along watercourses in the lower South-West, often in the shade of tall timber. On the south coast between Walpole and Cheyne Beach, east of Albany, it forms thickets near seepages.

In the Perth Metropolitan Region wonnich was collected in 1977 from a few plants at a single site in the lower Helena Valley by wildflower enthusiast Joanna Seabrook. By 1988 the mature plants had disappeared and only six young saplings remained. The plants have not been seen in more recent years. The site is privately owned, and the plants appear to have been lost as a result of disturbance.

The Helena River site is quite isolated. Wonnich is not otherwise known north of Pinjarra, where it was collected in 1927. It was also recorded from Wanneroo in 1900, but it is most unlikely still to exist there.

Wonnich is one of only two species in the genus *Callistachys*, the other occurring on Western Australia's south coast. Genetic studies have found, however, that three eastern Australian pea-plants in the genus *Podolobium* are related to wonnich, and should be transferred to *Callistachys*.

Ecological notes

Wonnich is killed by fire. Seedlings that germinate afterwards grow very rapidly. In January 1988 the young specimens mentioned above were more than 4 m tall, having germinated after a fire only two or three years before.

Growth habit

Typically growing in dense vegetation, wonnich is an upright, often very slender shrub when young. A young sapling is illustrated. When mature, wonnich is a small open tree. It grows to about 6 m in the valley of the Murray River, and to 10 m or more in the karri forest.

Associated life

The stems of wonnich are soft enough for native bees to burrow through their tissues and create their own nest-holes, rather than using holes already made by the larvae of beetles or moths. The female bee burrows in an old stem and makes several brood cells. In each, it lays an egg and deposits bee-bread, a mixture of pollen and nectar. The larva feeds and develops in the cell,

∧ *Young sapling, Helena Valley, 1988.*

and then pupates. The adult bee then chews its way out. Several species of jewel beetle, including the one illustrated, feed at the flowers.

Human uses

In the lower South-West, beekeepers make use of wonnich's pollen for building up broods of bees. In some years, wonnich provides a flow of nectar good enough to produce a crop of honey.

Collection and naming

Wonnich was collected in 1803 from plants growing in the garden of La Malmaison, in Paris. Its specific name, from the Latin *lanceolatus* 'shaped like a lance-head', refers to the narrow leaves with curved sides that taper to a point.

Distinctive features

Tall, robust shrub or small tree, growing on moist sites.

Leaves green, 5-14 cm long and ½-1½ cm wide, pointed; usually arranged in whorls of 3, sometimes 4, on the stem.

Flowers yellow to orange pea-flowers, in sprays at the ends of the branches, produced in spring to early summer.

Pods 10-15 x 5-7 mm, silky, slightly flattened.

Distinguished from river pea (p. 144) by the colour of its flowers, the arrangement of its leaves and the size of its pods.

Toobada, lesser bottlebrush

Callistemon phoeniceus

Toobada's bright red bottlebrush flowers in spring and early summer contrast strikingly with its blue-green foliage.

This round, shrubby bush has large leaves and a robust appearance. The thick, gnarled trunks of many natural specimens suggest that it is quite long-lived. It often grows in river beds, and can suffer serious damage from floods, but recovers by regrowing strongly from the base.

There are a number of Western Australian 'bottlebrushes', so called because of their dense cylindrical flower-spikes. The genus *Calothamnus,* commonly called 'one-sided bottlebrushes' because the flowers are usually concentrated along one side of the stem, is the largest, with over 40 Western Australian species. Another is the genus *Beaufortia,* with 20 Western Australian species.

The callistemons, often called 'true bottlebrushes', comprise about 30 species, occurring only in Australia and found mostly in the east. There are only two Western Australian species: toobada (*Callistemon phoeniceus*) and Albany bottlebrush (*C. glaucus*).

Of these, the former is the much larger. It grows up to 4 m, compared to the 1-2 m of Albany bottlebrush. The common name 'lesser bottlebrush' is therefore strange, and the Aboriginal name, 'toobada', is more suitable.

Occurrence and distribution

Toobada is wide-ranging, extending through the Wheatbelt, the Goldfields and beyond, from the Murchison River to east of Kalgoorlie, and to the south coast, except for the heavily forested south-west corner. It grows along watercourses and in depressions.

The Perth Metropolitan Region is at the edge of toobada's distribution. Here it grows in the Helena Valley downstream of Mundaring Weir, and in the Avon Valley in the vicinity of Avon Valley National Park.

Associated life

The flowers are a favourite source of nectar for honey-eating birds. They also strongly attract various insects, such as honeybees and various butterflies. On 23 October 2007, specimens in the Helena Valley were being visited by three or more species of lycaenid butterfly, particularly the brilliant blue satin azure.

A minute gall-wasp, black with a golden sheen, lays its eggs in the clusters of buds, where its larvae make a gall. Numerous black dots on the leaves, some with a white border, are scales, the secretions of tiny psyllid insects.

The larvae of ghost moths burrow in the stems of species of *Callistemon,* which may include toobada.

Collection and naming

Collected by James Drummond near Perth in 1839. Specific name after the Phoenicians, who discovered a purple-red dye, and refers to the colour of the flowers, described as a 'very rich deep crimson'.

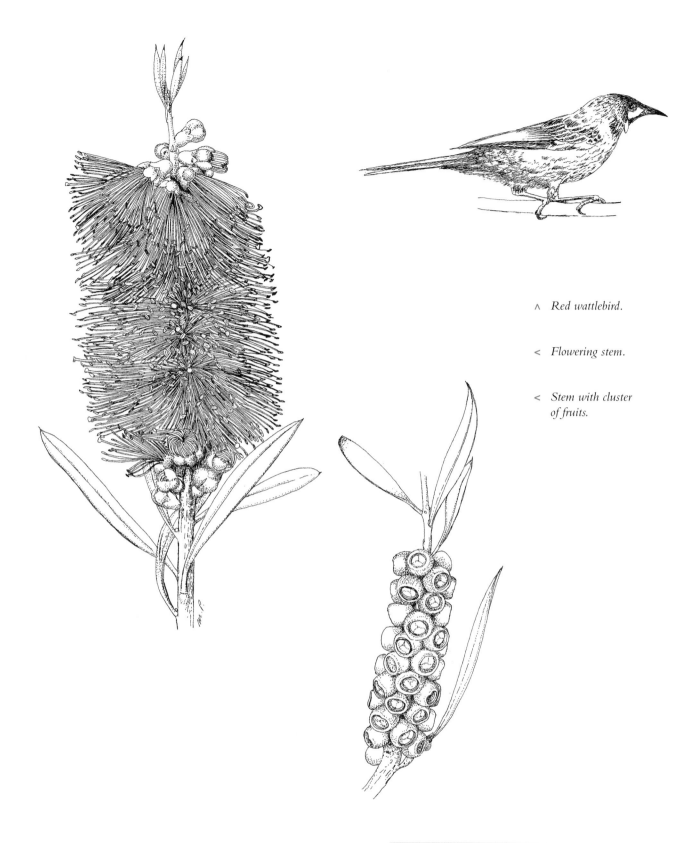

∧   *Red wattlebird.*

<   *Flowering stem.*

<   *Stem with cluster*
    of fruits.

Distinctive features

A shrub occurring in major river valleys of the Darling Scarp and Range, with blue-green leaves 4-12 cm long and prominent red flowers in spring and early summer, arranged in 'bottlebrushes'.

Rottnest cypress

Callitris preissii

∧ *Closed cone from top.*

The sharp outline and rich green foliage of Rottnest cypress immediately stamp it as a conifer.

There are 16 species in the genus *Callitris*, in Australia and New Caledonia, and six of these occur in Western Australia. Rottnest cypress occurs widely in southern Australia, often on sites too dry or infertile for other trees. In Western Australia and South Australia it grows on the coast and offshore islands, tolerating salt winds and limy soils.

Ecological notes

The pronounced shaft structure of most conifers is suited to trees competing in a forest (see p. 2). Rottnest cypress, however, has a more rounded, spreading form, to help it withstand salt winds. The main trunk often divides at the base into two or more main branches, and many of the lower side-branches develop strongly and tend upwards.

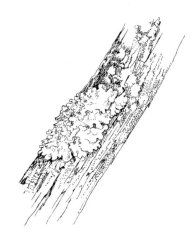

∧ *Lichen on cypress branch (x ½).*

Away from the ocean, Rottnest cypress can grow sparser and taller (as illustrated). At Peppermint Grove, on a steep east-facing limestone slope protected from sea winds, it can reach 10–15 m, much taller than coastal specimens, which are typically 5–10 m.

Another way Rottnest cypress protects itself near the coast is by forming thickets. It is killed by fire but the subsequent germination of seedlings can be prolific. The regrowth forms a thicket, the individual trees that develop within them being straight and unbranched, with a small crown of foliage. They grow quite slowly, owing to the intense competition. The height of these stands is even, as any projecting foliage is killed or damaged by the salt winds. It increases gradually with distance from the ocean.

Although dense thickets of Rottnest cypress gain height only slowly, isolated specimens develop quite rapidly. An old name for this species is *Callitris robusta*, meaning 'robust'.

Rottnest cypress used to be the dominant tree over much of Rottnest Island, as observed by the botanist Cunningham, who visited the island in 1822. Since then, human use of the island has almost caused the species to disappear. One main factor has been the increase in the frequency of fire: Rottnest cypress is readily killed by fire and needs long intervals between fires to mature and produce adequate stores of seed. Another has been the abundance of the quokka, which eats

∧ *Branch with young female cones.*

the cypress's seedlings. The cypress's abundance is now increasing again by the use of this species in plantations to restore Rottnest's tree cover, fenced to exclude quokkas.

Perth occurrences

The major populations of Rottnest cypress in the Perth area are now limited to Garden Island and Woodman Point. It also survives in Trigg Bushland and at Peppermint Grove, by the Swan River. As noted above, it is no longer abundant on Rottnest Island except in plantations.

Associated life

With its stiff stems and thick foliage, Rottnest cypress provides good places in which birds can nest or roost. Small mammals shelter in its dense thickets, in whose shade mosses and fungi flourish. Lichens grow on its trunk and branches.

Rottnest cypress produces a resin that deters insects. Nonetheless, green bugs (family Miridae) can be found in abundance on the foliage. These attract predators such as spiders, preying mantises and lacewings.

The cypress car weevil, a comparatively large species more than 5 mm long, is associated with this and other cypress species in western, southern and eastern Australia. The larvae live in the cones, one larva per cone, where they feed on the developing seeds. When mature they burrow into the soil to pupate.

Human uses

Rottnest cypress is commonly cultivated in parks and gardens. It is useful for planting near the coast, where it thrives.

Collection and naming

Collected by J.A.L. Preiss in 1839 at Rocky Bay, on the Swan River, and at Woodman Point. Specific name after Preiss, a German botanist who collected in Western Australia in 1839–41.

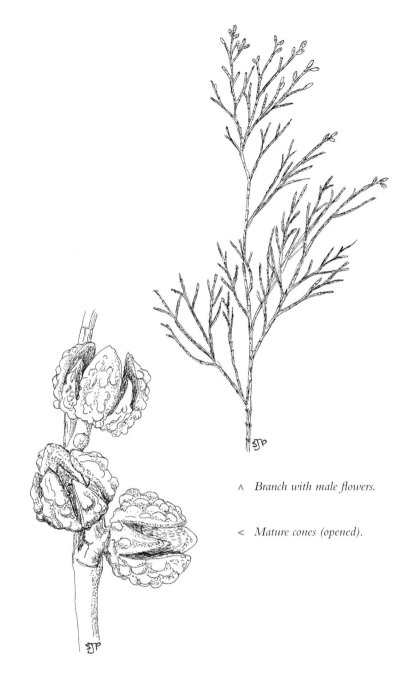

∧ *Branch with male flowers.*

< *Mature cones (opened).*

Distinctive features

A small tree, characteristically a cypress. Compact shape, often with a jagged outline. Young specimens are broadly flame-shaped. Dense foliage rich dark green (some specimens are paler and bluish).

Leaves tiny, lying flush with the stem.

Cones globular, 2½–3½ cm across. They have a warty surface, and consist of 3 large and 3 small valves.

Distinguished from swamp cypress (p. 52) by its occurrence near the coast and on offshore islands, its broader shape, and its larger cones with valves of two sizes.

Mouse-ears

Calothamnus
rupestris

The woolly fruit of this species has four lobes at the end, two of them turned back, like the ears of a fat little mouse. The species is commonly known as 'mouse-ears'.

Species in the genus *Calothamnus* are known as 'one-sided bottlebrushes'. Although both *Calothamnus* and *Callistemon* (the genus of true bottlebrushes) belong to the myrtle family, the two genera are not closely related. Although both have brushes of red flowers, there are notable differences. The flowers of true bottlebrushes are on the new growth, near the ends of the stems. Those of one-sided bottlebrushes form on the old wood, below the new growth, near the ends of the stems, and are often concentrated along one side of the stem. In mouse-ears and some other species, they are arranged in small clusters that hardly look like 'brushes' at all.

One-sided bottlebrushes are entirely Western Australian. There are over 40 species, all confined to the southern half of this State. The best known is the widely cultivated common one-sided bottlebrush (*C. quadrifidus*), whose distribution includes Perth.

The flowers of one-sided bottlebrushes are specially designed for pollination by birds. They attract honey-eating birds with their bright red colour, and reward them with copious amounts of nectar. The long stamens are fused for most of their length into bundles, and look like toothbrushes. The bird perches on the stem immediately below the flowers. As it probes a flower for nectar, the 'toothbrushes' deposit pollen on its head, its throat, or at the base of its beak. It then transports the pollen to other flowers.

Occurrence and distribution

Mouse-ears is largely confined to the Metropolitan Region. It occurs in the Darling Scarp from Red Hill to Martin, east of Gosnells, and other places in the Darling Range, such as Canning Dam, Karnet, Mt Solus and Mt Cooke. St Ronans and Boyagin Rock, in the western Wheatbelt, are the only places where mouse-ears is known to occur outside the Darling Range.

Granite is the chief soil-type, but in some places mouse-ears grows in laterite.

Canning Dam is one of the best sites for mouse-ears. Extensive stands grow on either side of Lady McNess Drive just below the dam, on granite slopes. Some splendid large specimens occur near Karnet, particularly just to the south, on North Road.

Appearance

Mouse-ears is a neat shrub 2-4 m tall. Its robust appearance is emphasised by its dark green foliage. Where it grows in the open, its branches spread wide but tend to curve upwards. They fork frequently, and form a dense mass. In stands, some specimens are less branched and more erect. Collectively, the dividing branches look like a net, and the species is sometimes also called 'cliff net-bush'.

Ecological notes

Mouse-ears does not always grow to its maximum size. On some sites, particularly near granite sheets, it is restricted by shallow soils. Moreover, it is killed by fire, and needs 10-20 years for the subsequent seedlings to grow to near full size.

Being a good coloniser of bare ground, mouse-ears can be found in quarries and on road verges in areas where it occurs; for example, along Kingsbury Drive between Karnet and Serpentine Dam.

Associated life

The flowers, from mid winter to late spring, are a popular source of food for red wattlebirds, brown honeyeaters and probably honey possums. Being dense and prickly, stands of mouse-ears provide good cover for brown and New Holland honeyeaters and the splendid fairy-wren.

Cultivation

Mouse-ears is not cultivated as much as several other one-sided bottlebrushes, but is occasionally grown. It is easily raised from seed, and thrives in gardens in the Darling Scarp. Being a dense bush, mouse-ears has potential for use as a windbreak. Horses will not eat its prickly foliage.

Collection and naming

Collected by J.A.L. Preiss in November 1839 among quartzitic rocks on the side of the Darling Range. Specific name, from the Latin *rupes* 'rock', refers to its rocky habitat.

∧ *Splendid fairy-wren.*

Distinctive features

Dense, usually spreading shrub, 2-4 m tall, growing in the Darling Range.

Leaves needle-like, dark green, crowded together on the stem, 2-3½ cm long, ending in a sharp point.

Flowers in small clusters, produced in mid winter to late spring; stamens rich pink, fused together into 4 bundles or 'toothbrushes', 2½-4 cm long.

Fruits 1-1½ cm across, covered in short, dense, silver hairs, with 4 lobes at the end, with the two thinner, opposite ones curled backwards.

Salt sheoak, cooli

Casuarina obesa

∧ *Mistletoebird.*

Like many sheoaks, salt sheoak occurs in an environment too harsh for most other plant species. It grows in or near saline wetlands, such as estuaries, where it has to withstand salty, waterlogged soil, and often salt winds as well.

Associated life

Salt sheoak supports a number of different insects, including a lemon-yellow long-horned beetle, with black wingtips.

In the Metropolitan Region two species of mistletoe, slender-leaved mistletoe (*Amyema linophylla*) and sheoak mistletoe (*Lysiana casuarinae*), grow on salt sheoak's outer branches. Mistletoes' berries are eaten by the mistletoebird, which is uncommon in the Metropolitan Region but found along the Swan and Canning rivers where salt sheoak grows. Two species of butterfly lay their eggs on slender-leaved mistletoe, the spotted jezebel (p. 200) and the satin azure.

On salt sheoak's trunk, particularly where it is protected from the sun and hot winds, lichens may be found.

Salt sheoak is less valuable to nesting waterbirds than many other wetland trees. It develops few, if any, of the hollows needed by hole-nesting ducks. It is little used by stick-nest builders, such as herons, in the Perth area, possibly because it has fewer horizontal branches than flooded gum or the paperbarks. Darters breed in branches of salt sheoak that droop over the edge of the Harvey River. They may well have bred in this way along quiet reaches of the Canning River in former times, when they were less disturbed.

Distribution

Salt sheoak is widely distributed across southern Australia. In eastern Australia a closely related species, swamp oak (*C. glauca*), occurs as well.

Occurrence in Perth

The occurrence of salt sheoak is determined by saline water at or near the surface. It is found along the lower Swan and Canning rivers, and in the Beermullah soils, near Bullsbrook and between Forrestdale and Mundijong.

Many of the sheoaks seen along the rivers nowadays, however, are not salt sheoak but the eastern Australian swamp oak, which was formerly planted extensively and is now spreading by natural reproduction. If not controlled this robust species is likely to displace salt sheoak.

Growth habit

Salt sheoak has a splitting structure, with gracefully flowing branches. The dispersed foliage and slender outer branches and twigs form intricate patterns. Specimens along rivers display an immense variety of form. Many often lean over the water to obtain extra light. Some, uprooted by erosion of the banks or by floods, continue to grow, sending up new branches. Some re-root where branches touch the soil, forming complex structures. By contrast, specimens on the Beermullah flats are upright, neat and much more uniform.

∧ *Stem with scale-leaves (x 6).*

Ecological notes

Like rock sheoak, salt sheoak is an outstanding coloniser. Young plants grow rapidly in disturbed areas. Many road verges in the Beermullah areas (for example, west of Byford) have been recolonised by dense stands of this species. In estuarine areas, it quickly establishes itself on bare silt, providing conditions that allow paperbarks and other plant species to grow.

Salt sheoak is killed by fire, and even–aged stands result from the subsequent regrowth.

Human uses

Salt sheoak is frequently planted in projects to restore the fringing vegetation of the Swan and Canning rivers. Unfortunately, however, swamp oak is often planted by mistake. It is important that people involved in planting or managing such areas should learn to distinguish one from the other. Swamp oak is larger and greener than salt sheoak, with a more jagged outline, and tends to have a shaft structure.

Although salt sheoak does not occur naturally round lakes or swamps on the western side of the coastal plain, it is often planted there in the mistaken belief that it does. Consideration should be given to removing such specimens, in order that the plantings should more closely reflect the natural vegetation.

Collection and naming

Salt sheoak was collected by J.A.L. Preiss in 1839 at the Swan River and Port Leschenault. Its specific name, from the Latin *obesus* 'plump', refers to the shape of the cones.

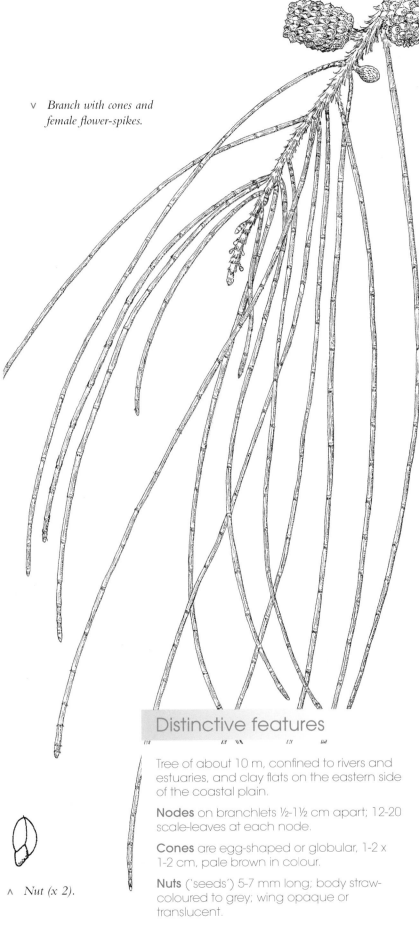

∨ *Branch with cones and female flower-spikes.*

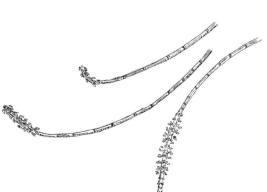

∧ *Male flower-spikes.*

∧ *Nut (x 2).*

Distinctive features

Tree of about 10 m, confined to rivers and estuaries, and clay flats on the eastern side of the coastal plain.

Nodes on branchlets ½-1½ cm apart; 12-20 scale-leaves at each node.

Cones are egg-shaped or globular, 1-2 x 1-2 cm, pale brown in colour.

Nuts ('seeds') 5-7 mm long; body straw-coloured to grey; wing opaque or translucent.

Tree smokebush

Conospermum triplinervium

∧   *A male smokebush bee (x 2).*

Masses of grey, white or blue flowers are borne above the foliage of smokebushes, and from a distance resemble smoke.

All 53 species of smokebush in the genus *Conospermum* are confined to Australia. Of these, 42 occur in Western Australia, the vast majority in the South-West.

Tree smokebush is the only species that grows into a tree, and in the Perth Metropolitan Region it can reach 4½ m. The habit is neat: the plant divides repeatedly into two or more equal branches. Foliage is retained only at the ends of the branches, and well developed specimens have an open appearance.

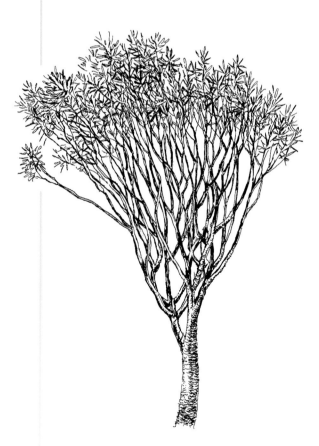

Associated life

Three species of tiny colletid bee are known to visit the flowers of smokebushes for pollen and nectar. Two of them visit tree smokebush, and are probably the main pollinators. On inserting their proboscises into the flower, they trigger an explosive mechanism that dabs them with an adhesive and showers them with pollen. The back legs of the females are specially adapted for carrying the coarse pollen-grains. The bees are well camouflaged against the woolly flowers of smokebushes: the male bees are densely clothed in white hair and have white eyes and milky wings.

Holes of different sizes in both the old stems and the young twigs indicate that at least two species of wood-boring insect use tree smokebush. Lichens grow on many of the stems.

Ecological notes

Glands on the tips of the leaves produce a sugary fluid. It is not known whether they attract useful insects. It is also possible that their purpose is to release surplus carbohydrates, salts or water.

Occurrence and distribution

Tree smokebush occurs in sandy soils from Kalbarri to Albany. On the Swan Coastal Plain it usually grows on sand over limestone. It is common in Kings Park, particularly along Forrest Drive, at the top of the escarpment.

Collection and naming

Collected in 1829 near King George Sound by William Baxter, who collected for a London nursery. Specific name, from the Latin *triplus* 'group of three' and *nervis* 'nerve', refers to the three prominent veins in the leaf.

< *Leaves and flowering branches (x ⅔).*

Distinctive features

Open shrub or small tree of neat habit, up to 4½ m high.

Leaves large, very variable in shape, 5-20 cm long and 2 mm-4 cm wide, tapering at the base and usually with three prominent parallel veins, but sometimes very narrow with veins scarcely visible.

Flowers tiny, white and woolly, in mid winter to late spring, on white, woolly stems above the foliage. At a distance these flowering stems give the effect of smoke.

Marri, red gum

Corymbia calophylla
(formerly *Eucalyptus*
calophylla)

Many people who grew up in Perth will know 'honkey nuts', the fruits of marri. These thick, woody, urn-shaped fruits are typical of eucalypts in the genus *Corymbia*.

The eucalypts in this genus are known also as 'bloodwoods', since they exude dark red kino or gum (hence marri's alternative name, 'red gum'). Marri's splendid autumn display of flowers clearly demonstrates another characteristic of the bloodwoods, the arrangement of their flowers in conspicuous terminal clusters. Marri's leaves are distinctive too. They have close, parallel veins almost at right angles to the midrib, and are held upperside up — not edge up, as in eucalypts in the genus *Eucalyptus*.

Only one other bloodwood occurs in the Perth Metropolitan Region: lesser bloodwood (p. 96), an attractively crooked smaller tree of the region's extreme south.

Cycle of growth/flowering/ fruiting

Marri begins growing in spring, earlier in the year than most eucalypts, and has largely finished growing by early summer, when the flower buds first appear. They develop rapidly, opening in February or March. Borne on branching stems at the end of the shoots, the flowers are held outside the foliage, and well displayed. The fruits take a year to mature. Whereas most other eucalypts retain their seed, marri sheds its seed over 12 to 18 months, after the fruits mature.

Associated life

The fruits, seeds, flowers, leaves and wood of marri are all important food sources for wildlife. The ringneck and red-capped parrots chew the soft, immature fruits. When the fruits are fully grown, the ringneck parrot chews off and eats the fleshy, outside parts.

The seeds are a major food of Baudin's black-cockatoo, Carnaby's black-cockatoo and various parrots. The red-capped parrot's beak is specially adapted for extracting seeds from the large fruits, and its distribution largely coincides with that of marri. It nips off the fruit, sticks in its long upper mandible, then revolves the capsule to pick out the seeds. This leaves a circle of imprints of the lower mandible just below the fruit's neck (see p. 20).

The flowers' abundant nectar and pollen attract many birds, such as purple-crowned lorikeets, silvereyes, red and little wattlebirds, and brown and New Holland honeyeaters, as well as insects such as bees, wasps, ants, beetles, butterflies and moths. In fruit-growing districts, parrots and silvereyes are much less apt to eat cultivated fruit when marri is flowering heavily.

A sampling of marri's foliage at Karragullen, north-east of Armadale, revealed an isopod, 62 species of spider and 380 species of insect.* If the invertebrate species associated with the bark are added, together with those that live in the leaf litter or topsoil under the tree (see p. 19), the number associated with marri is probably at least 800.

One of the many insects that eats marri's leaves is the larva of the Australian silkworm moth (sometimes called a 'woolly bear'). When fully developed, the larvae pupate in crevices in the bark, and the adults emerge in February to April, the right time of year to feed at the flowers.

The larvae of long-horned beetles and other wood-boring insects eat the wood, causing the characteristic bleeding of gum. In autumn, this gum attracts clusters of western brown butterflies.

Marri casts a heavier shade than do most eucalypts, and is of value to wildlife that seek shelter on hot days.

Stalked mistletoe readily grows on marri, augmenting marri's biological value by supporting additional birds and insects (see p. 22). On marri's trunk, particularly where it is protected from the sun or wind, lichens may be found.

Human uses

The Aboriginal people soaked marri blossoms in water to make a sweet drink. They also ate a sugary substance exuded from the trunk, and insect larvae found under the bark; and they ate the seeds and the gum as cures for diarrhoea.

Marri is one of the major honey plants of the South-West. The pollen is used for building up bee colonies, and the honey is excellent. Flowering is sparser the year after a season of prolific flowering, when the fruits are developing. Marri generally flowers prolifically every third or fourth year, but produces enough blossoms in between to make it fairly dependable for beekeepers.

Because it provides good shade, marri is valuable on farms as shelter for stock. The wood is strong and easily worked. With its light yellowish colour and attractive gum veins, it is popular for furniture.

(continued overleaf...)

< *Australian silkworm moth.*

∨ *Stem with immature fruits.*

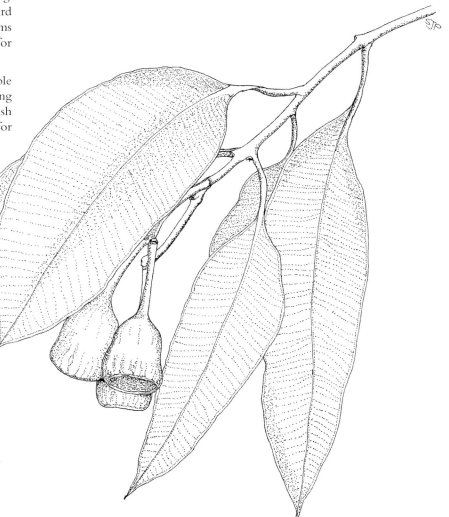

Corymbia calophylla
(formerly *Eucalyptus
calophylla*)

∧ *Seeds.*

Ecological notes

Marri's seeds, said to be larger than those of any other eucalypt, produce robust seedlings with a good survival rate. They compete well with weeds and soon develop a lignotuber, enabling them to resprout after fire. Thus marri's ability to reproduce is scarcely inhibited by human disturbance, and it regenerates well on road verges and waste land.

The regeneration is usually dense. On the coastal plain, where the vegetation is mostly woodland, marri often forms localised patches of forest. In the Darling Range, marri combines in a forest with jarrah or yarri.

In the tuart belt, tuart has traditionally dominated marri by growing larger and faster, despite producing fewer seedlings. In today's bushlands, however, it is often only marri's robust seedlings that are able to compete with weeds and survive.

Species of native *Quambalaria* fungus are associated with marri's branches or young leaves. One of them, *Q. coyrecup*, is responsible for marri canker, causing wounds to develop on the twigs, branches or trunks of stressed marri trees. The fungus can kill susceptible trees or large sections of them, by girdling trunks or branches. In areas where marri occurs, the fungus is readily transferred to any planted specimens of red-flowering gum, which have little resistance to the disease.

Until the 1970s, the fungus played a useful role in eliminating weak marri trees, reducing competition for the healthy trees, which resisted the disease. Since that time, however, many specimens of marri throughout its range have become susceptible, dying or losing large branches. Most of the affected trees are along roadsides or on farms; fewer trees are affected in bushlands.

Clearly, many marri trees in recent times have become stressed, losing their resistance to the disease. The stress is very likely from the more arid conditions that are developing, as a result of global warming.

Growth habit

As might be expected of a tree that normally grows in a forest, marri is tall (over 30 m in the Darling Range) and tends to adopt the shaft habit of growth (see p. 2). Where there is room, however, the side-branches spread wide. The heavy clusters of fruits strongly influence marri's appearance. After the tree flowers prolifically, the fruits weigh down the branches. The next shoots grow up and out, producing a curve. Wiggly branches are a feature of marri.

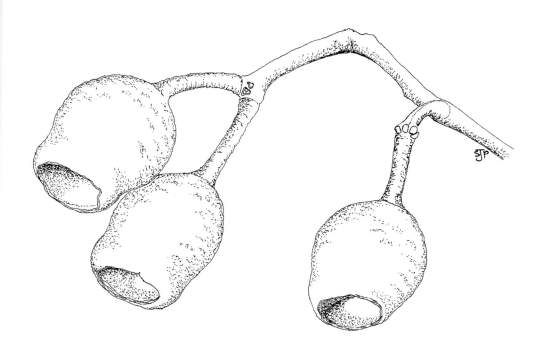

> *Mature fruits.*

Distribution

Marri is abundant throughout the lower South-West. It is less common north of Perth and more confined to river valleys, but occurs as far north as the Murchison River. Although it grows in a variety of soils, it prefers those that are moderately fertile, and hence is more localised in occurrence than jarrah on the coastal plain round Perth.

Collection and naming

Collected about 1839 at Augusta by Georgiana Molloy, a pioneering settler there. She made notes on many plant species and sent them, together with pressed specimens and seeds, to England for scientific study. The specific name refers to the similar appearance of the foliage to that of a tropical plant in the genus *Calophyllum*.

★ Recher, H.F. *et al.*: see 'Works consulted'.

∧   *Mature buds.*

<   *Immature buds.*

Distinctive features

Large tree, widespread and common.

Bark grey, rough and flaky; often exudes a reddish-brown gum from the trunk or branches.

Leaves green to dark green above, pale below. Veins at 50-70° to midrib, densely packed.

Flowers produced in mid summer to late autumn, held in branching stems above the foliage.

Fruits large, urn-shaped, 3½-4 cm long and almost as wide. Seeds black.

Lesser bloodwood, mountain marri

Corymbia haematoxylon (formerly *Eucalyptus haematoxylon*)

∧ *The western gerygone, which feeds in the foliage of this and other eucalypts.*

Lesser bloodwood could be described as a caricature of marri in miniature. The weight of its fruits strongly influences the development of its branches, which seem to wander in all directions. Even the trunk is often crooked or leaning. The character of this little tree is further enhanced by its reddish-brown bark, often flaky in texture.

Occurrence and distribution

Lesser bloodwood occurs in the Whicher Range, south of Busselton, and northwards in the Darling Scarp and the adjacent range and coastal plain, becoming more and more scattered.

Its northernmost occurrences are east of Keysbrook, in the extreme south of the Metropolitan Region, where it can be seen on Kingsbury Drive west of Scarp Road, and on Gobby Road (about 2 km south of Kingsbury Drive).

A closely related species, *Corymbia chlorolampra*, occurs much further north. This many-stemmed mallee is found inland from Jurien Bay, near Mt Lesueur, 200 km north of Perth, growing at the foot of scree slopes below lateritic breakaways. This suggests that at one time lesser bloodwood may have extended much further north.

Appearance

Being a bloodwood related to marri, lesser bloodwood has quite similar leaves, flowers, fruits and bark. And both species commonly exude dark red gum from the trunk and branches. The difference between the two in size, however, is quite striking: marri is a large tree but lesser bloodwood is, at most, 10 m tall.

Human uses

Beekeepers use lesser bloodwood for its pollen and honey, particularly in the Capel area, where it is abundant.

Associated life

Like marri, lesser bloodwood supports the wood-boring grubs of long-horned beetles. Their tunnelling causes gum to bleed from the trunk or a branch, and sometimes a branch is ringbarked and killed.

A showy display of flowers in mid summer attracts honeybees, native bees, wasps and ants. Among the fruits that subsequently develop, dead ones may be found, suggesting use by a weevil.

Lesser bloodwood's foliage supports some psyllids and brown lacewings but does not appear to be used by many other insects. 'Bites' out of some of the leaves suggest the red-legged weevil.

Ecological notes

South of the Metropolitan Region, lesser bloodwood often grows as an understorey tree with marri and jarrah. It tolerates partial shade reasonably well, perhaps because its leaves are held upper side up, rather than edge up.

Common name

Since the Darling Range and the Whicher Range can hardly be called mountains, the alternative common names for this species, 'mountain marri' and 'mountain gum', are misleading. 'Lesser bloodwood' is more suitable, since this species grows in regions where marri, a much larger bloodwood, grows too.

Collection and naming

Collected in 1912 at Happy Valley, north of Jarrahwood, by W. Donovan, a forest ranger. The specific name, from the Greek *haima/haimatos* 'blood' and *xylon* 'wood', refers to the red, or blood-coloured, timber.

< *Seeds.*

Distinctive features

A small, crooked tree of the Darling Scarp in the extreme south of the Metropolitan Region.

Bark rough, reddish-brown.

Leaves dark green above, pale beneath; veins crowded together, almost at right angles to the midrib.

Flowers produced in summer, held in branching stems above the foliage.

Fruits large and oval or urn-shaped, 2-3 x 1½-2½ cm; opening 5-10 mm across.

Seeds reddish-brown.

Distinguished from marri (p. 92) by its smaller size, its smaller fruits with narrower openings, and its reddish-brown seeds.

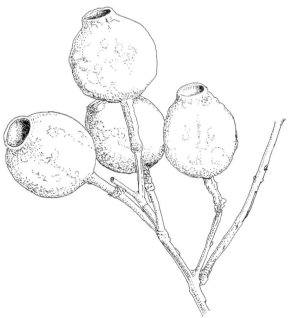

∧ *Fruits.*

Coast hop-bush

Dodonaea aptera

∧ *Harlequin bug on fruit (x 2).*

With its bright mid green to dark green foliage, coast hop-bush is quite a striking shrub of the coastal limestone, where it extends from Geraldton to Canal Rocks, south of Yallingup. It is also found on a number of islands, such as Rottnest and Garden and some of the larger islands of the Houtman Abrolhos.

There are about 70 species of hop-bush (genus *Dodonaea*). All are endemic to Australia except sticky hop-bush (p. 102), which occurs throughout the tropics. About 35 species occur in Western Australia.

Occurrence near Perth

Coast hop-bush has declined in the Perth area. On the Perth mainland, one of few places where it can still be found is the limestone slope down to the river at Peppermint Grove, below the Esplanade. Another is the west side of Aquinas Bay in Manning.

Associated life

The foliage of coast hop-bush supports an abundance of looper caterpillars, leaf-hoppers, booklice and spider-mites. These attract predatory invertebrates such as spiders, lacewings and ladybirds.

In late spring and early summer an orange, green and blue harlequin bug visits coast hop-bush to suck sap from the fruits.

A case-moth, beautifully camouflaged, has been found on the bark.

The circular shape of boreholes in some of the branches suggests that they were made by the larva of a moth, rather than a beetle. Large holes near the base of the plant suggest use by wood moths or swift-moths.

Appearance

The strong green of coast hop-bush's foliage is supplemented in spring to early summer by its decorative pinkish-brown fruits. This species forms a spreading shrub up to 3½ m, usually with several stems arising from the ground. Young plants are fairly dense and bushy, and older plants more open. The grey bark is rough and stringy.

Ecological notes

Most species of hop-bush are killed by fire, and coast hop-bush is probably no exception. Frequent burning could explain its disappearance from some localities. If the intervals between fires are not long enough, seedlings cannot grow to maturity and shed sufficient seed.

Human uses

This bright, robust shrub is biologically valuable for the abundance of life it supports. It should be planted a lot more in its natural belt of occurrence, on the coastal limestone.

Collection and naming

Collected by J.A.L Preiss in 1839 at Arthur Head, Fremantle, and at Rottnest and Garden islands. Specific name, from the Greek *a* 'without' and *pteron* 'wing', refers to the wings on the fruit, which are very small compared to those of other hop-bushes.

< *Stem with male flowers.*

< *Stem with fruits.*

Distinctive features

Shrub up to 3½ m tall, growing on limestone.

Bark stringy.

Leaves mid to dark green; broad, 2-7 x 1-3 cm, with leaf-stalks.

Branchlets without hairs.

Fruits four-angled, 5-7 x 6-8 mm, brown when mature, in spring to early summer.

Perth hop-bush

Dodonaea hackettiana

∧ *Lichen on branch.*

Perth hop-bush was at one time thought to be completely restricted to the Perth area. It was first collected in Kings Park in 1904 by J. Sheath, the park's superintendent. Small populations also occur round Jandakot, such as in Thomsons Lake Nature Reserve, and southwards towards Kwinana and Medina. A few specimens grow at Woodman Point and in Kensington.

In 1980, a search revealed only about 2,000 reproductively mature plants, and the species was declared rare. New populations were subsequently discovered in the Gingin Shire, and on several nature reserves, enabling its removal from the list of rare flora.

Ecological notes

Perth hop-bush grows on both wetland and dryland sites, and on soils ranging from Quindalup sand (at Woodman Point) to Bassendean sand (in Kensington). Given this adaptability, it is surprising that it is not more abundant.

Perth hop-bush seems to be an opportunist. Its seeds, encased in the fruits, probably persist for many years, waiting until certain conditions (such as fire or soil disturbance) trigger germination. In many places where it is most abundant the soil is periodically disturbed by rabbits, horses or vehicles. On the other hand, Perth hop-bush is killed by fire, and successive fires at short intervals could have eliminated it from some areas.

Appearance

Perth hop-bush is an elegant upright shrub or small tree to 4 m or more. Its fairly wide angle of branching, often 45-60°, gives it a spacious look. Abrupt bends in older branches are probably derived from this habit. The pinkish-red and yellow fruits are often borne in great profusion. When they mature, in late spring, they give the plant a rich hue.

Associated life

Perth hop-bush attracts harlequin bugs, sometimes in large numbers. In October 1987, for instance, in Thomsons Lake Nature Reserve, many were observed sucking the sap from the fruits. Up to 100 bugs were seen on specimens that were fruiting heavily.

Lichens, such as the one illustrated, can sometimes be found growing on Perth hop-bush's branches.

Naming

Specific name after Sir John Winthrop Hackett, who was the proprietor and editor of *The West Australian* and the first Chancellor of The University of Western Australia.

<   *Flowering branchlet.*

<   *Fruits.*

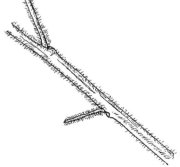

∧   *Stems with rows of hairs (x 2).*

Distinctive features

An erect shrub or small tree to 4 m or more.

Leaves 3-6 cm long, narrow, smooth in outline, without leaf stalks but tapering to the stem.

Branchlets with 2 or 3 rows of dense white or brown hairs.

Fruits prominently 3-winged, 9-13 x 12-17 mm, yellow to red or orange-brown when mature.

Sticky hop-bush

Dodonaea viscosa
subspecies
angustissima

Sticky hop-bush is the only hop-bush (genus *Dodonaea*) whose distribution extends beyond our shores. Indeed, it is more widely distributed than any other species in this book, occurring in most of the hot and temperate parts of the world.

Human uses

Sticky hop-bush is used for a number of purposes. In some countries it is planted to control erosion or reclaim marshlands. In Africa it is used as a hedge in dry areas. Sticky hop-bush is often cultivated as an ornamental plant in this country. It is not, however, the local form that is used for this purpose, but an exotic form with purplish leaves, from the south island of New Zealand.

The wood is hard and close-grained and, in countries such as India, is used for engraving and turning, and for making tool handles. The leaves contain an alkaloid, used for a wide range of medicinal purposes in many countries.

The name 'hop-bush' is Australian. The early European settlers used the capsules as a substitute for true hops in making yeast and beer. This species is called sticky hop-bush because of its sticky leaves.

The subspecies *angustissima*

Sticky hop-bush has many forms — not surprising for such a wide-ranging plant. The form that occurs in the Metropolitan Region is the subspecies *angustissima*, which occurs over much of this continent, including arid, inland regions.

Occurrence in the Metropolitan Region

Sticky hop-bush is not common in the Metropolitan Region. It is known from Wooroloo Brook, where O'Brien Road crosses it, just east of Walyunga National Park.

Appearance

In the Metropolitan Region, sticky hop-bush is a graceful shrub or small tree, 3-4 m tall, similar in many ways to Perth hop-bush. Specimens sometimes occur in close stands, where they grow very sparse and slender.

Associated life

Like other hop-bushes, sticky hop-bush attracts harlequin bugs. The nymphs, and those of leaf-hoppers, suck sap from the stems.

Other insects associated with the foliage or stems include small green bugs, of at least two species. Few moth caterpillars can be found but the cocoon of one species is illustrated. Elliptical brown scales on the stems of the new growth are visited by meat ants. A smaller species of ant appears to be attracted to the sticky substance on the leaves.

Insects do not appear to visit either the male or the female flowers.

Collection and naming

Collected by H. Sloane in the early eighteenth century in Jamaica. Specific name, from the Latin *viscum* 'bird-lime' and *-osus* 'abounding in', refers to the sticky leaves. The name of the Perth variety is from the Latin *angustissimus* 'very narrow', and refers to the shape of the leaves.

∧ *Moth cocoon on stem (x 2).*

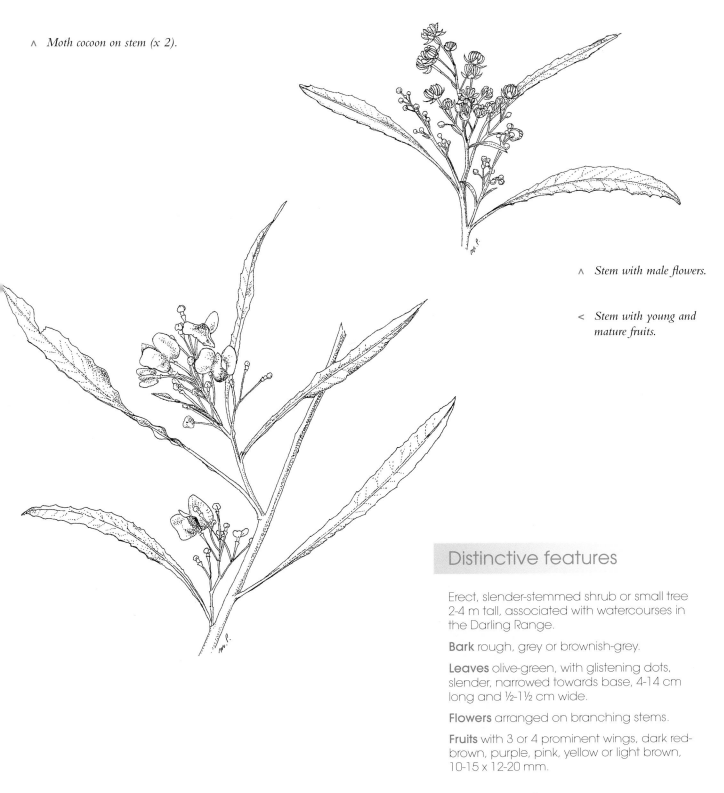

∧ *Stem with male flowers.*

< *Stem with young and mature fruits.*

Distinctive features

Erect, slender-stemmed shrub or small tree 2-4 m tall, associated with watercourses in the Darling Range.

Bark rough, grey or brownish-grey.

Leaves olive-green, with glistening dots, slender, narrowed towards base, 4-14 cm long and ½-1½ cm wide.

Flowers arranged on branching stems.

Fruits with 3 or 4 prominent wings, dark red-brown, purple, pink, yellow or light brown, 10-15 x 12-20 mm.

Powderbark

Eucalyptus accedens

This smooth-barked tree grows mostly on the outer fringes of the jarrah forest.

Powderbark is often confused with another smooth-barked tree, wandoo (p. 136), which is common in this area. The fact that powderbark is often called 'powderbark wandoo' adds to the confusion. The name is inappropriate, especially as a northern form of wandoo, in the Dandaragan area, has powdery bark. Powderbark and wandoo are not closely related. Botanically, powderbark is closer to butter gum (p. 116).

Apart from having different buds and fruits, powderbark and wandoo can be distinguished by rubbing the trunk. If your hand comes away coated with powder, the tree is powderbark. Both trees shed their bark in autumn. Wandoo's new bark is cream, whereas that of powderbark is apricot. Even when the colour of the bark fades, powderbark's bark is always the brighter, since it greys less with age. Moreover, the two species prefer different soils: powderbark inhabits the rocky lateritic breakaways, whereas wandoo usually occupies the clayey valleys.

In habit of growth, these two species are remarkably similar (though both are very varied). If you examine their wonderfully detailed crowns, in time you may pick out subtle differences.

Growth habit

Many populations of powderbark have been cut for timber, and the regrowth trees are small and slender. Mature specimens can reach 30 m. Some are stout, but stunted, probably because of the rocky terrain.

∧ *Echidna.*

Human uses

Powderbark's major commercial use nowadays is in beekeeping. Although powderbark has only a limited flow of honey, the pollen is excellent, and very useful for building up and maintaining bee colonies in summer and autumn.

Associated life

Mature and old powderbark trees develop hollows used for shelter and nesting by lizards, birds and bats. Fallen branches decay to form hollow logs, which make important refuges for lizards, snakes and echidnas.

Powderbark has fewer insects than wandoo associated with its bark, or otherwise found on its trunk. This is because of its powder. The powder adheres to the body surfaces of insects such as ants, particularly round their mouthparts, causing them discomfort and preventing them from climbing the trunk. This is probably the powder's main purpose. Various ant species tend colonies of sap-sucking bugs, in order to drink their sugary secretions. Since few ants can climb the tree, there are few of them in the canopy to protect the bugs, whose numbers are reduced by predation.

Distribution

Powderbark grows mainly in the western Wheatbelt and the adjacent eastern edge of the jarrah forest, where it extends from Three Springs to Pingelly. It can be found in many nature reserves in this region. The closest to Perth are those in the shires of Toodyay, Northam and York.

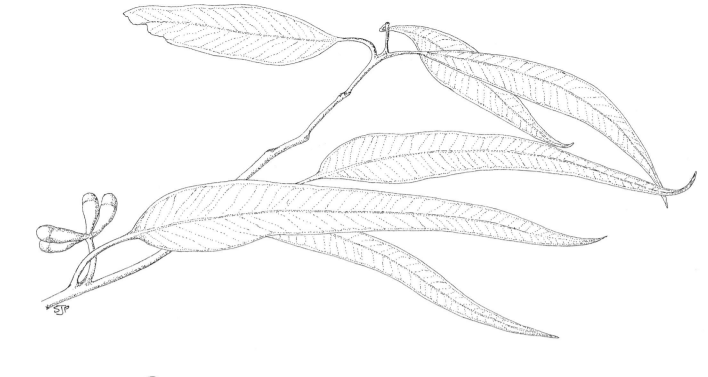

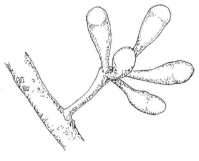

∧ *Buds.*

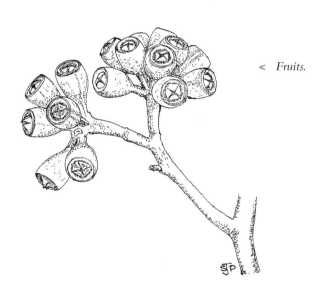

< *Fruits.*

Occurrence in the Metropolitan Region

Powderbark occurs in places in the Avon Valley and the Darling Scarp north of Greenmount, and can be found in Walyunga and John Forrest national parks.

Collection and naming

Collected by W. V. Fitzgerald in 1903 near Pingelly. Fitzgerald published a number of scientific papers, including 'The Botany of the Kimberleys'. The specific name is Latin for 'approaching' and refers to the botanical similarities between this species and *Eucalyptus redunca* and *E. foecunda* (as previously recognised as a widely occurring species; see p. 110).

Distinctive features

Medium to large tree growing on rocky laterite of the Darling Range.

Bark smooth and powdery. New bark in autumn apricot-coloured, often with dark flecks; fades to creamy white by summer.

Leaves dull on both sides.

Bud-caps hemispherical, shorter than floral tube.

Fruits turban-shaped, 7-10 x 5-7 mm.

Yanchep mallee

∧ *Pixie-cap
caterpillar.*

Many eucalypts grow not as a tree, with a single stem, but as a mallee, a shrub with several stems. These eucalypts develop, just below the ground, a large woody tuber, known as a lignotuber. Mallees begin life with a single stem. When, however, this stem is killed in a fire, or is eaten or dies in a drought, the plant sprouts from its lignotuber and produces more than one stem. As the plant develops, the lignotuber grows, and the plant is capable of producing a larger number of new stems whenever the old ones are destroyed. For some species of mallee eucalypt, specimens may occasionally be found arranged in a circle perhaps as large as 50 m in diameter. For some of these stands it has been determined that the specimens are genetically identical, formed from the gradual expansion of the lignotuber, which after a time rots away in the centre. Such a stand, therefore, may comprise an individual plant thousands of years old!

In Perth's coastal limestone belt grow three mallee eucalypts: Yanchep mallee, Fremantle mallee (p. 110) and rock mallee (p. 128). A further species, limestone marlock (p. 108), will sometimes grow as a mallee, if its main stem is entirely killed in a fire. For many years, however, Fremantle mallee was the only true mallee known from this region. It is only in more recent years that rock mallee and Yanchep mallee have been found here.

Mallees are more typical of drier regions. In general they do not grow in the wetter, densely forested regions, no doubt because eucalypts need plenty of sunlight and cannot tolerate being overshadowed.

The three Perth mallees all grow in shallow soils over limestone, where taller vegetation cannot develop.

Yanchep mallee derives its common name from its occurrence in the Yanchep area. It was not until 1992 that it was described and named *Eucalyptus argutifolia*. Before that, it was known as *Eucalyptus* aff. *obtusiflora*. The 'aff.' stands for 'affinity', and refers to Yanchep mallee's similar appearance to Dongara mallee (*Eucalyptus obtusiflora*). Yanchep mallee has broader and greener leaves than Dongara mallee, which occurs further north, from Walebing (near Moora) and Dongara to the Murchison River.

Occurrence

Yanchep mallee has a very limited occurrence, comprising scattered spots between Wanneroo and the Hill River. As mentioned above, it grows in limestone, on soils too shallow for larger eucalypts. The soils in which Yanchep mallee grows are particularly shallow, where the surrounding vegetation is low shrubland or thickets of parrotbush or chenille honey-myrtle.

Because of its limited occurrence, Yanchep mallee is recognised as a threatened species, being declared as 'rare flora' under State legislation. No-one may destroy, dig up, cut or injure plants of this species without the written consent of the Minister for the Environment. It is also listed as 'vulnerable' under the Commonwealth's Environmental Protection and Biodiversity Conservation Act.

Growth habit

Yanchep mallee is sparse and slender-stemmed, and varies from less than 2 m to 4 m tall, depending on the depth of soil.

Ecological notes

After recovering from fire, by resprouting from its lignotuber, Yanchep mallee produces its first flower buds within 3 or 4 years.

Yanchep mallee typically spreads by an expansion of its lignotuber, as described above. Specimens comprising a number of stems over an area of 3-4 m by 3-4 m may be found, but the species is too young for specimens to have formed the large rings referred to above.

In one population of Yanchep mallee that was studied, the plants flowered profusely but produced no seeds. Most of the other populations, however, are known to produce an abundance of viable seed.

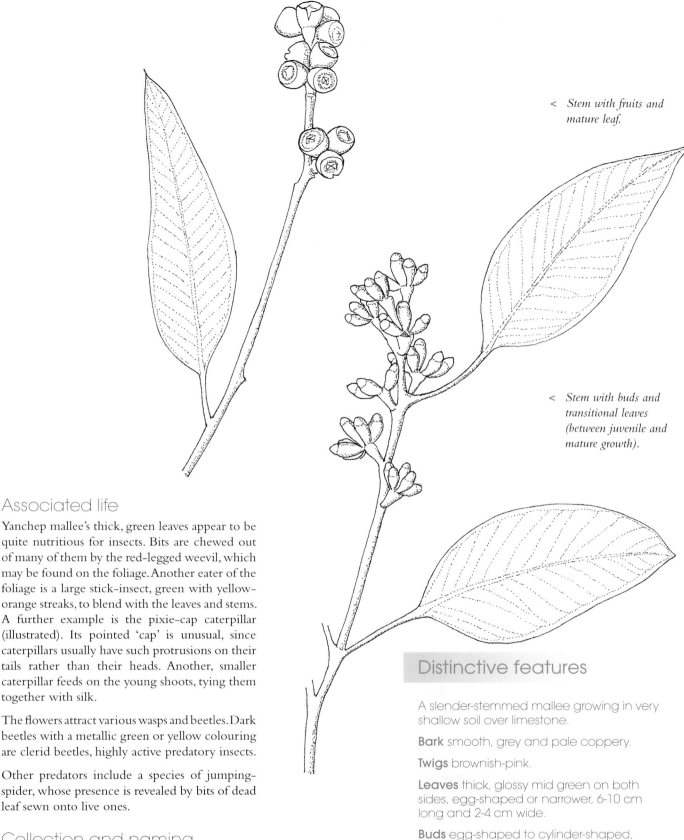

< *Stem with fruits and mature leaf.*

< *Stem with buds and transitional leaves (between juvenile and mature growth).*

Associated life

Yanchep mallee's thick, green leaves appear to be quite nutritious for insects. Bits are chewed out of many of them by the red-legged weevil, which may be found on the foliage. Another eater of the foliage is a large stick-insect, green with yellow-orange streaks, to blend with the leaves and stems. A further example is the pixie-cap caterpillar (illustrated). Its pointed 'cap' is unusual, since caterpillars usually have such protrusions on their tails rather than their heads. Another, smaller caterpillar feeds on the young shoots, tying them together with silk.

The flowers attract various wasps and beetles. Dark beetles with a metallic green or yellow colouring are clerid beetles, highly active predatory insects.

Other predators include a species of jumping-spider, whose presence is revealed by bits of dead leaf sewn onto live ones.

Collection and naming

Collected in 1987 by M.I.H. Brooker and S.D. Hopper from Parrot Ridge, near Yanchep. The specific name, from the Latin *argutus* 'clear, bright, sharp' and *folium* 'leaf', refers to the contrasting appearance of this species to Fremantle mallee, when the two are seen in proximity.

Distinctive features

A slender-stemmed mallee growing in very shallow soil over limestone.

Bark smooth, grey and pale coppery.

Twigs brownish-pink.

Leaves thick, glossy mid green on both sides, egg-shaped or narrower, 6-10 cm long and 2-4 cm wide.

Buds egg-shaped to cylinder-shaped, about 10 mm long and 5-6 mm wide; bud-cap hemispherical.

Flowers white, in autumn.

Fruits cup-shaped to cylinder-shaped, 7-9 x 6-8 mm.

Limestone marlock, redheart

Eucalyptus decipiens

In some ways limestone marlock resembles tuart. Its bark, though coarser, has a similar colour, and both species are often densely foliaged and have a splitting, spreading habit. Limestone marlock, however, is much smaller than tuart, only 10-15 m high, and branches lower down. And there is no mistaking the different sizes and forms of the buds and fruits.

Limestone marlock is so named because its occurrences in the Perth area and to the north are often on shallow soils over limestone. To the south of Perth, it occurs on various soils, including sandy clay and gravelly loam, and may also be found on winter-wet sites. The alternative common name, 'redheart', refers to the reddish colour of the wood.

Human use

Limestone marlock flowers over an extended season, with a peak in spring. It produces good honey and pollen, and beekeepers use it northwards from Yanchep. Its use is limited, however, owing to its very scattered occurrence, in small stands.

Associated life

Many insects use limestone marlock's foliage, stems or branches. The larger foliage insects include bushcrickets, or katydids, and gum-leaf grasshoppers. An orange species of sawfly lays pods of eggs, inserting them between the leaf surfaces. In late spring or early summer the adults may be seen clinging to the leaves, guarding their eggs or young larvae. Known as 'spitfires', the larvae stay close together, exuding unpleasant liquids if threatened.

At least two types of white, cottony scale may be found on the leaves, and may be attended by ants.

Several different types of gall may be found on the leaves or stems. White galls on the leaves are made by tiny *Fergusonia* flies, and slender peg-like galls by a scale insect. Brown thickenings of leaves are caused by the tiny larvae of gall-wasps, and thickened and rolled leaves by another gall-wasp. A further species of gall-wasp makes sausage-shaped swellings on the side stems. On the main stems, green or woody thickenings indicate additional species of gall-forming insects. One of the insects responsible for leaf galls, a tiny scale insect (*Eriococcus* sp.), is a favourite food of ringneck parrots in autumn.

The insects that use the stems or branches include a moth larva that burrows into the stem and emerges at night to eat the leaves. Its presence is revealed by a sac at the entrance of its burrow, made of leaf fragments and faecal pellets cemented together. Brown stains on the branches, and holes of a finger's thickness in the larger branches, are further signs of the larvae of moths or beetles. Slender ichneumon wasps can sometimes be seen searching the branches for moth larvae. These parasitic insects have long ovipositors to reach larvae burrowing in the wood.

Distribution

Limestone marlock is widely distributed, occurring in various places between Shark Bay and Bremer Bay. In the northern parts of its range it is found fairly near the coast, whereas in the south it extends to areas further inland, such as near the Stirling Range.

Occurrence in the Perth Metropolitan Region

Limestone marlock occurs in various scattered spots on Perth's coastal limestone. There is a good stand in City Beach, north of Oceanic Drive, in Bold Park. Another good stand is in Hamilton Hill, a few hundred metres south of Manning Lake. In Sorrento, a few specimens can be found in the south-west corner of Robin Reserve.

It also occurs in a spot on the eastern side of the coastal plain, in the north-western corner of Passmore Street Bushland, Southern River, among jarrah and marri trees. Here it grows on the Muchea Limestone, scattered deposits associated with former lakes or springs, along a line from Muchea to Benger, west of the Darling Scarp.

v   *Ringneck parrot.*

∧ *Stem with leaves, buds, flowers and fruits.*

Ecological notes

In the particular spots where limestone marlock is found, the soil is too shallow, dry or infertile for other, taller trees to grow. Limestone marlock therefore has no need to grow tall, and instead spreads out. Many of the spots are fairly exposed to sea winds, where the trees often grow in groups, protecting one another: their combined dense, rounded canopy deflects the salt winds.

In a severe fire, limestone marlock is burnt to the ground. However, it has a well developed lignotuber, from which it regrows vigorously to form a mallee.

Usefulness for cultivation

Limestone marlock is better adapted than most eucalypts to coastal conditions. It should be considered for parks near the ocean, where its heavy foliage can provide good shade. Its moderate size is an advantage where space is limited, although spreading side-branches can sometimes get in the way, particularly if they droop under the weight of heavy masses of buds and fruits. It grows vigorously in its early years, at a rate comparable to that of many much larger eucalypts.

Collection and naming

Collected in 1833 at King George Sound by Baron von Huegel, who visited south-western Australia that year and made extensive botanical collections. The specific name is Latin for 'deceiving', and refers to the similarity of this species to swamp gum (*Eucalyptus ovata*), a tree of south-eastern Australia.

Distinctive features

A small to medium-sized tree, sometimes a mallee, growing on the coastal limestone.

Bark rough, grey.

Leaves shiny, grey-green. Juvenile leaves heart-shaped.

Fruits hemispherical, 4-6 x 5-6 mm, valves usually protruding.

Fremantle mallee

*Eucalyptus
foecunda*

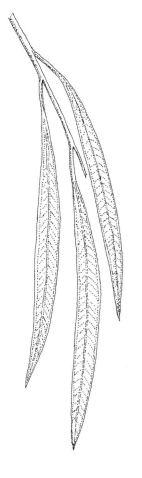

Fremantle is now so urbanised that it is hard to imagine a plant of special interest being named after it. But Fremantle mallee, which is quite uncommon in the Metropolitan Region, was first collected in the Fremantle area. A few specimens still survive there, particularly in Locke Crescent Bushland, East Fremantle.

Fremantle mallee grows on shallow soils over limestone. A large part of Fremantle has limestone near the surface and must have had an interesting vegetation (see p. 30).

Distribution

Several mallees that are botanically similar extend widely through the drier parts of southern Australia. For quite some time they were combined under the name *Eucalyptus foecunda*, but they are now recognised as seven or more distinct species. The name *E. foecunda* now refers only to Fremantle mallee, which grows on coastal limestone from Yalgorup National Park to Lancelin.

Occurrence in Perth

Fremantle mallee is limited to a few of the many limestone hills along the above stretch of coastline. There are two populations in Bold Park: one is south of Reabold Hill; the other is on the park's northern boundary, beside The Boulevard, opposite the entrance to the Wembley Golf Course. A few specimens have been retained in gardens in Sorrento. A larger population in Sorrento was destroyed when a new housing estate was created.

Ecological notes

Foecunda means 'fruitful' and refers to the large clusters of buds, flowers and fruits. The buds assume a bright brownish-orange colour as they near maturity. The buds of the southern population in Bold Park can be seen as masses of colour from the top of Reabold Hill, about 500 m away.

Each year's buds take about two years to mature, so small young buds and larger older buds, or small buds and flowers, are found on each mature specimen. As fruits of different ages are present on the trees as well, yearly growth can be measured.

Fremantle mallee regrows from its lignotuber after fire. By examining the different ages of buds and fruits it is often possible to estimate the time of the last fire (allowing for no buds being produced in the first two years after the fire). On sites protected from fire, Fremantle mallee may grow larger than is normally seen, with a single stem.

Individual specimens of Fremantle mallee flower in different seasons. Thus a population can produce nectar over long periods. If several apparently different specimens grouped together are flowering all at once, they are probably all part of just one specimen, connected by a large underground lignotuber (see p. 106). This may be the case for the stand south of Reabold Hill.

Associated life

The flowers' abundant nectar is sought by honey-eating birds. The flowers also attract wasps, bees, ants, moths and beetles, which include at least five species of jewel beetle.

Holes seen in some of the buds are probably made by a brown weevil about 2 mm long, which has been found in the vicinity. Its larvae, feeding inside the buds, would probably be the cause of the frequent dead buds often seen among the live ones.

The foliage supports leaf-hoppers, small native cockroaches and numerous booklice. Swellings on the stems contain tiny off-white larvae, probably of a sawfly. Psyllid insects (*Chaetophyes* sp.) on the stems produce hard, whitish scales, which attract ants.

On the larger stems with rough bark, swellings indicate the larvae of wood moths.

Collection

Collected by J.A.L. Preiss in 1839 from limestone slopes near Fremantle.

∧ *The jewel beetle* Stigmodera elegans.

Distinctive features

A mallee, usually less than 5 m tall, growing in shallow soil over limestone.

Bark thin, rough and grey.

Leaves glossy, green, comparatively small and narrow, 7-10 cm long and about 1 cm wide.

Bud-caps conical.

Fruits pear-shaped, 3-6 x 3-6 mm.

Tuart

Eucalyptus gomphocephala

Many Perth people will have heard of tuart. It is the largest tree on the coastal plain and the most typical eucalypt of the coastal dunes and limestone soils along Perth's coast. It is an impressive tree in many respects, and one that the inhabitants of Perth's coastal suburbs can take a pride in identifying as their own.

In the Metropolitan Region, specimens of tuart can be found that are more than 30 m tall, or 2 m thick near the base. Marri and jarrah grow taller in favourable high-rainfall sites in the South-West, but nothing like as large as tuart on the coastal plain.

Tuart is not only majestic but also graceful. It typically adopts the splitting habit of growth, described on page 2, dividing into several major branches. The branches are nicely spaced apart, and in healthy trees flow gracefully. Tuart's foliage, particularly on trees growing close to the ocean, is often denser than that of most eucalypts.

As well as from its size and habit, tuart can be recognised by its colouring. Its grey-green foliage is glossier than that of most of Perth's eucalypts. And its bark, compared with that of Perth's other rough-barked species, is noticeably the palest. Tuart's bark is often mottled, with paler patches where small areas of the surface bark have been shed. Or it can be a pale, off-white colour throughout. Generations ago, when Perth was much smaller, these pale-barked trees were much more numerous and visible. They were readily recognised, and were called 'white gums', a name preserved in the name of the suburb White Gum Valley.

Associated life

Tuart is one of Perth's most biologically valuable trees. Hollows in mature and old trees are used by tree-martins, red-capped parrots and other native animals. In bush round Perth, dead hollow trunks harbour ringneck parrots, kestrels, sacred kingfishers, brushtail possums and falsistrelle bats.

Tuart's value to insects — and thus to the general ecology — is especially important. Jarrah and marri are each known to support some 800 species of invertebrate. Tuart, since it grows in more fertile soils, is likely to support even more. Insects use virtually every part of the tree, the foliage and bark being particularly important. The bark is also favoured by fence skinks and marbled geckoes for foraging or shelter.

Although most of tuart's associated insects hardly suppress its vigour, the tuart longicorn can have a major effect. Its larvae are grubs that feed under the bark in the smaller, outer branches, causing sap to flow and leaving brown stains. In large numbers they can ringbark branchlets, resulting in dead clumps of foliage. The tree recovers by shooting from below where the damage occurred. The grubs are eaten by black-cockatoos, which locate them by listening to their tunnelling, and are also destroyed by a parasitic wasp.

Another insect that can have quite a visible effect is the scale insect *Maskellia globosa*. It causes irregular swellings along the stems where it is present, and distortions of the stems and leaves.

Tuart buds lying on the ground show the presence of the tiny tuart bud-weevil. The female makes a hole in the cap of an unopened bud and lays its eggs. The larva grows inside the bud, and eventually eats its way to the base. It pupates there, and the adult weevil cuts its way out.

The trunk of a rain-soaked tuart may sprout a spectacular assortment of fungi, such as myriads of tiny, soft shells, and giant-sized bright orange

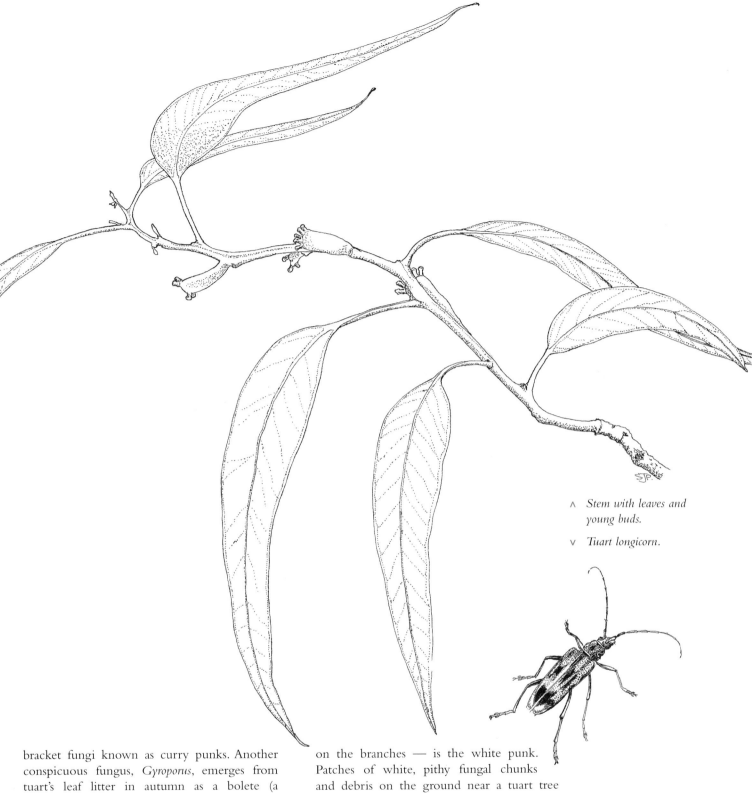

∧ *Stem with leaves and young buds.*

∨ *Tuart longicorn.*

bracket fungi known as curry punks. Another conspicuous fungus, *Gyroporus*, emerges from tuart's leaf litter in autumn as a bolete (a mushroom with pores). These fruiting bodies are quite large and robust, and if touched will instantly turn a vivid purple.

Large bracket, or pore, fungi may be found on tuart at any time of year. They can grow up to a metre wide and weigh more than 10 kg. A specimen sent to the Bureau of Animal Populations, Oxford, Great Britain, in 1958 yielded 27,000 insects, mainly fungus beetles and fly larvae.

One type of large bracket fungus often seen on tuart — either low on the trunk or high up on the branches — is the white punk. Patches of white, pithy fungal chunks and debris on the ground near a tuart tree are created by cockatoos: they often peck at the punks, dislodging chunks of various sizes. It is not known whether the birds eat the fungus or simply enjoy pecking at its pithy flesh. Eventually the punks, whether pecked at or not, break cleanly off the tree and fall to the ground, where they lie for months or years. During that time a succession of insects, including flies, worms and beetles, inhabit the punks, which become increasingly ragged and bleached as they decay.

(continued overleaf...)

*Eucalyptus
gomphocephala*

Occurrence and distribution

Tuart is almost entirely restricted to a narrow coastal strip 5-10 km wide, from Jurien Bay to the Sabina River, near Busselton.

Tuart grows mostly on brown or yellow sand over limestone, but also on white coastal sand. Its occurrence is fragmented in the northern part of its range, but south of Yanchep it forms an almost continuous strip. In some places, such as near rivers, it occurs a little further inland. Near the Canning it can be found in Riverton (for example, along High Road) and near the Murray at Ravenswood. Tuart also used to grow near the Swan in Belmont. A fine old tree that stood in Abernethy Road was probably the last remnant of this population.

The most inland natural occurrence of tuart used to be at Guildford, on the eastern side of the coastal plain, where plant specimens were collected in 1937. This population comprised a stand of just five trees, which differed from normal tuarts in having red, rather than yellow, heartwood. Unfortunately these 'red tuarts' were apparently destroyed, and no trace of them has since been found.

Ecological notes

Tuart has an almost linear, north-south occurrence. It becomes progressively larger in size as one heads south, and the climate becomes cooler, moister and more humid. In the north the trees are quite small, often less than 10 m tall. The largest trees are in the extreme south of tuart's range, in Tuart Forest National Park, at Ludlow, east of Busselton. In 1952 the tallest were 140 feet (42.7 m) tall.

It is interesting that tuart should grow much taller near Busselton than near Perth, since Busselton, in the rain-shadow of the Leeuwin-Naturaliste Ridge, receives no more rainfall than does Perth. Busselton's climate is nonetheless moister, as a result of cooler temperatures and greater humidity. Moreover, in the Busselton region the water-table is generally higher, and the limestone is derived from marine fossils. Such soils support larger trees than do the terrestrial limestone soils of the Perth area.

Unlike many of Perth's eucalypts, tuart is decidedly a fast grower, particularly where planted outside its natural range, and thus away from many of its associated insects. In 1958 a small group of

specimens was planted in Fred Jacoby Park, Mundaring, probably from seed germinated in 1957. Fifty years later, in 2007, the height of one of them was measured as 41 m, almost as tall as the tallest trees in Tuart Forest National Park.

Tuart is one of Australia's toughest eucalypts in withstanding the salt winds close to the ocean. Here one might expect small, shrubby eucalypts to do best, since they will receive the most protection from the surrounding shrubby coastal wattles. It is the massive tuart, however, that grows closest to the ocean on Perth's coastal plain. Tuart enhances its ability to survive in this environment by spreading out and developing thick foliage, often in a continuous broad canopy. It branches low, often right at the base, into two, three or several main stems. Since most salt winds come from the south-west, growth is inhibited on that side, and the trees are asymmetrical, with most of their growth on their north-eastern side.

In a few places near the coast, such as south-west of Yanchep, and at Dalyellup, south of Bunbury, tuart responds to the salt winds by growing as a mallee.

Another factor affecting tuart is depth of soil, its size being limited where the limestone is close to the surface.

Tuart roots may be seen hanging through the roofs of limestone caves, or protruding from stalactites or stalagmites. They can also form small dense lumps of roots and rootlets on the cave's floor, beneath drip-points or in other moist places.

Unlike most Perth eucalypts, tuart does not develop a true lignotuber, and relies mostly on its bark to protect it from fire. Many saplings are killed, but some recover by shooting from a slight swelling at the base of the stem.

The tuart longicorn, referred to above, severely affected many tuarts throughout much of Perth's tuart belt in the 1960s and 1970s, and for a number of years the trees died back faster then they could recover, becoming stag-headed. Many have since made a splendid recovery, although in places the trees remain under heavy attack.

Conservation concern

Since the 1990s, many tuart trees in a large area south of Mandurah have died or died back severely. The community and the Government have been greatly concerned about this problem,

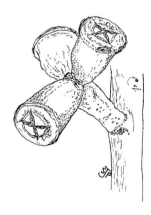

^ *Fruits.*

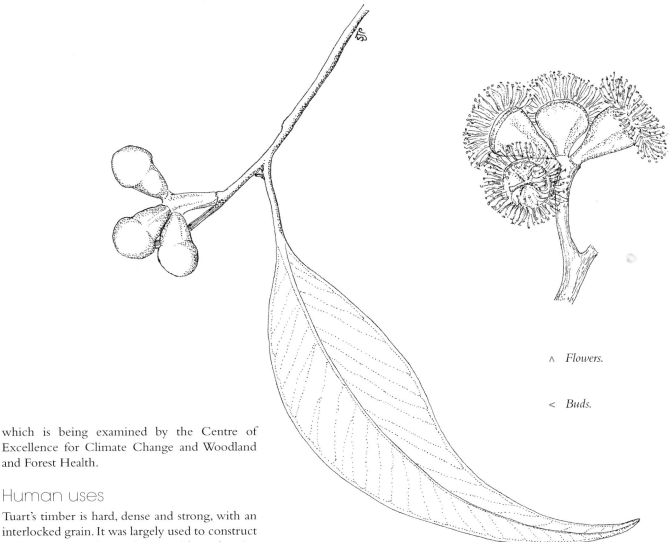

∧ *Flowers.*

< *Buds.*

which is being examined by the Centre of Excellence for Climate Change and Woodland and Forest Health.

Human uses

Tuart's timber is hard, dense and strong, with an interlocked grain. It was largely used to construct railway wagons, where it had to withstand strains and abrasions. It is no longer available, since the forest at Ludlow from which it was cut is now the Tuart Forest National Park.

Although tuart's pollen is of poor quality, its honey has a pleasing flavour and candies well. Its production is limited, however, because of the destruction of many buds by the tuart bud-weevil.

Tuart is widely cultivated in southern Australia and many countries overseas, and is especially valued in the Mediterranean for its high tolerance of salt winds and alkaline soils. In Perth it is sold in nurseries, and in recent years has been planted by local governments in parks and open spaces. Where space permits, this distinctive tree should be grown in its natural belt of occurrence for its beauty and its biological and heritage value.

Collection and naming

Collected in 1801 at Geographe Bay by Leschenault de la Tour, a naturalist on Baudin's expedition of 1800-04. Specific name, from the Greek *gomphos* 'club' and *kephale* 'head', refers to the rounded, swollen bud-cap.

Distinctive features

Large tree, usually occurring within 10 km of the coast, or near estuaries.

Bark pale, grey and rough; smaller branches often stained brown.

Foliage greyish mid green, shiny.

Bud-caps hemispherical, 10-12 x 8-10 mm, much broader than the rest of the bud.

Fruits bell-shaped to cylindrical, 12-20 mm.

Butter gum, Darling Range ghost gum

Eucalyptus laeliae

∧ *Sawfly.*

This tree, with its pure white bark, is named after Laelia, one of the vestal virgins. On a summer's day, the powdery bark gleams white in the sunshine. In autumn, however, the old bark is shed, and the new bark is creamy in colour, which accounts for the common name.

Growth habit

Butter gum is renowned for its beauty. Its graceful habit complements its white trunk and branches. Its well developed bole divides fairly evenly into several gracefully curving major branches. Butter gum is less open than most eucalypts. Its foliage, instead of being concentrated into clumps, is dispersed through the crown.

The flowers, in late summer and autumn, are small and almost hidden by the growth of leaves in summer. In years of good flowering, however, almost all the tree's energy is put into producing buds and flowers. Buds are numerous and leaf-growth minimal, so the flowers are well exposed. In most years the occasional specimen flowers prolifically, but it is not known how often a year occurs when nearly all the trees flower well.

Butter gum will grow to 30 m, especially south of Perth, but is usually smaller. Since it grows in association with granite, its size is probably often limited by the shallowness of the soil.

Occurrence and distribution

Butter gum is confined to the Darling Range between the Helena Valley and Harvey, 135 km to the south. It occurs on the sides of granite hills, usually in the Darling Scarp. In the Helena Valley, in the extreme north of its range, butter gum grows on the north side of the valley but not the south. The north is the cooler side, since it faces south. Aridity, therefore, may be the main factor that limits butter gum's extension northwards.

There are butter gums in Kalamunda National Park, and in Serpentine National Park on hillsides above Serpentine Falls. They also grow along Gobby Road in the Shire of Serpentine-Jarrahdale, which runs east from the South-Western Highway 1½ km north of Keysbrook. Just outside the Metropolitan Region, there are stands on the south-western slopes of Mt Cooke. This tree should not be confused with another eucalypt that occurs in most of these places, wandoo (p. 136).

Associated life

Butter gum's foliage shows use by many insects and spiders. Brown patches on leaves are produced by a leaf-miner. Leaves sewn together indicate other moth larvae, and 'bites' out of leaves suggest the red-legged weevil. Another weevil, of salmon colour, chews holes in the leaves. Leaves bent over twice indicate crab spiders. Spherical orange-and-white scales on the leaves, made by psyllid insects, attract meat ants. Small hard galls on the leaves are caused by coccid bugs. Football-shaped swellings on the small stems, 2–3 cm long, are made by the females of bugs in the genus *Apiomorpha*.

The foliage is also a favourite food of sawfly larvae, commonly known as 'spitfires'. They feed at night, and during the day huddle together on a stem for protection, in clusters of up to two or three dozen. When disturbed, they all raise their heads and tails, tap their tails and eject from their mouths a thick yellowish fluid that smells strongly of eucalyptus. The larvae descend in a group to the ground to pupate. They bury themselves a few centimetres below the surface near the base of the tree and construct a communal nest of hexagonal cells, like honeycomb.

On some of butter gum's stems are woody galls, hollow inside. Some may be found picked apart, probably by a parrot.

Many different insects use the trunk. Tiny holes in the bark that produce sap stains are made by moth larvae. Springtails and the larvae of case-moths shelter under the bark. On dead wood, various fungi may be found, such as a small orange bracket fungus.

In the Helena Valley, New Holland honeyeaters commonly visit butter gum when it is in flower.

Older specimens of butter gum develop many hollows useful to wildlife. The larger ones are used by possums, whose scratchings may be found on the tree's trunk.

Collection

Collected in 1966 on Whittakers Hill Road, 1.8 km south-east of North Dandalup, by Leslie McGann, a field officer with the Forests Department.

∧ *Stem with leaves and buds.*

< *Fruits.*

Distinctive features

Medium to large tree growing on granite slopes of the Darling Scarp.

Bark smooth, powdery, white through most of the year; creamy-white when shed in autumn.

Foliage dull, grey bluish-green.

Bud-cups hemispherical or conical, shorter than the floral tube.

Fruits almost cylindrical, about 6 x 5 mm; valves protrude slightly.

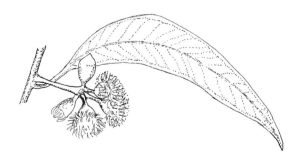

∧ *Flowers.*

Salmon white gum

Eucalyptus lane-poolei

This small tree stands out with its bright colouring. Its smooth bark is white to pale pink (pinkish-orange in autumn, when the old bark is shed), except for decorative patches of flaky brown bark near the base. The foliage is a quite bright mid green.

Growth habit

Salmon white gum is spreading, sometimes irregular in shape. Its many branches often twist and turn under the weight of its buds and fruits, for it flowers prolifically. Some old specimens are a gnarled tangle of branches.

The well developed lignotuber ensures that the tree survives fire. Even in the absence of fire, strong new branches are often sent up from below ground.

Distribution

Salmon white gum ranges from Pinjarra to Cockleshell Gully, near Jurien Bay, but the localities at which it grows are scattered.

Occurrence in Perth

Salmon white gum is uncommon in the Metropolitan Region, occurring in a few places in the Darling Scarp, but mostly on the eastern side of the coastal plain, such as south of Armadale, north of Keysbrook, and between Mundijong and Byford. A number of these populations are near the Perth-Bunbury railway. With their brightly coloured bark in autumn, these little trees are a striking sight from the train.

Salmon white gum favours the flat, clayey Guildford soils. So do marri and wandoo, which, being much larger, can crowd out salmon white gum. Perhaps this is why it is most abundant on waterlogged sites, where the other species are less common.

Since the Guildford soils are choice farmland, the remnant populations of salmon white gum in the region are almost all on private land. It is poorly represented here in reserves.

Associated life

The foliage of salmon white gum supports an abundance of insects and spiders. Leaf-hoppers are numerous, and predatory insects such as lacewings may be seen. Brown blisters on leaves containing oval holes are made by the tiny larvae of leaf-miner moths, and leaves sewn together or covered in frass (insect waste) indicate other moth larvae. White, cottony growths on leaves are the sugary secretions of lerp insects. Leaves bent over twice show the presence of crab spiders. On the new leaves, a leaf beetle protects itself by resembling an orange gall.

A small bug sucks sap from the small stems and secretes a honey-dew. It often causes a swelling, or gall. A long-horned beetle bores into the outer branches, causing sap to flow from them.

The secretions and sap flows attract ants. The common meat ant and related species often run up and down the branches. At least two further species of ant nest on the tree, one in cracks under the bark and the other on the smaller stems, using plant material it sticks together.

Many more insects are attracted by the prolific flowers. After flowering, the tree produces masses of fruits. Some swell into galls, suggesting the presence of a weevil. Dead buds with holes in them suggest another weevil, the hole being where the adult has emerged after pupating within the bud.

Human uses

The pollen and honey of salmon white gum are of good quality, but of insufficient quantity for the commercial beekeeper. This is because the species is not abundant, and because the different individual trees flower at different times. Flowers have been recorded from July to December, but

< *Common meat ant (x 2)*.

also from February to May. It appears that, at any time of year, some specimens can be in flower.

Salmon white gum is cultivated here and there. It has proved to be very adaptable, and has the advantage of its very moderate size. It is biologically valuable in supporting many different insects. This distinctive, brightly coloured little tree should be planted much more to give a sense of place to suburbs on the alluvial soils of the eastern side of the coastal plain. Where there are no overhead wires it should be considered as a street tree.

Collection and naming

Collected in 1919 at Beenup (now Byford) by C.E. Lane-Poole, Conservator of Forests from 1916 to 1921. Specific name after Lane-Poole.

Distinctive features

A small to medium-sized tree (10-15 m) of the Darling Scarp and the eastern side of the coastal plain.

Leaves mid green, slightly glossy.

Bark smooth. New bark, in autumn, salmon-pink or pale orange, gradually fading to near-white.

Fruits almost spherical to a broad turban-shape, 1-1½ cm across. The four valves protrude prominently.

Jarrah

Eucalyptus marginata

Renowned for its timber, jarrah is Perth's most famous eucalypt. It is abundant on the Darling Plateau, where much of the land is State forest or national park. It has mostly been cut for timber, and the slender trees we see today are subsequent regrowth. In the original virgin forest, many trees were up to 2 m thick and more than 30 m tall.

Jarrah is adapted to agriculturally poor soils, and is a principal tree of both the laterites of the Darling Plateau and the porous sands of the coastal plain. On the plain it occurs as a smaller, more branching tree to 15 m or so. It is less common on the more fertile soils of the Darling Scarp or the alluvial, eastern side of the plain.

Much of the jarrah forest of the plateau is affected by root-rot, caused by the water-mould *Phytophthora cinnamomi*. It is believed to have evolved in south-east Asia, and to have been introduced to Western Australia. It attacks the root systems of shrubs and trees, killing susceptible species. The disease is often called 'dieback', because it causes jarrah trees to die back gradually, from the ends of the branches. The infertile lateritic soils have made jarrah susceptible. Many of the forest's understorey plants, however, are even more so, dying within months, rather than the years it takes jarrah. On most sites on the western side of the coastal plain, where conditions are less suitable for the disease, jarrah does not succumb.

Associated life

A sampling of jarrah's foliage at Karragullen, north-east of Armadale, revealed an isopod, 59 species of spider and 386 species of insect.★ If the invertebrate species associated with the bark are added, together with those that live in the leaf litter or topsoil under the tree (see p. 19), the number associated with jarrah is probably at least 800.

The foliage of jarrah on the coastal plain often turns brown in spring, when the jarrah leaf-miner is active. The larva of this moth eats the tissue between the outer layers of the leaf, leaving reddish-brown patches. It also makes small, oval-shaped holes. The mature larva cuts out the outer leaf layers and cements them together to form a sac, in which it falls to the ground. It then burrows into a crack to pupate. In the tree, the larvae are eaten by birds such as pardalotes, thornbills and parrots, and destroyed by a small wasp. On the ground they are eaten by ants, beetles and earwigs.

The tree recovers by producing a fresh summer crop of leaves. If the balance of nature has been upset, however, the trees may suffer severe attack over many years, which may cause them to go into a decline.

The red-legged weevil, associated with a number of eucalypts in the Metropolitan Region, particularly likes jarrah leaves. Sawfly larvae, commonly called 'spitfires', are often found on jarrah. Their habits are described on p. 117.

Jarrah flowers in the warm days of late spring and early summer. Many adult insects appear at this time and visit the flowers for pollen or nectar, including two common butterflies, the Australian painted lady and the western brown.

Forms of jarrah

On the coastal plain jarrah has green foliage, but on the Darling Plateau blue-green. The green-leaved form has 'two-sided' leaves: green and shiny on one side and pale green and dull on the other. The blue-leaved form has dull leaves, much the same colour on both sides.

The blue-leaved form is found in the northern jarrah forest of the Darling Plateau and the Dandaragan Plateau. The green-leaved form occurs more widely, including the heavily forested areas of the lower South-West.

> *Typical specimen growing on the coastal plain.*

The green-leaved and blue-leaved forms are recognised subspecies, with the subspecies names of *marginata* and *thalassica* respectively. A further form of jarrah is of much more restricted occurrence, being confined to the foot of the Darling Scarp between Perth and Serpentine; it can be seen along the South-West Highway south of Byford. It is quite distinctive in its small size (usually less than 8 m tall) and compact habit, with narrow leaves. It is not currently, however, recognised as a subspecies.

Growth habit

Jarrah is thought to live for 400 years or more. A mature jarrah has a solid, woody appearance, which can give a satisfying feeling of permanence.

On the coastal plain, jarrah usually occurs as a quite open woodland, associated chiefly with banksias and sheoaks. Most of the individual jarrah trees thus receive plenty of light. They do not need to grow tall, and their height is often less than 15 m. As they grow older they become stout and spreading — but their structure varies, and each tree tends to be of quite distinctive appearance. Old specimens are especially beautiful for their complexity and detail.

On the Darling Plateau, jarrah's habit is much more determined. The forest trees compete for light, and jarrah typically progresses from a seedling to a mature tree in several well defined stages. Seedlings that survive the intense competition for light, moisture and nutrients in the forest develop lignotubers (swellings at the base of their stems), which send out a number of dwarf stems to form a low shrub. In a dense forest, this form will often be maintained for decades, as the diameter of the lignotuber gradually increases. When the lignotuber is about 10 cm thick, a single shoot will dominate and develop into a sapling with a crown of small branches, which are shed as the tree gains height.

As the tree develops, it will often pass through the stages shown here. At the 'pole' stage, the larger lower branches are retained for some time before being shed. In the 'pile' stage, the tree begins to

form branches that will persist. As these and later branches develop, the structure of the mature tree is formed.

Seasonal growth and flowering

Jarrah's flowers are well displayed along the ends of its twigs. Its main growth is in summer, when flower buds are produced in the axils of the new leaves. Some buds are shed, in varying proportions from year to year. Those retained develop strongly the following spring, when they can be seen as yellow or orange patches in the foliage, and come into flower in spring or early summer. This happens before the summer growth of leaves, so the flowers are not hidden by the new leaves. A year later, the fertilised flowers form mature fruits.

Heavy budding and fruiting are at the expense of new leaves, so after heavy flowering the trees are left with very thin crowns once the older leaves have been shed. The foliage normally thickens again after the fruits have matured.

(continued overleaf...)

> *Stages of the development of jarrah in a forest: shrub, sapling, pole, pile, mature tree.*

Jarrah (continued)

∧ *Red-legged weevil.*

Distribution

Jarrah ranges widely through the wetter South-West, eastwards to the western Wheatbelt and Cheyne Bay on the south coast. Its main belt extends north to the Julimar forest in the Darling Range and Wannamal in the Dandaragan Plateau. On the western coastal plain, jarrah extends just beyond Yanchep. Several specimens can be found on the highway north of Yanchep National Park, at Jarrahs End picnic area.

A few isolated populations occur beyond jarrah's general range (for example, at Mt Lesueur in Lesueur National Park and at Jilikin Rock in the Shire of Kulin). This suggests that the tree's range extended much further in previous eras, presumably when conditions were much wetter.

Health concerns and remedies

As noted above, many jarrah trees on the Darling Plateau die from attack by the root-rot water-mould. Sadly, nowadays, many jarrahs in bushlands on the coastal plain are dying too. Some die quite suddenly. Others appear to do so but then recover by shooting from their lignotubers. The collapse of such trees is initiated by stress, perhaps from a rapidly dropping water-table, or the effect of some pathogen. That lowers their resistance to the common eucalypt longicorn, whose larvae tunnel in the trunk, under the bark, and in large numbers soon ringbark the tree.

In suburban Perth, many of the jarrah trees that survive are in grassed parks. In some of them the jarrahs do splendidly well. In others, however, particularly in the more coastal suburbs, the trees lose vigour, their foliage becomes quite yellow and they may die back. This is because the bore water pumped from places in the limestone belt is too alkaline for these trees, making it difficult for them to take up iron: they are suffering from a type of chlorosis. Researchers at Murdoch University and staff of the Botanic Gardens and Parks Authority are studying this problem. It appears that the trees can be helped by implanting iron into them. Another approach is to obviate the need for so much watering, by removing the lawn from round the trees and converting the area to a garden bed, with native shrubs.

Human uses

Jarrah is world-renowned for its beautifully grained, rosy-red timber. It is strong and hard, but quite easily worked. It is also durable and fairly fire-resistant. The Aboriginal people used it for making spear-throwers. Before concrete and bitumen were used to surface roads, many famous roads in cities such as London and Berlin were paved with jarrah blocks. Nowadays the timber is used chiefly for high-quality wooden furniture.

In years of good flowering, jarrah provides a flow of honey. Beekeepers find its highly nutritious pollen useful for maintaining bee colonies.

It is only in more recent years that jarrah has begun to be cultivated. Many of the trees planted along the northern part of Perry Lakes Drive, City Beach, are jarrah, as are many of those along the west side of Murdoch Drive, Winthrop, where it abuts Piney Lakes Reserve. Although slow-growing if overshadowed, jarrah trees in the open develop strongly.

On the Cottesloe and Karrakatta soils of the western coastal plain jarrah is unlikely to succumb to the water-mould. Here its moderate size makes it more suitable for growing in urban areas than most of the eastern Australian eucalypts commonly planted.

As noted above, jarrah in grassed parks may suffer from chlorosis, but this problem can be remedied. Jarrah may also do poorly where the topsoil has been removed or built up, or where large pathways or other hard structures have been

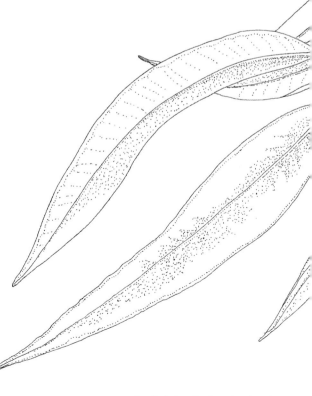

built close to the trees. Despite these problems, cultivated jarrah trees often do very well. Jarrah should be grown much more. No eucalypt is more typical of Perth than this tree, which is much heard of but poorly known by the general community.

Collection and naming

Collected in 1799 from a specimen cultivated in Kew Gardens in England, by W.T. Aiton, Royal Gardener at Kew. Specific name, from the Latin *marginatus* 'having a border', refers to the thickened, reddish margins of the leaves.

★ Recher *et al.*: see 'Works consulted'.

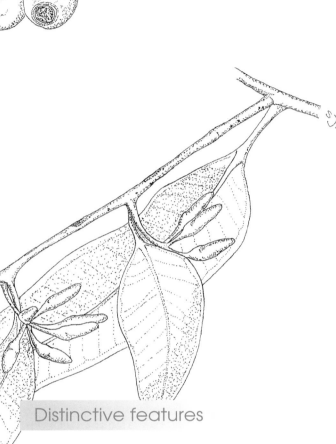

Distinctive features

A medium to large tree, widespread on the sands of the coastal plain and the laterite of the Darling Plateau.

Bark grey, brown in the furrows, stringy; strips can easily be pulled off, revealing a reddish colour.

Leaves green and shiny on one side, pale and dull on the other (green-leaved form); or dull blue-green on both sides (blue-leaved form).

Bud-caps narrowly conical, longer than the floral tube.

Flowers in spring or early summer.

Fruits globular to cup-shaped, 12-15 x 12-15 mm.

Seeds black, 5-6 mm long.

Bullich

Eucalyptus megacarpa

^ *Purple-crowned lorikeet.*

Resemblances can be misleading. The buds and fruits of bullich are similar in shape to those of the commonly cultivated Tasmanian blue gum, especially in having smooth, broad, incurved valves. But the two species are not closely related.

Bullich has closer links to several eucalypts of the south coast of Western Australia, such as crowned mallee and Mt Le Grand mallee.

Appearance

Bullich is also known as 'swamp karri'. Although bullich is smaller than karri, it is similar in its bark and habit of growth. Its slender branches are straight or curve smoothly upwards, and the foliage of its open canopy is concentrated in tight clumps at the ends of the branches. These features distinguish it from Perth's other smooth-barked eucalypts.

The new bark is pale orange-yellow and the oldest bark is mid grey. Bullich sheds its bark incompletely each year, in summer, giving a mottled effect. The smooth bark and strong growth habit make it a striking tree.

Associated life

Bullich's foliage is well used by insects, as evidenced by the various marks found on the leaves and stems. Many leaves have bits eaten out of them. Scribbly marks on some are made by an insect larva, probably of a moth, or possibly a fly. Scales on the stems are attended by ants, and other scales may be found on the leaves. On the young shoots, leaf-beetles or their larvae may be found.

Many smooth-barked eucalypts contain hollows used by birds and other animals. So might bullich, especially when damaged by fire.

The purple-crowned lorikeet, New Holland honeyeater and red wattlebird feed from the flowers — which also attract honeybees, and no doubt native bees and wasps.

Occurrence and distribution

Bullich grows in moist places in the high-rainfall region of the lower South-West. Near the south coast it is often found on hills where there is runoff from granite slopes; elsewhere it is found mainly in low, swampy sites. It occurs east to Albany and the Stirling Range, and north to the Jarrahdale area, with an isolated population near Mundaring.

In the Perth Metropolitan Region bullich occurs in several places near Karnet. There is a good stand on Bee Farm Road, by a small clearing a kilometre south of Albany Highway, about 4 km north of Gleneagle.

The Mundaring population is located in Mundaring National Park, on the upper western and south-western slopes of a hill north of McCallum Road, Sawyers Valley. This is an interesting occurrence. It is more than 35 km north of the nearest known population, on Bee Farm Road. Moreover, it grows here scattered among jarrah trees, in what does not appear to be a moist site but an otherwise typical area of jarrah forest, on lateritic soil. There is one mature to old tree, which has resprouted from its base, its main stem being reduced by fire to a blackened stump. All the remaining bulliches are slender and noticeably younger, and may be its descendants. Many have produced new stems or branches after damage from fire. Among them are many saplings, showing that bullich is continuing to increase at this site.

Ecological notes

The bark of bullich does not resist fire as well as that of other forest eucalypts, such as jarrah or marri. In a severe fire, many bullich trees are reduced to stumps. They recover by sprouting strong branches from their lignotubers (see p. 6). In addition, many seedlings germinate and grow strongly.

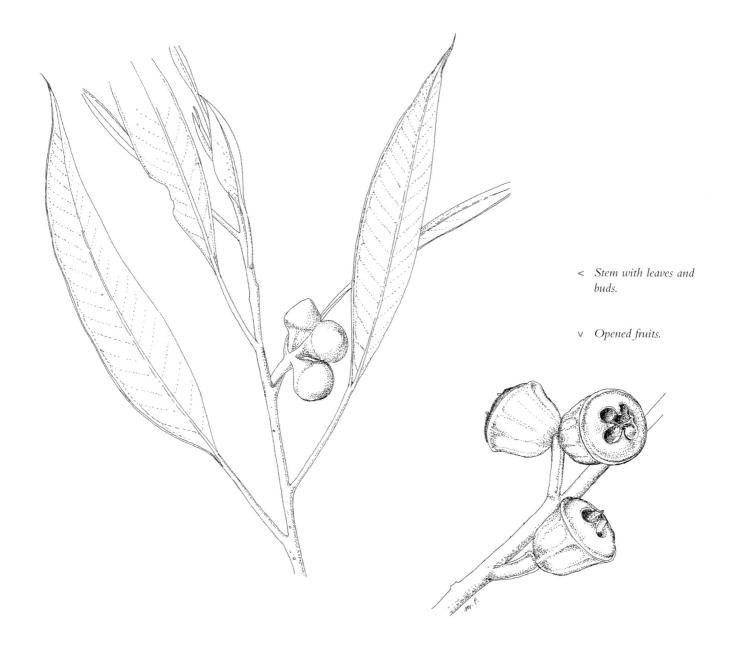

< *Stem with leaves and buds.*

v *Opened fruits.*

Fire has affected the trees in many places in the forest; few old trees can be found that are undamaged.

Human uses

The pollen and nectar produced by bullich are useful to beekeepers, but the species is rarely found in stands large enough to produce a honey crop.

Collection and naming

Collected in 1858 near Wilson Inlet by George Maxwell, who accompanied the botanist Baron von Mueller on a number of collecting journeys. Specific name from the Greek *mega* 'large' and *karpos* 'fruit'.

Distinctive features

Medium to large tree (up to 25 m) growing in valleys in the Darling Range, in the extreme south of the Metropolitan Region.

Bark smooth; shed incompletely each summer, leaving patches of old bark. New bark pale yellow-orange or pale apricot, fading to off-white, and later darkening to grey.

Leaves dull, a soft blue-green to green.

Buds in groups of no more than 3. Bud-cap hemispherical, of similar size to floral tube.

Fruits comparatively large, 17-20 x 20-24 mm, roughly globular in shape. Valves very thick, incurved.

Yarri, blackbutt

Eucalyptus patens

This impressive rough-barked tree grows in fertile valley soils of the Darling Range. It is called 'blackbutt' for its fire-blackened trunk. This, however, is misleading: the term 'blackbutt' normally refers to eucalypts with pale, smooth bark and a 'stocking' of darker, rough bark at the base (e.g. several Goldfields species). 'Yarri', believed to be the Aboriginal name, is preferred.

∧ *Sittella.*

Growth habit

Like jarrah and marri in the Darling Range, yarri is a large, tall tree, which can grow up to 45 m in the lower South-West. Yarri is more graceful than jarrah, and its heavier foliage and thicker branches give it a solid look. This is accentuated by the furrowed bark.

In the forest yarri grows tall and straight. Many of the fertile sites on which it occurs, however, have long been cleared for agriculture. Thus yarri is often found today as isolated trees in fields. In this environment it spreads out, like the specimen illustrated, and often develops particularly thick branches and dense foliage.

Associated life

Yarri produces abundant summer blossoms, and large numbers of birds feed at them and on the insects they attract. Honeyeaters, rosellas and ringneck parrots are frequent visitors.

The furrowed bark of yarri harbours many insects, which are sought by sittellas as they hop along the branches. It is interesting that grey fantails, which normally catch insects in the air, have been observed on yarri branches behaving like sittellas.

Since yarri occurs on more fertile soils than jarrah or marri, it is likely to have even more insects associated with its foliage.

Ecological notes

The Darling Range is well stocked with trees, and in the valleys, where yarri occurs, there are many tall to medium shrubs. Yarri's large, broad juvenile leaves, held flat, absorb light efficiently, allowing the seedlings to develop where light is limited. In saplings these leaves are gradually replaced by the mature leaves. These, like those of most eucalypts, are elongated and hang downwards.

Human uses

Yarri's timber is of high quality. Except for its pale yellow-brown colour, it has similar characteristics to jarrah. It has never been available in large quantities, however, owing to yarri's limited occurrence.

Yarri's excellent pollen is available shortly before marri comes into flower. Beekeepers use it to build up their broods of bees ready to harvest the nectar-flow from marri.

Occurrence and distribution

Yarri is a tree of the wetter South-West. From the south-west corner of the State, it extends northwards as far as the Avon River.

In the Metropolitan Region yarri can be found, mixed with marri or flooded gum, along many rivers and streams in the Darling Range, such as below Canning Dam, Serpentine Dam and Mundaring Weir. A most unusual occurrence, unfortunately destroyed by land development, was on the coastal plain in Canning Vale, north-west of the intersection of Nicholson and Ranford roads.

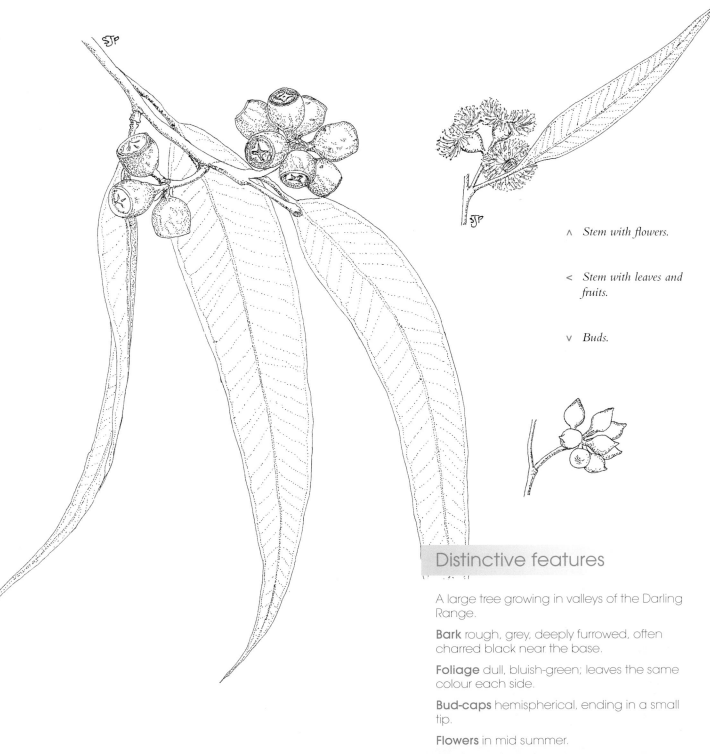

∧ *Stem with flowers.*

< *Stem with leaves and fruits.*

∨ *Buds.*

Distinctive features

A large tree growing in valleys of the Darling Range.

Bark rough, grey, deeply furrowed, often charred black near the base.

Foliage dull, bluish-green; leaves the same colour each side.

Bud-caps hemispherical, ending in a small tip.

Flowers in mid summer.

Fruits turban-shaped to globular, 10-16 x 10-16 mm.

Seeds brown, 2-3 mm long, 'D'-shaped.

Distinguished from jarrah (p. 120) by its more furrowed bark, broader buds and smaller, brown seeds.

Collection and naming

Collected by Augustus Oldfield in the 1840s at the Harvey River. Oldfield collected eucalypts and other plants in the coastal belt from King George Sound to the Murchison River, and across the Nullarbor Plain to Adelaide. The specific name is Latin for 'spreading'.

Rock mallee

Eucalyptus petrensis

Like Yanchep mallee (p. 106), rock mallee has been botanically described and named only in recent years. It was first collected in 1972 in Yalgorup National Park, south of Mandurah, but was mistaken for limestone marlock (p. 108). In 1987 it was recognised as distinct, but was not named until 1993.

Rock mallee's common name refers to its occurrence on very shallow soils over limestone, often with the rock cropping out at the surface.

Occurrence and distribution

Rock mallee extends from Yalgorup National Park, south of Mandurah, to north of Jurien Bay. In the Metropolitan Region an easy place to find it is in Bold Park, where it occurs on a limestone ridge just south-east of the Bold Park Swimming Pool. It may also be found in other parts of the park where it was planted in the past.

Less accessible populations of rock mallee occur in Yanchep National Park and on a limestone ridge to the east, and near Shire View Hill, Nowergup.

Associated life

When flowering prolifically, rock mallee may attract an abundance of white-cheeked honeyeaters. The flowers also attract wasps, honeybees and native bees.

An ant-like wasp observed on rock mallee belongs to the family Mutillidae. Wasps in this family are known as 'velvet ants', because of the resemblance of the wingless females to hairy ants. These wasps parasitise social wasps or bees.

White and orange scales, produced by a scale insect on the plant's stems and leaves, are attended

∧ *White-cheeked honeyeater.*

by ants. The larva of a species of moth sews the shoots together with silk. Crescent-shaped nicks in the leaves suggest the presence of a weevil.

Wood-boring insect larvae make holes in the branches, some of which are later taken over by ants.

Appearance

Rock mallee is a spreading, smooth-barked mallee with crooked stems; its height, 1-4 m, depends on the depth of the soil. The old bark is grey and hangs down in long strips in autumn, when it is shed, to reveal the coppery, or pale coppery, new bark.

This species is distinguished from limestone marlock by its smaller size, smooth bark, earlier flowering season and stalked buds and fruits.

Collection and naming

Collected in 1988 by M.I.H. Brooker near Seabird. Specific name, from the Greek *petra* 'stone' or 'rock' and Latin *-ensis* 'native of', refers to the stony place where this species was collected.

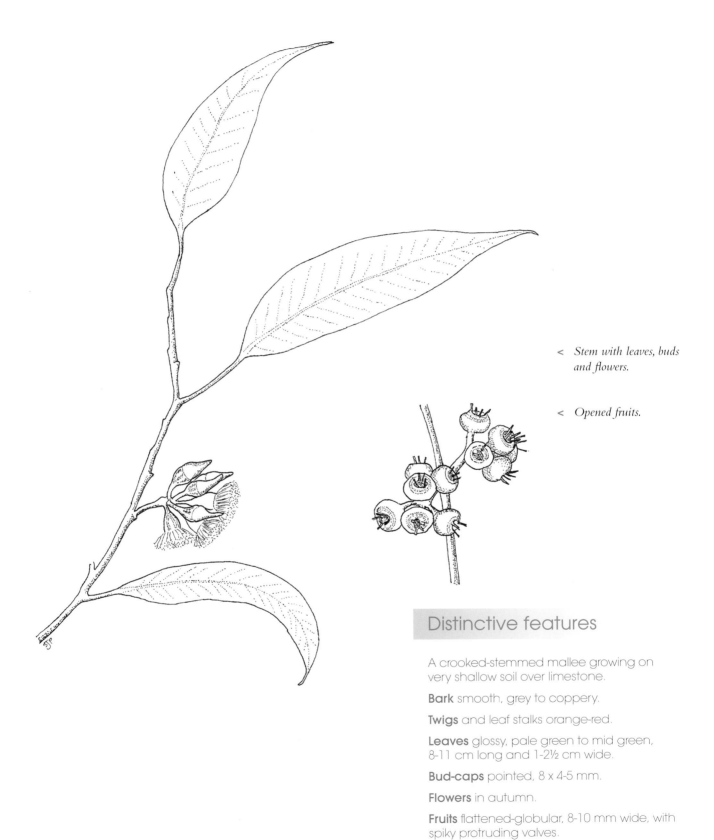

< *Stem with leaves, buds and flowers.*

< *Opened fruits.*

Distinctive features

A crooked-stemmed mallee growing on very shallow soil over limestone.

Bark smooth, grey to coppery.

Twigs and leaf stalks orange-red.

Leaves glossy, pale green to mid green, 8-11 cm long and 1-2½ cm wide.

Bud-caps pointed, 8 x 4-5 mm.

Flowers in autumn.

Fruits flattened-globular, 8-10 mm wide, with spiky protruding valves.

Flooded gum, moitch

Eucalyptus rudis

Perth has its share of bizarre trees. Christmas tree is an obvious example — not to mention balga, if it can be called a tree. But it also has graceful trees, and flooded gum, when healthy, is a splendid example.

Flooded gum tends to split, often from near the ground, into more or less equal branches. The branches flow gracefully and form a rounded outline. The foliage is more dispersed than that of most other eucalypts. Rather than being a bold pattern of branches and clumps of foliage, flooded gum's crown makes a fine pattern of twigs and leaves.

Strangely, flooded gum has little reputation for beauty, although its close relative the river gum, a larger tree with thicker branches and heavier foliage, is much admired. Flooded gum should be equally valued; less for its grandeur, more for its grace and delicacy.

Occurrence

As might be expected from its common name, flooded gum usually grows on land that is periodically flooded. This includes the flood-plains of the Swan and Canning rivers, as well as round lakes and swamps. On the more fertile soils, however, such as those in the Darling Scarp, it occurs also on higher ground.

Common names

'Flooded gum' is the best-known common name. 'Moitch', an Aboriginal name, has the advantage of avoiding confusion with an eastern Australian eucalypt also called flooded gum.

A further name, 'blue gum', refers no doubt to the blue-green foliage. It is hardly used nowadays but is preserved in a place-name, Blue Gum Lake, in Mt Pleasant. Most of the flooded gums that used to grow there were drowned when storm water was channelled into what was then a swamp, converting it into a lake. Various eucalypts from eastern Australia were planted on the lake's northern side, but flooded gums and other wetland vegetation may be seen in a small bushland on the southern side.

Associated life

Flooded gum is one of the most ecologically valuable trees in the Metropolitan Region, for two reasons. Firstly, it occurs along watercourses, which, in today's highly cleared landscapes, form many of the most important wildlife corridors, or 'greenways'. The value of such corridors in facilitating the dispersal of animals, plants and fungi is explained on page 33.

Secondly, flooded gum itself is of outstanding value to other life. No other Perth tree supports such an abundance and diversity of insects and spiders. For this reason, the trees are well visited by birds of many different species.

The myriad of leaf-miners, scale insects, aphids and bugs supported by flooded gum's foliage are eaten by predatory insects such as ladybirds, praying mantises and lacewings, as well as birds such as pardalotes, thornbills, silvereyes and western gerygones. Other insects bore into the wood; the trunk is used by a particularly large species of long-horned beetle.

Additionally, many insects use flooded gum's bark. The larvae of a beautifully coloured jewel beetle, the southern fire-banded melobasis, tunnel under the bark, where the adult beetles are sometimes found. The adults are otherwise not often seen, but probably spend their time in flooded gum's canopy, feeding on the leaves. Some species of wasp build mud nests in cracks in the bark. Web-spinning insects make silk tunnels on the bark and in crevices. Scorpions and crickets shelter under the bark.

The conk fungus *Phellinus* sp. can sometimes be

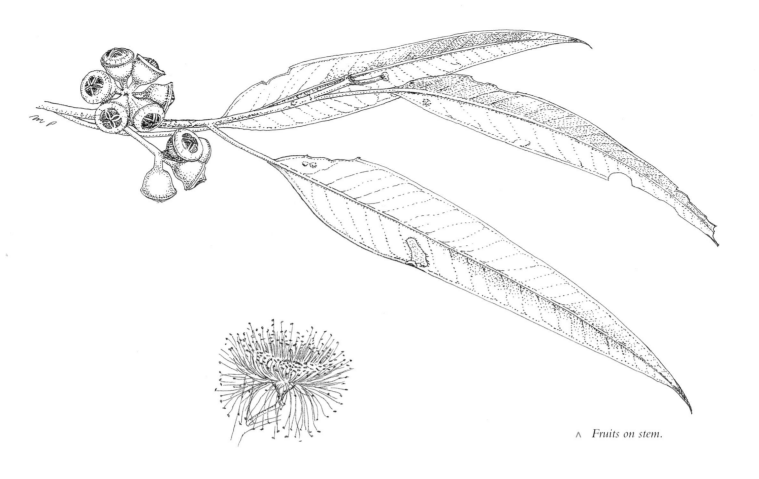

∧ *Fruits on stem.*

found attached to the trunks or lower branches of older specimens of flooded gum.

Flooded gum flowers over an extended period, from winter to early summer, and is an important source of food for nectar-feeding insects and birds. Assassin bugs hunt other insects on the flowers.

By the Swan and Canning rivers, and lakes such as Bibra Lake, North Lake and Booragoon Lake, flooded gum is vitally important to waterbirds. Mature and old trees develop hollows at the base of large branches, which are ideal nesting-sites for ducks such as the black duck, grey teal and wood duck. Many trees have numerous horizontal forking branches, used by bird species that build nests of sticks, such as the darter and white-faced heron. The dead branches are used for nesting and roosting by cormorants, egrets, herons and ibises.

Many other species of wildlife use flooded gum's hollows, including bats, possums, kingfishers, pardalotes, owls and parrots. In the 1960s Major Mitchell's cockatoo nested in flooded gums along the Swan River. This bird had otherwise long since disappeared from Perth.

Flooded gum is also of value in controlling erosion. With its good regeneration and rapid growth, it can re-establish cover quickly in disturbed areas, thus helping to stabilise the soil along watercourses.

Ecological notes

Since flooded gum supports so many insects, it is not surprising that the trees can suffer badly if the ecological balance is upset. From time to time they are affected by a superabundance of psyllid bugs. There are numerous Australian species of psyllid, of which many are associated with particular species of eucalypt. These small insects suck the sap from the leaves or young stems. Some species roam freely whereas others, including the main one affecting flooded gum, live under a cover, called a scale, or lerp, formed from a waxy, sugary substance that the insect excretes. At times the psyllids may be so abundant that the dead patches caused by their feeding combine over the whole leaf, causing it to drop from the tree. In these circumstances, the tree loses vigour and dies back.

(continued overleaf...)

Eucalyptus rudis

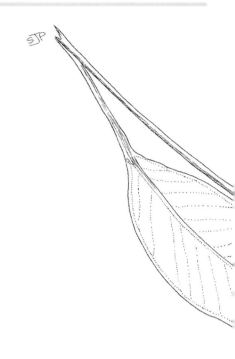

Human changes to our landscapes have resulted in many outbreaks of these insects, and many flooded gums, particularly in highly cleared agricultural areas, are suffering so badly that their future survival may be threatened. In some places, where agricultural landscapes have been converted to urban ones, the psyllid numbers have decreased and the trees have greatly recovered.

In urban areas the threat to flooded gum is more from its widely planted relative, river gum, mentioned above. River gum is not natural to Perth, but occurs widely along river systems elsewhere in Australia. Many forms of this variable species continue to be planted, often in mistake for flooded gum! Where flooded gums occur, there is the danger that the two species may produce hybrids, with the loss of flooded gum's genetic integrity. At many such sites the river gums are reproducing, but their seedlings are being mistaken for those of flooded gum (despite their distinctive longer juvenile leaves) and being allowed to develop into trees. Since they carry fewer associated insects than they do in their natural environments, these river gums grow vigorously and outcompete flooded gum — and thus at many sites pose a threat to flooded gum's future survival. In view of flooded gum's immense biological value, consideration should be given to setting up a deliberate, effective program to tackle this issue.

Occurrence, variation

Flooded gum is widely distributed over the south-west corner of the State, from Dongara to east of Albany. It varies in appearance from place to place, even in the Metropolitan Region. Near lakes such as Perry Lakes, it is usually a compact tree 15 or 20 m tall, but along the Swan River at Guildford it is larger and stouter, more like river gum. Specimens on the coastal plain have rough bark on the trunk and lower main branches, but smooth bark over the greater part of the tree. In places in the Darling Range, however, the trees have more rough bark than smooth.

North of Perth flooded gum becomes more and more like river gum, and the two species intergrade. North of Geraldton most specimens are regarded as being river gum. To preserve the different forms it is important not to plant non-local forms in their vicinity, where they might compete or interbreed with the local form.

Human uses

The Aboriginal people used to eat the lerps referred to previously, as well as the insects underneath. In those times, when the ecology was better balanced, that food was not very plentiful.

Flooded gum's honey is pleasant, but the tree is most useful to beekeepers as a source of pollen for building up hives.

Flooded gum is now being planted in many places by rivers and lakes to restore their fringing vegetation — although often, as already mentioned, river gum is planted by mistake.

Flooded gum is of more convenient size than many of the eucalypts from eastern Australia so commonly planted in Perth's parks and open spaces. It is readily raised from seed and healthy saplings grow remarkably quickly. Flooded gum should be cultivated more, to provide a richer habitat for wildlife in our city.

Collection and naming

Collected by Baron von Huegel in 1833 at King George Sound. The specific name is Latin for 'rough', but the Latin description does not state to what this refers.

∧ *Striated pardalote.*

< *Stem with leaves and buds.*

Distinctive features

A medium to large tree (up to 25 m) growing in clayey soil or by rivers or lakes, or in damplands.

Bark rough on the trunk and lower branches; smooth and grey-white on the upper branches.

Foliage dull, bluish-green or grey-green.

Bud-caps conical.

Fruits hemispherical to broadly turban-shaped, about 5 x 8 mm, with valves prominently projecting.

Pricklybark, coastal blackbutt

Eucalyptus todtiana

∧ *An ichneumon wasp, which visits the flowers.*

The thick, rough bark of this species is composed of fine, tough fibres that stick into your hand if it is rubbed hard on the tree; hence the name 'pricklybark'.

Pricklybark's attractively stunted form reflects its occurrence on Perth's infertile Bassendean sands. In the sandy country north of Perth, pricklybark is the chief shade tree, where it provides important shelter on farms.

Appearance

Pricklybark is only 9-15 m tall. It often grows in places too infertile or dry for large trees to develop, and its associated trees are chiefly banksias. To obtain plenty of sunlight, it need only grow taller than the banksias, and it often barely does.

Although not tall, pricklybark is a stout, spreading tree. Its branches often droop, weighed down by large clusters of fruits. Its pale green or bluish-green foliage combines agreeably with its grey to brown bark, yellow-orange after fire.

Distribution

Pricklybark extends from the Murray River, east of Mandurah, to the Arrowsmith River, near Dongara. The further north one goes, the more widespread its occurrence. South of the Swan River it is confined to Bassendean sands. At Karrinyup it is found at the corner of North Beach Road and Marmion Avenue, in Karrakatta sand, and at Yanchep it occurs also in Cottesloe sand.

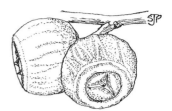

∧ *Fruits.*

Its absence from the more fertile soils further south probably illustrates competition among eucalypts: larger species dominate and exclude it.

Ecological notes

Pricklybark survives fire well; if badly damaged it develops new branches from near the base or from a lignotuber. Since pricklybark is not tall, the new branches do not have far to grow before their foliage becomes part of the tree's main canopy. Even if the original trunk is reduced to a stump, the tree still recovers. The size of some such stumps suggests that pricklybark is long-lived.

Associated life

Various marks on pricklybark's leaves betray the presence of various insects. Brown patches with oval holes in them are made by a leaf-miner. Brown blisters indicate the larva of the leaf-blister sawfly. Mature leaves sewn together with silk are the work of a moth larva, and large chunks cut out of a leaf suggest the red-legged weevil.

A crab spider lives in an enclosure in a leaf, which it makes by bending it over twice and fastening and sealing it with silk. It leaves a section of a join unsealed, through which it ambushes small insects that come by.

A very visible feature on pricklybark's stems are large spherical galls, sometimes almost the size of ping-pong balls. These are made by the females of an eriococcid bug, a species of *Apiomorpha*, which reside inside them.

Dead stems hollowed out may be caused by the larvae of a long-horned beetle or a weevil, which burrow in pricklybark's stems.

Pricklybark's abundant flowers in late summer are an important source of nectar for honey-

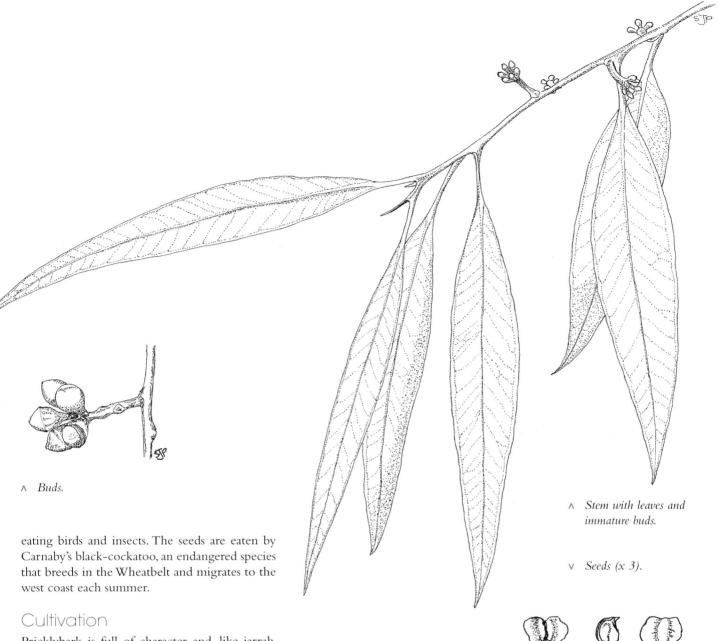

∧ *Buds.*

∧ *Stem with leaves and immature buds.*

∨ *Seeds (x 3).*

eating birds and insects. The seeds are eaten by Carnaby's black-cockatoo, an endangered species that breeds in the Wheatbelt and migrates to the west coast each summer.

Cultivation

Pricklybark is full of character and, like jarrah, should be grown a lot more to give us a sense of place. It is a hardy tree, withstanding dry conditions, and has the further advantage of small size, enabling its use where space is rather limited. Slow-growing and floriferous when mature, pricklybark nonetheless grows strongly as a sapling if planted in an open position.

Also like jarrah, pricklybark may not thrive in grassed parks in the more coastal suburbs, where the irrigation water can be too alkaline. Ways of addressing this problem are given on page 122.

Collection and naming

Collected in 1877 near the Greenough and Arrowsmith rivers by Baron von Mueller, a botanist, explorer and geographer who wrote and published extensively. Specific name after Emil Todt, an artist who drew some of the species for Mueller's *Atlas of Eucalypts*.

Wandoo, white gum

Eucalyptus wandoo

Wandoo is known best as a tree of the Wheatbelt and the drier, eastern side of the jarrah forest, where it stands out with its smooth, white, mottled bark. But it also occurs in the Darling Scarp, and even on the coastal plain. On the plain it is confined to the alluvial soils, near the scarp.

Wandoo does not have the mass of marri or jarrah. Whereas marri's trunk can thicken to 2 m, that of wandoo does not reach much more than 1 m. Wandoo nonetheless grows tall, to 30 m.

The trees with which wandoo is likeliest to be confused in the Perth area are powderbark, butter gum and salmon white gum. Wandoo is a much larger tree than salmon white gum and, unlike powderbark and butter gum, does not have powdery bark.

If wandoo saplings are present, they at least can be readily distinguished from the saplings of other smooth-barked trees — by their rough bark. This is a most unusual feature: there is probably no other Western Australian example of a smooth-barked eucalypt with rough-barked saplings. It is more usual for smooth-barked eucalypts to develop some rough bark in old age, at the base.

Associated life

Wandoo is one of south-western Australia's most biologically valuable trees. It grows in more fertile soils than jarrah or marri, and its foliage is correspondingly richer in associated insects. In the Wheatbelt and eastern side of the jarrah forest, its conservation value is increased by its widespread occurrence.

Tree sampling at Dryandra has shown that wandoo supports a great abundance of insects and spiders. The insects include native cockroaches, thrips, beetles and flies. Wandoo's smooth bark offers less refuge than rough bark. Many different insects and spiders can, however, be found on the trunk and branches, comprising many that use the tree's canopy or the ground environment, as well as those that depend primarily on the bark for their food and shelter.

One of the more conspicuous insects is a species of sawfly (*Perga* sp.), notable in that the adult guards its eggs and also its young larvae. The larvae, known as 'spitfires', stay together for their protection, ejecting through their mouths unpleasant liquids when threatened. The adults are all female, the eggs developing without the need for fertilisation.

∧ *Gould's wattled bat.*

Other insects leave conspicuous signs of their presence. Along wandoo's branches, paper-ants construct their paper-like shelters, underneath which they tend sap-sucking scale insects. The larvae of the wandoo longicorn tunnel under the bark, horizontally or obliquely across a stem or branch, leaving telltale scars. Where the larvae are numerous they may kill the branch by ringbarking it.

Wandoo's blossoms appear in various seasons, depending on the year and locality. Their copious nectar is a good source of food for wildlife.

Wandoo woodland is a particularly good habitat for birds. Not only is there an abundance of food in the form of invertebrates and nectar, but there are also numerous hollows for the various bird species that use them. Many are created by a termite that attacks the trees and hollows out the limbs, sending large branches crashing to the ground. Here they remain for many years, since the dead wood is termite-resistant. Valuable hollows are thus provided both in the trees and on the ground.

The hollows are used also by snakes, lizards and mammals. In the Darling Scarp, mammals using the hollows in the trees include the wambenger, Gould's wattled bat, the white-striped free-tailed bat, the inland free-tailed bat and other small bat species. Snakes and lizards, and the echidna, mardo and chuditch, use the hollow logs. Most of these mammals are now endangered or uncommon. The brush-tailed possum uses hollows both in the tree and on the ground.

The State's faunal emblem, the numbat, still survives in the wandoo woodland east of the Darling Range, especially in the Dryandra woodland, west of Narrogin.

Regeneration and development

The densest and most vigorous regeneration of wandoo is on ashbeds after a fire. The young saplings develop quite quickly until slowed by the competition between them.

In a forest dominated by mature trees, however, a wandoo seedling may develop like jarrah, becoming shrubby and remaining so for several years while its lignotuber develops, before sending up a vigorous shoot to form a sapling. The sapling commonly grows up without branching for several more years to form a 'pole'. As noted above, these early stages are unusual in having rough bark, quite unlike the smooth, mottled bark of the mature tree.

Thereafter, the tree develops to less of a pattern than do most other eucalypts. Wandoo woodland is beautiful for the great variety in the forms of the individual trees, whose well developed crowns are full of interesting detail. Branches often have wiggles or abrupt bends, which may result from the weighing down of the foliage during times of prolific flowering, or from regrowth where branches have been shed.

Human uses

The Aboriginal people ate the roots, which were sweet and juicy. They located water in tree-hollows by observing a discoloration of the bark. They collected it by making a hole in the tree with a hammer, then carefully closing it again. This use of wandoo was no doubt more important in the dry Wheatbelt than near Perth.

Wandoo was once south-western Australia's main source of honey, mild in flavour and of excellent quality. Most of it came from areas with good agricultural soils, which are now largely cleared. The chief remaining areas of wandoo, on the eastern side of the jarrah forest, are less dependable for honey.

Wandoo's timber has a light brown or yellowish-brown colour. It is hard and strong, and is considered one of the world's most durable timbers. Metal bolts in the wood do not produce any chemical reaction, and so have a very long life. The wood, moreover, resists termites, and was popular for strainer posts and floor stumps. Its availability for commercial use is now limited.

(continued overleaf…)

Eucalyptus wandoo

Occurrence and distribution

Wandoo extends north to Three Springs, south to the Kalgan River and inland to a line running through Kellerberrin and Corrigin. East of this line occurs a similar, related species, Wheatbelt wandoo (*Eucalyptus capillosa*), differing in its orange new bark, yellowish-green foliage, and hairy, smaller-leaved seedlings. The ranges of the two overlap in places, with wandoo occurring on duplex soils and Wheatbelt wandoo on hills and rocky country.

Wandoo is fairly common in the Darling Scarp, and can be found in Walyunga National Park, Kalamunda National Park and the western part of John Forrest National Park. On the coastal plain it grows on the alluvial Guildford and Swan soils, and can be found at Upper Swan and between Armadale and Cardup.

Conservation concern

At various times in the past, wandoo trees in some areas have died back, most of them later recovering. Since the mid 1980s, however, this phenomenon has occurred over a wider area than ever before, including much of the western Wheatbelt. It has also been unusually severe. In places, there are signs that the trees are recovering — but over much of the large area affected they have continued to die back progressively. Some have died, and many others have very little live growth.

Insects and fungi are involved. Fungi invade the holes formed by wood-boring insect larvae, and affect the wood to the extent that it can no longer conduct water to the foliage. That the trees can be damaged so severely, however, shows that their resistance is low. They are suffering stress, probably as a result of the drying climate.

The community and the Government have been greatly concerned about this problem, which is being examined by the Centre of Excellence for Climate Change and Woodland and Forest Health.

Collection and naming

Collected by A. Oldfield in 1840 near the Kalgan River.

The specific name is Aboriginal.

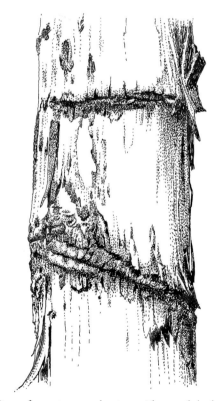

∧   *Stem of a wandoo sapling, showing its rough, flaky bark.*

∧   *Stem of a mature wandoo tree, with smooth bark. The two scars are made by the larvae of the wandoo longicorn. The tree is producing new bark to repair the damage, most noticeably along the lower scar, towards the left.*

< *Stem with leaves and buds.*

Distinctive features

A medium to large tree growing on clayey soils, largely restricted in the Perth area to the Darling Scarp and eastern side of the coastal plain.

Bark smooth; off-white to grey when old, creamy-white when new (in autumn), but always mottled with patches of old bark. Saplings have a rough, often flaky, bark, grey to brownish in colour.

Foliage dull, bluish-green.

Bud-caps narrow and pointed, as long as or longer than the rest of the bud.

Fruits pear-shaped or cylindrical, 6-10 x 5-8 mm.

Distinguished from powderbark (p. 104) and butter gum (p. 116) by its powderless bark and long, pointed bud-caps. Saplings distinguished by their rough bark.

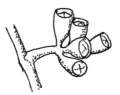

∧ *Cluster of fruits.*

Broom ballart, native cherry

*Exocarpos
sparteus*

∧ *A species of
shieldbug.*

Ballarts are plants in the genus *Exocarpos.* All are semi-parasitic and, like quandong (p. 200), belong to the sandalwood family. The leaves, or in this case the green stems, manufacture food by photosynthesis, but the roots also feed from those of other plants. The 'broom' in 'broom ballart' probably refers to the willowy appearance of this species, reminiscent of broom (*Cytisus scoparius*), a common pea-plant of Britain and Europe. It is less likely that the 'broom' would relate to any use of this species by early European settlers for making brooms, since broom ballart's green stems are quite flexible, and probably not stiff enough for the purpose.

Like most of the other members of the genus *Exocarpos,* broom ballart has very small leaves. In fact the leaves are usually absent, except on the branchlets that bear flowers. What appear as small leaves are normally leaf-like bracts.

There are about 26 species of *Exocarpos,* from Indonesia and nearby areas to New Zealand and Hawaii. Four occur in Western Australia.

Occurrence and distribution

Broom ballart has a wide distribution, growing in all of Australia's mainland states. In Western Australia it extends along the coast from Exmouth to Israelite Bay and occurs on a number of islands off the west coast. It also extends through much of the interior.

In the Metropolitan Region it grows chiefly in the coastal dunes and on limestone. It also occurs in wetland vegetation near lakes. There are many fine specimens near Thomsons Lake, and a few can be found near lakes Joondalup and Goollelal.

Growth habit

On sites near the ocean, or on shallow soils over limestone, broom ballart is a small to medium shrub, usually only 1-2 m tall.

On wetland sites, however, it grows much taller — commonly to 4 m; and sometimes, when among taller vegetation, to about 7 m. It is erect and graceful, splitting into fairly equal branches that curve upwards and form a smooth, rounded shape.

Ecological notes

On specimens growing close to the ocean the green stems are thick. This is a form of succulence, and is a common reaction of plants that grow in salty environments, such as samphire and pigface.

The taller specimens that grow near lakes evidently grow quite fast. In a dense regenerating stand of coojong and broom ballart 3-4 m tall at Blue Gum Lake seen in 2008, the broom ballarts were almost as tall and large as the specimens of coojong, a species known for its very rapid growth.

Associated life

Broom ballart's foliage is rich in insects. Moth caterpillars are numerous, as are leaf-hoppers and shieldbugs. Another bug betrays its presence by producing a white cushion-scale on a stem. Other foliage insects include lycid and clerid beetles.

In mid to late spring, when hoverflies are abundant, many can be seen in the vicinity of broom ballart, settling here and there to lay eggs. This may reflect the presence of insects suitable as food for their larvae, such as aphids. Other predatory insects include assassin bugs and damselflies. Damselflies that settle on broom ballart are well protected, their slender bodies mimicking the plant's slender stems. Also attracted to broom ballart are parasitic insects, such as tachinid flies.

The larvae of a tiny wasp feed inside broom ballart's developing fruits, causing them to swell into galls. Fruits that develop normally are eaten by ringneck parrots, and probably other birds.

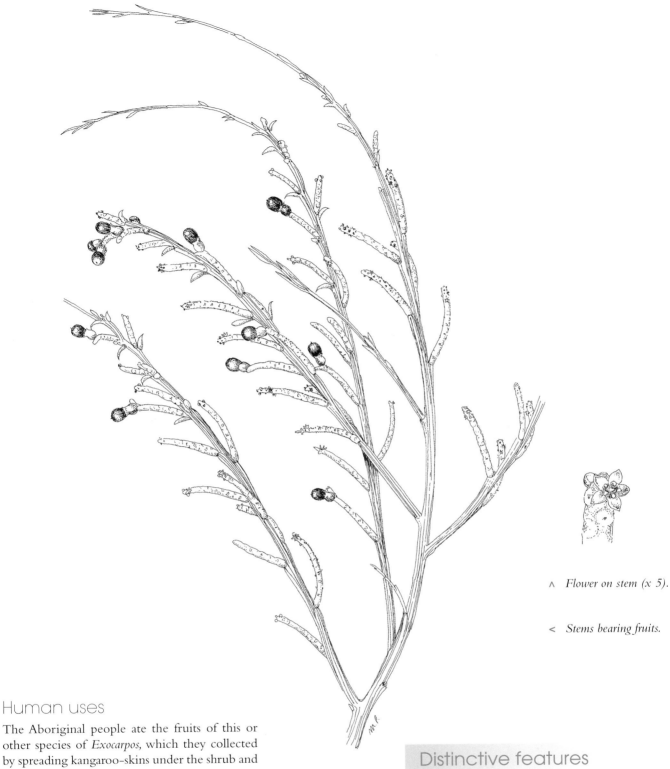

∧ *Flower on stem (x 5).*

< *Stems bearing fruits.*

Human uses

The Aboriginal people ate the fruits of this or other species of *Exocarpos*, which they collected by spreading kangaroo–skins under the shrub and then shaking it.

Because of its many associated insects, broom ballart should be considered for use in revegetation projects. Unfortunately, however, little is known about how to propagate it.

Collection and naming

Collected by Robert Brown in 1802 at King George Sound. Specific name from the Latin 'esparto', kinds of Spanish grass used for making paper and rope.

Distinctive features

Shrub up to 4 m, yellowish-green in colour. Branches tend upwards but branchlets often droop. Generally leafless; leaves that do occur on flowering branchlets are small with no leaf-stalk. Stems ribbed.

Flowers tiny (about 1 mm across), usually yellow or yellowish-green, sometimes white.

Fruits egg-shaped drupes, 4-5 mm long, red or pink in colour.

Heart-leaf poison

Gastrolobium bilobum

Heart-leaf poison is soft and succulent, but deadly to many grazing animals. Despite its toxicity it may have helped save some of our native animals, such as the woylie, from extinction.

The woylie, a small wallaby formerly found in most parts of southern Australia, became extinct in New South Wales, Victoria and South Australia, but has survived in Western Australia. A thick understorey of poison-plants in parts of this State's South-West has protected it from the fox, an introduced predator that has contributed to the woylie's disappearance over most of its range.

Heart-leaf poison is one of the most toxic plants of the genus *Gastrolobium*, many of which are known as 'poison-plants' or 'poisons'. This large genus is entirely Australian, and nearly all of the 109 species occur in Western Australia. They contain fluoroacetate, a chemical in compound 1080, which is used to kill foxes and rabbits. In the early days of European settlement, these plants killed large numbers of domestic stock.

Ecological notes

Many shrubs defend themselves against grazing animals by being tough, spiny or poisonous. But as poison-plants evolved, many different mammals, birds and reptiles evolved a resistance to their poison. Brush-tailed possums and southern bush-rats in south-western Australia are highly resistant to fluoroacetate, whereas animals of the same species in eastern Australia, where the poison is absent, are much more susceptible.

Various underground fungi attach themselves to heart-leaf poison's roots, an association that greatly stimulates the plant's growth. The woylie digs up and eats the nutritious fungi, and the spores are deposited in its faeces. The spores are thus dispersed, and also, by passing through the animal's digestive tract, primed for germination. The woylie may therefore be important in the survival of the fungi, and hence also the poison-plant. It is not known whether the woylie's absence in the Perth Metropolitan Region contributes to the lower numbers of the poison-plant here.

In the Perup forest, east of Manjimup, thickets of heart-leaf poison are vital to the survival of another wallaby, the tammar, now found in few places in mainland Australia. The thickets grow from the prolific germination of seedlings after fire. After five years they help protect the tammar from foxes and native predators such as wedge-tailed eagles. After 25 to 30 years, however, the plants begin to die, and the thicket gradually loses its value as cover. Thickets in the Perup forest are now burnt individually, over a cycle of 25 to 30 years, so that there are always suitable thickets for the tammar.

Associated life

The woylie, tammar and other mammals use the thickets for food or shelter. The common bronzewing eats the seeds. If a cat or dog then eats the bronzewing, it can have fits and die in convulsions.

Appearance

Heart-leaf poison is an erect bush with a splitting habit of growth. In spring, its green foliage is dotted with small, dense clusters of orange flowers.

Occurrence and distribution

Heart-leaf poison occurs in the south-west corner of the State, north to Perth and east to Wagin, and along the south coast as far as Cape Arid. It grows chiefly in valleys or near granite rocks.

∧ *Woylie.*

In the Perth Metropolitan Region it can be found by the Helena River in Paulls Valley, by the Canning River near Araluen, and in gullies in Kalamunda National Park.

Collection and naming

Collected in 1802 from King George Sound by Peter Good, a gardener with Robert Brown on the voyage of Matthew Flinders in the *Investigator*. Specific name, from the Latin *bi* 'two' and *lobus* 'lobe', refers to the leaf, which has two lobes at the end.

Distinctive features

Erect shrub to 3 or 4 m growing in the Darling Range.

Bark grey-brown.

Leaves dark green above, pale below, 2-6 x 1-2 cm, indented at the end.

Flowers produced in spring, pea-shaped, yellow with red markings, arranged in small, dense clusters at the ends of the stems.

Pods 7-10 x 4 mm, pointed.

River pea

Gastrolobium ebracteolatum (previously *Oxylobium lineare*)

River pea's flowers are quite variable in colour, being red or yellow or a combination of the two, with a yellow standard petal and red or reddish wings and keel. A similar combination of red and yellow is found for other pea-plants, some of which are known as 'bacon-and-eggs'.

A genetic study of pea-plants in the genus *Gastrolobium* and their relatives has determined that the genus should include many plants in related genera, including river pea. Thus river pea's generic name has changed from *Oxylobium* to *Gastrolobium*. Its specific name, *lineare*, has changed too, because the name *Gastrolobium lineare* had been used already for another species.

Ecological notes

Being legumes, pea-plants are highly nutritious to kangaroos, wallabies and other animals. Many plants in the genus *Gastrolobium*, such as heart-leaf poison (p. 142) are highly toxic. River pea, apparently, is not — nor does it have the spines or prickles that protect other pea-plants.

Unlike other pea-plants, such as heart-leaf poison and prickly mirbelia, river pea does not form

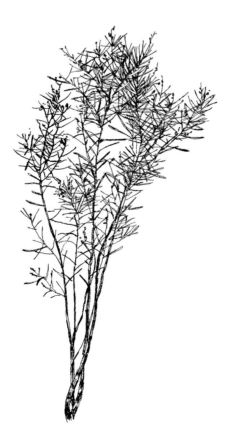

thickets. It is likely that many of its seedlings are eaten and only the odd one here and there survives.

Perhaps it does not need as much protection from being eaten as other pea-plants. It grows on moist sites, where the often thick, shrubby vegetation may shield it from grazing animals. Moreover, once mature, river pea is tall and spindly, and its foliage is out of most animals' reach.

Like many wetland pea-plants, river pea is killed by fire.

Growth habit

River pea is extremely sparse, with slender stems and little foliage. By putting on new growth it extends its stems where it can emerge through the canopies of its associated shrubs.

Occurrence and distribution

From the State's south-west corner, river pea extends northwards to Perth. There are also isolated occurrences well to the north, on the Murchison River near Kalbarri, and near Mt Lesueur.

In the Metropolitan Region, river pea grows mainly along watercourses in the Darling Range. Specimens are scattered, and not readily found. A few grow in Serpentine National Park, by the river below the falls; and in Paulls Valley, along the Helena River.

On the coastal plain, river pea probably used to occur quite extensively along the Swan and Canning rivers. There are old collections from the Swan in Bayswater and Guildford, and the Canning in Kelmscott, as well as from the Swan Estuary in Melville and Como. The clearing or disturbance of much of the vegetation fringing the rivers will have caused this quite delicate plant to disappear from many places. It still occurs by the Swan River in Success Hill Reserve, Bassendean. By the Canning it is found here and there in the Waterford bushland and in a wetland at the northern end of Sandon Park, Salter Point. Here it grows mostly among rushes, under stands of modong, freshwater paperbark or flooded gum.

There are also some recordings of river pea from the eastern chain of the Beeliar wetlands. Until recently it could be found along the swampy drainage-line in North Lake that crosses Farrington Road west of Bibra Drive.

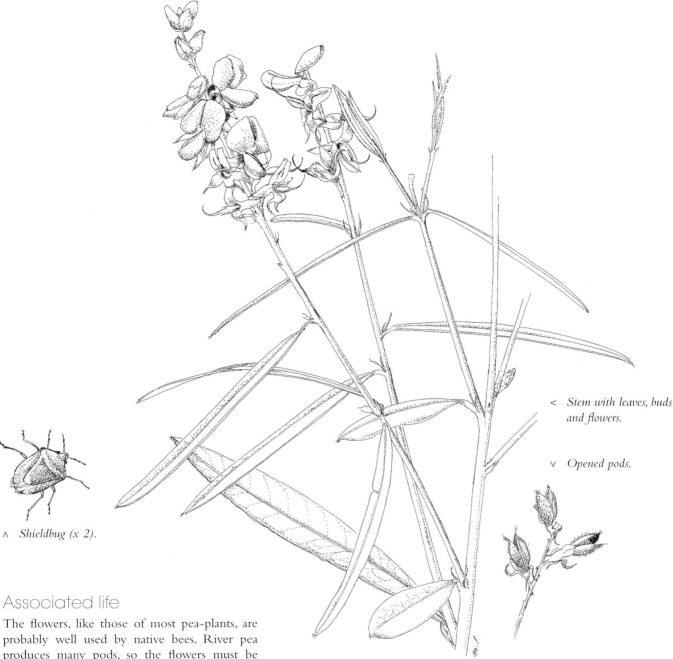

< *Stem with leaves, buds and flowers.*

∨ *Opened pods.*

∧ *Shieldbug (x 2).*

Associated life

The flowers, like those of most pea-plants, are probably well used by native bees. River pea produces many pods, so the flowers must be readily fertilised. A green species of shieldbug (illustrated) has been taken from the foliage.

Some planted specimens die or die back extensively. The dead stems reveal many tiny borer holes, 1-2 mm across, and the base of a dead specimen had extensive borer tunnels. The sites where some specimens are planted, drier and more exposed than those of the natural occurrence of this species, may cause the plants stress, lowering their resistance to the wood-borers.

Collection and naming

Collected by Baron von Huegel in 1833 from Western Australia. Specific name, from the Latin *e* 'without' and the later Latin *bracteolaris* 'bracteoles', refers to the absence of bracteoles, small bracts (leaves) on the stalk of a flower or at the base of the calyx.

Distinctive features

Slender, erect shrub growing on moist sites, up to 3 m, or taller where growing among taller shrubby vegetation.

Leaves very narrow, 5-16 cm long and usually less than 1 cm across, widely and irregularly spaced along the stem, sometimes with occasional opposite pairs.

Flowers pea-shaped, red, red and yellow or yellow, produced from spring to mid summer.

Pods 7-10 x 3-5 mm, silky, oval-shaped, slightly flattened.

Distinguished from wonnich (p. 80) by the colour of its flowers, the arrangement of its leaves and the size of its pods.

Valley grevillea

∧ *Caterpillar of* Oenochroma *sp., a species of geometer moth, on leaves.*

The name 'valley grevillea' is suggested for this moisture-loving species. It is found on the floors and sides of valleys in the wettest part of the South-West, from Mundaring to the south coast, west of Albany.

There are about 360 species in the genus *Grevillea*. It is almost exclusively Australian, but a few species occur in Indonesia, Papua New Guinea or New Caledonia. Over 230 species — nearly two thirds the total — occur in Western Australia.

Appearance

On shallow soils among granite rocks on valley sides, valley grevillea is a bushy, spreading shrub about 2 m tall.

On the valley floor, growing under eucalypts among tall shrubby vegetation, it is sparser and taller, occasionally seen as a slender tree of 9 or 10 m.

Valley grevillea's small, yellowish flowers blacken as they age. Unlike the showy flowers of many grevilleas, they are quite inconspicuous. '*Diversifolia*' means 'variable-leaved', and leaves on the one plant may have two distinct shapes. Some

are narrow and oval; others have three lobes at the end. The length and width of these lobes vary too. Seedlings have only the first type of leaf.

Ecological notes

Observations suggest that valley grevillea grows vigorously and is short-lived. It is killed by fire.

Associated life

Valley grevillea's foliage supports numerous mites, spiders and tiny weevils. Larger insects include beetles and moth larvae and a green species of katydid. One of the beetles, a black species with a purple and green sheen, belongs to the family Lagriidae, of which the larvae feed on rotting wood and the adults on plants. The moth larvae include those of a geometer moth (illustrated) and a smaller species that makes a protective cover by fastening leaves together.

On the fine stems, camouflaging brown scales are common, and minor swellings may be found, suggesting use by tiny insect larvae. Cracks in the stem with gum leaking out of them are probably caused by moth larvae. Large and small holes observed in the bases of dead specimens suggest various wood-boring insect larvae.

The flowers of valley grevillea appear to be visited only by tiny native bees, which are probably the pollinators.

Thickets of valley grevillea are likely to be important cover for birds. New Holland honeyeaters have been seen in them.

Localities in the Metropolitan Region

Valley grevillea can be found in the Helena Valley from Mundaring Weir down to the suburb of Boya; several specimens grow just below the bridge on Mundaring Weir Road. It is abundant along the Serpentine River below the falls in Serpentine National Park.

Collection and naming

Collected by J.A.L. Priess in 1839 at the Vasse River. Specific name, from the Latin *diversus* 'different' and *folium* 'leaf', refers to the plant's variable leaves.

< *Stem with leaves, flowers
and fruits.*

Distinctive features

Dense, spreading shrub to 2 m, on side of
valley, or slender, erect shrub or tree to 6 m
or more, on valley floor.

Branchlets covered in hairs that lie along
the stem.

Leaves narrow-oval or wedge-shaped, 3-8½
cm long, sometimes with 3 lobes at the
end.

Flowers produced throughout the year,
inconspicuous; yellowish, aging to black.

Smooth grevillea

Grevillea manglesii

Smooth grevillea has no hairs on the leaves or stems, hence its common name, although several other grevilleas in the Perth Metropolitan Region have hairless stems too. It is found in valleys in the Darling Range.

Associated life

The tiny white flowers, on long stalks, are designed for pollination by insects. They attract hoverflies and large numbers of native bees, such as the tiny black colletid bee illustrated. Scorpion flies are sometimes seen round the flowers, hunting small insects.

The foliage supports small bugs, such as heteropterans and psyllids, and numerous booklice. The abundance of small insects attracts numerous spiders, many of them green to match the foliage. Young spiders would find the spines on smooth grevillea's leaves useful for attaching their line of web, when they cast themselves off to disperse.

Ecological notes

Smooth grevillea is killed by fire but reproduces readily. Both the seedlings and the mature plants are robust and vigorous. The species is probably short-lived.

Appearance

Smooth grevillea is loose and spreading. It grows to 2-4 m tall, sometimes taller if shaded in a dense forest. Some stems grow out a long way without branching, and bend towards the horizontal, contributing to the spreading habit.

Occurrence and distribution

Whereas valley grevillea is often concentrated along watercourses, smooth grevillea extends more up the sides of valleys. It is confined to the Darling Range, and extends from Wooroloo Brook to the Murray River and east to North Bannister.

In the Metropolitan Region it can be found in such places as the Helena Valley, below Mundaring Weir; and the valley of Wooroloo Brook where O'Brien Road crosses it, east of Walyunga National Park.

Collection and naming

Collected by James Drummond, probably in 1839, from near Perth. Specific name after the naturalist Captain James Mangles.

∧ *Colletid bee (x 2).*

< *Stem with leaves, buds,
flowers and fruits.*

Distinctive features

Spreading, open shrub to 4 m, broader
than tall. Smooth, hairless branches and
stems.

Leaves 2-5 x 1½-5 cm, spiny, variable. All
divide into 3 lobes; in some each lobe
divides into 2 or 3.

Flowers produced from mid winter to mid
spring, tiny, white, on stalks ½-2 cm long, in
clusters at the ends of the stems or in the
leaf-axils.

Corkybark

Gyrostemon ramulosus

This distinctively coloured small tree has bright green fleshy foliage and pale brown bark. The spreading crown above its short bole reveals a lovely pattern of straight or gently curving branchlets, each supporting a puff of foliage. Its light, corky bark is quite rough in texture, being longitudinally ribbed.

The gyrostemon family, to which corkybark belongs, is confined to Australia but covers almost the entire continent. It is most typical of arid regions. The genus *Gyrostemon* contains 12 species and occurs in all Australian states. Like sheoaks, the gyrostemons have separate male and female flowers, and each corkybark plant bears flowers all of the one sex.

Corkybark is chiefly found in drier, inland parts of Australia. It is distributed extensively, covering parts of South Australia, Queensland and the Northern Territory, as well as Western Australia.

In Western Australia, corkybark occurs in the northern and central Wheatbelt, the Goldfields and the far interior, and extends north to the Kimberley. Perth is the southernmost limit of corkybark's distribution on the Swan Coastal Plain.

Associated life

The larvae of long-horned beetles burrow into the dead wood of older trees, and a small species of native bee lays its eggs in the tunnels they leave. The female flowers produce sticky secretions, which attract large numbers of ants.

In the northern Wheatbelt the emu eats the fruits, and thus disperses the seeds. This probably happens also in the north of the Metropolitan Region, where the emu still occurs in places such as Yanchep National Park.

Occurrence in the Metropolitan Region

Corkybark is uncommon in the Metropolitan Region, where it occurs mostly in the coastal dunes or on limestone. Some well developed specimens grow near Lake Nowergup in the south-east of Nowergup Nature Reserve. There is a good population in Trigg Bushland, on the dune ridge bordering Karrinyup Road, and a few specimens occur in Bold Park, near Stephenson Avenue.

In the 1980s there were one or two specimens at Alfred Cove, but the species seems to have disappeared from this site. This was possibly corkybark's only occurrence on the Swan Coastal Plain south of the Swan River.

Cultivation

Although interesting and distinctive, this small tree has hardly been cultivated. It can be grown from either seed or cuttings. As a small plant it needs protection from snails, which find its succulent stems and leaves very appetising.

Collection and naming

Collected from islands off Shark Bay in 1803 by naturalists on Baudin's expedition. Specific name from the Latin *ramosus* 'bearing many branches' and *-ul-*, a diminutive: the plant was described as having a large number of thin branches.

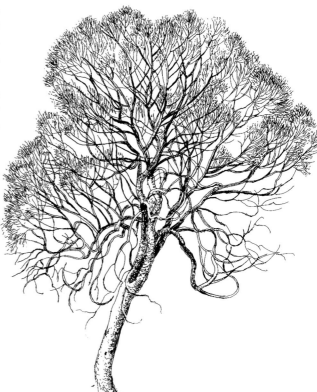

∧ *Emu.*

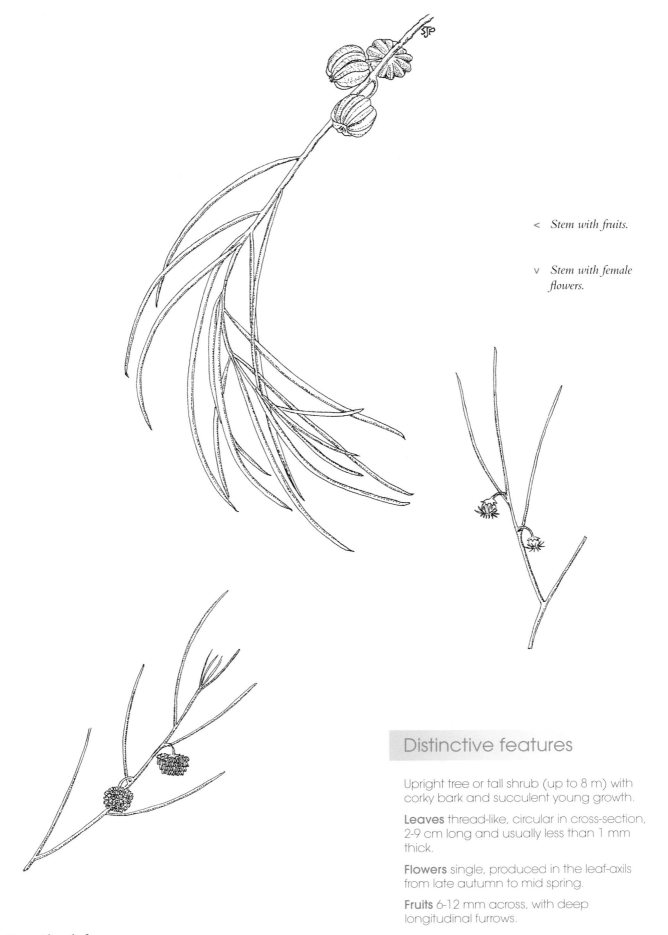

<   *Stem with fruits.*

v   *Stem with female*
     flowers.

Distinctive features

Upright tree or tall shrub (up to 8 m) with corky bark and succulent young growth.

Leaves thread-like, circular in cross-section, 2-9 cm long and usually less than 1 mm thick.

Flowers single, produced in the leaf-axils from late autumn to mid spring.

Fruits 6-12 mm across, with deep longitudinal furrows.

∧   *Stem with male flowers.*

Snail hakea

Hakea cristata

The large, snail-shaped fruit of this plant has given rise to the suggested name 'snail hakea'.

It has the smallest natural distribution of any species in this book, even smaller than that of Yanchep mallee. It extends north to Bullsbrook Nature Reserve, south to Kalamunda National Park, west to the Darling Scarp at Swan View and east to the Helena River south of The Lakes. It has a range of about 40 km from north to south, and of about 30 km from west to east.

Snail hakea grows predominantly on granite hills and granitic soils of the Darling Scarp and the sides of river valleys. It also grows on laterite. There is no obvious reason why its range extends no further.

Hakeas are shrubs or, rarely, small trees, which belong to the banksia family. About 150 species are known, all of which are confined to Australia. Most of these, more than 100 species, occur in Western Australia, the vast majority in the south-western part of the State, but several in the north or the dry interior.

Localities

An easily accessible population grows along the Toodyay Road, about 7-9 km from its junction with the Great Northern Highway. Snail hakea can also be found in the western parts of Kalamunda and John Forrest national parks.

Associated life

The leaves are host to two types of scale insect. One produces small, white, oval scales (pictured), the other more elongated scales. Leaves sewn together are the work of a moth associated with hakeas (see p. 19).

The New Holland honeyeater and the yellow-throated miner have been seen at the flowers.

Appearance

Several stems arise from a rootstock below ground, and spread outwards to form a broad shrub, usually no more than 3 m high.

Snail hakea is open rather than bushy. This habit, together with the irregular distribution of foliage and wiggly stems, forms a delightful silhouette. The wiggles are usually caused when the main shoot is eaten and a side-shoot takes over. This has happened repeatedly in the specimen illustrated.

Ecological notes

Snail hakea's underground rootstock enables it to survive fire. Where one plant has several stems, they probably originated as new shoots from the rootstock after fire, since in cultivation this species generally develops a single stem.

The size of the rootstocks of many natural specimens, evidenced by the spacing of the stems leaving the ground, suggests that the species is long-lived.

Collection and naming

Collected by Charles Fraser in 1827 at the Swan River. *Cristata*, Latin for 'crested', refers to the two crests on the fruit.

∧ *White scales on leaf.*

< *Stem with leaves, flowers and a fruit.*

Distinctive features

Open shrub of the Darling Scarp and Range, with smooth, chestnut-brown bark.

Leaves blue-green, 5-8½ x 3-7 cm, the entire margin prickly-toothed.

Flowers white, in clusters in the leaf-axils, produced in late autumn to early spring.

Fruits large, 4½-5 x 3-3½ cm, and snail-shaped.

Harsh hakea

∧ *Single flower (x 2).*

Hakea prostrata is an unlikely name for a tree or tall shrub. *Prostrata* (Latin for 'prostrate') is generally given only to mat-plants, or plants whose branches run along the ground. This was its growth habit where harsh hakea was first collected, from heath vegetation on the south coast. In this environment, salt spray readily kills foliage, forcing the plants to grow low, spreading and dense for mutual protection.

In the Perth area unburnt specimens typically grow as small trees up to 5 m, often slender and upright. Very young plants, however, often send out horizontal branches that run close to the ground. The prickly leaves give harsh hakea its common name.

Occurrence and distribution

Harsh hakea is widely distributed in the south-west of Western Australia, from Kalbarri to Israelite Bay.

This species is not particular about soil. In the Metropolitan Region it occurs widely both on the coastal plain and in the Darling Range, avoiding only the infertile Bassendean sands and some wetland soils. It is perhaps most abundant in the coastal limestone belt.

Ecological notes

On undeveloped land so degraded that only a few original plant species remain, there is a good chance that harsh hakea will be one of them, particularly if the soil is Cottesloe or Karrakatta. This species is one of Perth's toughest plants. If damaged, it will readily resprout from its rootstock, and it reproduces well if given time between fires to produce seed. The seedlings are hardy.

In Perth bushlands, harsh hakea often has several stems, showing that it has been burnt and resprouted. If it is only about a metre tall, that suggests there has been insufficient time since the last fire for it to reach full size, unless it is growing in extremely shallow soil.

Human uses

In the bushlands where it occurs, harsh hakea is a useful plant to use in closing unwanted tracks. It can be planted at each end of the track to provide a stout, prickly barrier, which will resprout after fire. To preserve the local form of harsh hakea, seeds for this purpose should be collected from within the bushland.

Associated life

Patches of dead leaves, with silken webbing and large amounts of brown frass, are a sign of the marbled concealer moth. The larvae feed in winter and spring, and the adult moths emerge in summer. The moth belongs to the genus *Thalamarchella*, which is confined to the south-west of Western Australia.

Other insects are associated with other various parts of harsh hakea. The larvae of another moth bore into the stems, betraying their presence by the brown frass with which they cover their exit-holes. Tiny nitidulid beetles, the size of a match-head, enter the bases of the flowers to eat the petals. Native bees and other insects visit the flowers for their nectar. The seeds are eaten by insects and birds such as Carnaby's black-cockatoo.

Collection

Collected in 1802 by Robert Brown, botanist of the Flinders expedition, on "sterile hills" at King George Sound.

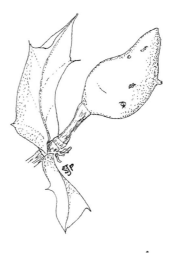

Closed and opened fruits.

∧ *Marbled concealer moth on underside of leaf of harsh hakea, with frass produced by the larvae of this moth species (x 2).*

Distinctive features

Shrub or small tree of the coastal plain and Darling Range.

Bark rough, grey-brown.

Leaves pale green to bluish-green, stalkless, with 2 lobes at the base, embracing the stem, 3½-6½ x 1½-3½ cm, prickly. .

Flowers creamy-white, produced in late winter or spring.

Fruits 2-3 x 1-2 cm, beaked, rather rough or with a few prickles.

Two-leaf hakea

Hakea trifurcata

Two-leaf hakea is unusual in having two distinct types of leaf. Most of its leaves are divided into slender segments, but oval-shaped leaves are scattered among them.

Ecological notes

The oval leaves resemble the fruits in shape and colour, and possibly serve to confuse seed-eating insects, a theory supported by the fact that two-leaf hakea does not produce any oval leaves until it is sexually mature and flowering.

The oval leaves are produced in the new growth in late winter to early spring, the later growth producing only divided leaves. Some specimens have a particularly high proportion of oval leaves, possibly because they finish growing early.

Compared with other hakeas, the fruits of two-leaf hakea have thin walls, and they remain green rather than turning brown. Whereas the fruits of most hakeas retain their seeds for many years, often until the branch dies, those of two-leaf hakea open and shed their seeds within a year.

Two-leaf hakea is vigorous, and probably not long-lived. It is killed by fire, and relies for its survival on the seedlings that germinate the following winter. These grow much faster than those of most other shrub species, and soon develop a spreading habit.

Associated life

Two-leaf hakea flowers prolifically in winter and spring, and is a rich source of pollen and

∧   *Carnaby's black-cockatoo.*

nectar. Its flowers attract large numbers of insects, including butterflies, various wasps, the honey-bee, several species of native bee and the brilliant green wolf-beetle. Carnaby's black-cockatoo eats the seeds.

Human uses

Two-leaf hakea is an excellent source of pollen for building up bee colonies in winter, immediately before parrotbush produces its main flow of nectar. A crop of honey can be produced too, but it is not of good quality.

Occurrence and distribution

Two-leaf hakea has an extensive range, from north of Geraldton to east of Esperance. It grows on a number of soil-types in the Metropolitan Region, particularly on shallow soils. On the coastal plain it is found on the coastal limestone, where it is common in bushlands north of Wanneroo. It also occurs on granite in the Darling Scarp, and in gravelly soils adjacent to the Scarp.

Appearance

Given room and light, two-leaf hakea is a large, spherical shrub. In scrub vegetation it tends to spread to fill whatever space is available. On the coastal plain it is often less than 3 m tall, but in the Darling Scarp it is commonly 3-3½ m.

The strongly scented cream flowers are in numerous small clusters among the foliage. From a distance, the flowering shrub is dull cream in colour, since the masses of flowers are seen through a 'screen' of divided leaves.

Collection and naming

Collected by A. Menzies in 1791 at King George Sound. Specific name, from the Latin *tres* 'three' and *furca* 'fork', refers to the leaves, many of which are divided into three segments.

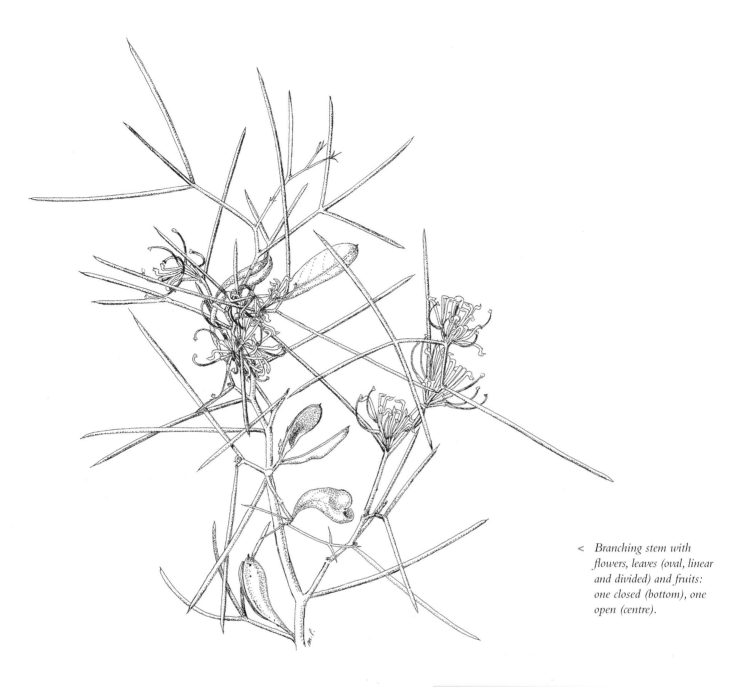

< *Branching stem with flowers, leaves (oval, linear and divided) and fruits: one closed (bottom), one open (centre).*

Distinctive features

Large, fairly dense, spreading shrub of the coastal plain and Darling Scarp.

Leaves of two sorts: one oval-shaped, 3½-5 cm long; the other linear or divided once or twice into linear segments. On most specimens the divided leaves are the more abundant.

Flowers white or pinkish, held in small clusters in leaf-axils near the ends of the stems; produced in winter or early spring.

Fruits green, sometimes brown, slightly curved, 2-2½ cm long and about ½ cm or more wide.

Grey stinkwood

Jacksonia furcellata

Like many other jacksonias, grey stinkwood is virtually leafless, with leaves reduced to minute scales, and their function taken over by green branchlets. This characteristic, an adaptation to living in an arid environment, is shared by many Western Australian plants.

The genus *Jacksonia,* in the legume family, is entirely Australian. Of its 74 species, 56 occur in Western Australia, mostly in the South-West.

Appearance

Grey stinkwood is usually a shaggy, upright small tree to 8 m. One or more shrubby forms less than 2 m are found here and there, notably in the Rockingham area. Its branchlets are grey-green, owing to a dense cover of minute silky hairs. The smaller stems divide frequently and give the effect of grey-green foliage. Green stinkwood (p. 160) has much darker and greener stems, lacking the silky hairs.

Ecological notes

The seeds of many members of the legume family are dispersed by ants, which gather and store them in their nests in order to eat the fleshy, oily appendages. This is probably true of grey stinkwood, since most seedlings germinate in open areas, where ants often build their nests.

Seeds stored in ants' nests, or buried by leaf-litter, can be dormant for years. The heat of a bushfire will crack the stored seeds, allowing them to germinate; and the summer sun, over one or more summers, will crack seeds brought to the surface in spots where the soil is disturbed. The seedlings are particularly hardy and grow rapidly.

Grey stinkwood is an outstanding coloniser of waste land, and many plants have established themselves along the Kwinana and Mitchell freeways. By contrast, it is uncommon in undisturbed bush.

The tall form of grey stinkwood is killed by fire, but its seedlings develop rapidly, and specimens only two or three years old can produce large amounts of seed. At least some of the shrubby forms can resprout after fire from a rootstock.

Associated life

Many insects besides ants make use of grey stinkwood. Tiny female gall-wasps chew holes in the stem in which to lay their eggs. The grubs tunnel in the stem, and the plant produces a gall, apparently in response to a chemical they produce. When fully grown they pupate and emerge as wasps. The size of the exit-holes in disused galls shows how small these wasps are.

Beetle-pruned branches are often found. The larva of a species of long-horned beetle cuts the branch off shortly before pupating below the cut (compare the jewel beetle that tunnels in coojong, pp. 48-9).

Jewel beetles take nectar from the flowers, and native bees pollen. A species of weevil eats the petals. Holes in the seed-pods are made by a species of weevil, whose larvae eat the seeds. Such pods are often taken over by tiny spiders.

Distribution

Grey stinkwood has a wide range in the South-West, from near Geraldton to near Esperance, and is particularly evident in the coastal strip of sandy soils. It is very common on the Swan

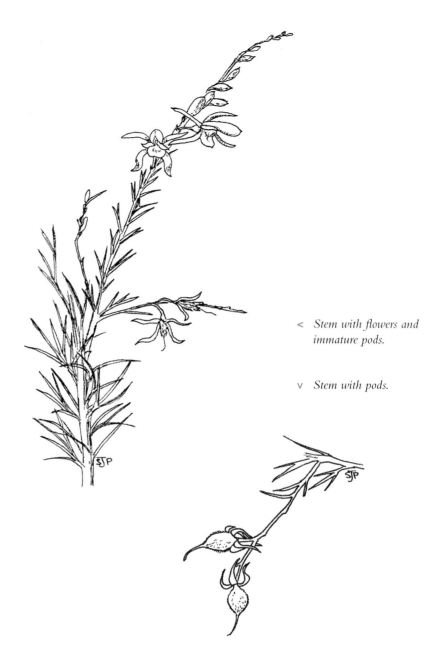

< *Stem with flowers and immature pods.*

∨ *Stem with pods.*

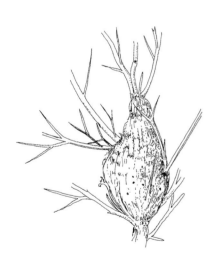

∧ *Gall on stem.*

Coastal Plain. Its abundance on many sites is no doubt the result of human disturbance.

Collection and naming

Collected from specimens cultivated at Malmaison and Navarre, Paris, in 1813. Specific name, from *furca* 'forked' and *-elle-*, a diminutive, refers to the forked branchlets.

Distinctive features

Upright shrub or small tree. Leafless.

Stems silky and pale, grey-green, the smaller stems frequently dividing into twos or threes and crowded together.

Flowers pea-shaped, yellow and orange-red, produced from late winter to early autumn.

Pods a slightly flattened egg-shape or narrow egg-shape, 6–10 mm long, covered in dense short hairs.

Green stinkwood, kabbur

Jacksonia sternbergiana

∧ *Long-tailed pea-blue.*

This species is aptly named. When its wood is burnt, particularly when still green, it smells like a urinal.

Like grey stinkwood, green stinkwood is virtually leafless. The two can be readily distinguished, however, by their colour and habit. Green stinkwood's 'foliage' (the green branchlets at the ends of the branches) is mid green, whereas that of grey stinkwood is a much paler grey-green.

Green stinkwood is more spreading than grey stinkwood, and develops into a stouter tree. It presumably lives longer. And whereas grey stinkwood's branchlets divide frequently to form a dense network, those of green stinkwood are long and flexible and often bend under their own weight.

Green stinkwood can be confused with swishbush (p. 206) or *Daviesia divaricata,* another green, leafless pea-plant. It can be distinguished from the latter by its more irregular outline, its softer, more flexible branchlets, its elliptic pods, and its longer period of flowering.

Associated life

Green stinkwood is one of Perth's most important shrubs for animals. Its flowers are produced for most of the year, and are a major source of pollen and nectar for insects. Several species of native bee visit the flowers. One of the largest, the black jacksonia bee, is perhaps the chief pollinator. It pushes open the keel of the flower with its legs, showering its thorax with pollen, which it transfers to the next flower it visits.

At least three species of butterfly breed on green stinkwood: the long-tailed pea-blue, fringed heath-blue and western jewel. The larvae of the first two feed on the buds and flowers. The adults of the pea-blue — small and grey-brown with a blue sheen — are often seen flying near this plant during the warmer months. The western jewel is brilliantly marked, with areas of iridescent blue on the upper side of the wings and broad pale green spots on the underside. Its larvae, which feed on the surface of the plant's stems, have an association with ants; the butterfly is found only north of the Swan River, in bushlands where the right species of ant are present.

Other insects use the foliage or wood. The crusader bug and the adults of two species of jewel beetle (*Astraeus flavopictus* and *Melobasis lathami*) feed on the foliage. *Astraeus flavopictus* was one of the first beetles to be described in Australia, and is the type species for the genus. The larvae of both species of jewel beetle tunnel in the branches.

Broken branches severed by a straight cut (see Fig. 24, p. 18) are caused by a species of long-horned beetle. The beetle is probably the same as or similar to the one that uses grey stinkwood. Ants and the solitary carpenter bee later use the disused tunnels for nesting. The adult bee makes a cocoon and stuffs it with pollen and nectar for the larvae to feed on.

In disturbed areas green stinkwood forms dense stands, which provide good cover and abundant food for insectivorous birds.

Ecological notes

Both species of stinkwood are good colonisers of disturbed land. Unlike the tall form of grey stinkwood, green stinkwood resprouts from a rootstock after fire, and is one of the few native species that thrive in unmanaged suburban bush remnants subject to frequent burning and other abuses.

Occurrence and distribution

Green stinkwood ranges from near Kalbarri east to York and south to Katanning.

In the Metropolitan Region it occurs in almost all soils, but favours the more fertile. Its abundance compared with that of grey stinkwood gives a rough idea of how fertile the soil is. Sites with only green stinkwood are usually the most fertile, those with only grey stinkwood the least.

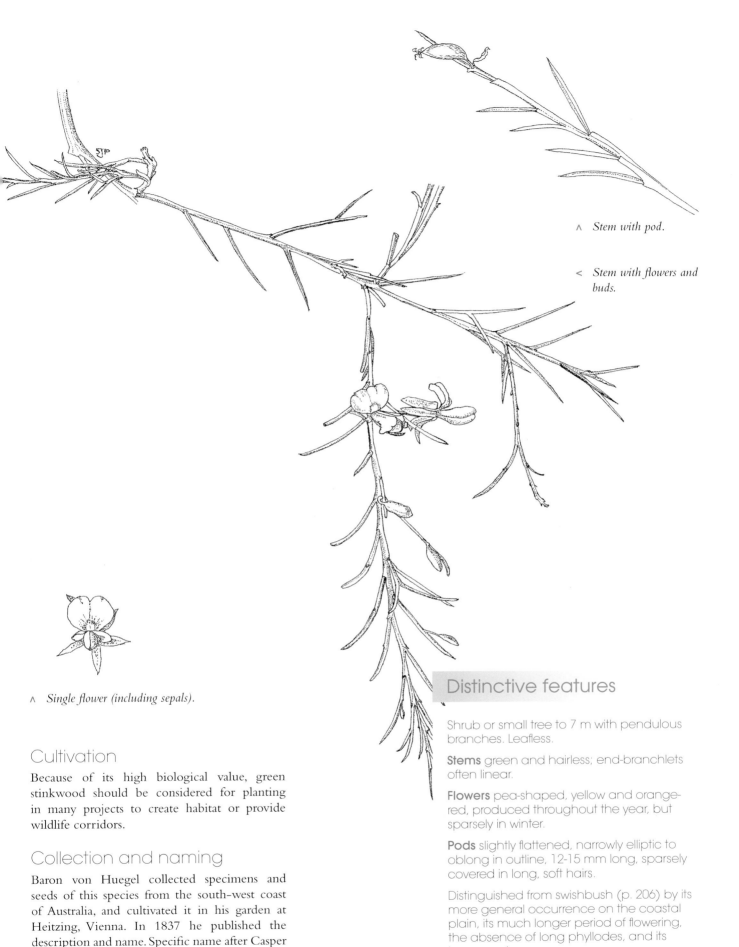

∧   *Stem with pod.*

<   *Stem with flowers and buds.*

∧   *Single flower (including sepals).*

Cultivation

Because of its high biological value, green stinkwood should be considered for planting in many projects to create habitat or provide wildlife corridors.

Collection and naming

Baron von Huegel collected specimens and seeds of this species from the south-west coast of Australia, and cultivated it in his garden at Heitzing, Vienna. In 1837 he published the description and name. Specific name after Casper von Sternberg, a Czech naturalist, founder of the National Museum in Prague.

Distinctive features

Shrub or small tree to 7 m with pendulous branches. Leafless.

Stems green and hairless; end-branchlets often linear.

Flowers pea-shaped, yellow and orange-red, produced throughout the year, but sparsely in winter.

Pods slightly flattened, narrowly elliptic to oblong in outline, 12-15 mm long, sparsely covered in long, soft hairs.

Distinguished from swishbush (p. 206) by its more general occurrence on the coastal plain, its much longer period of flowering, the absence of long phyllodes, and its larger pods.

Kingia, bullanock

Kingia australis

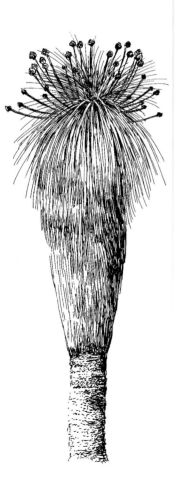

Kingia and balga (p. 208) look rather alike. Both have clusters of long, slender leaves, and trunks built from the accumulation of leaf-bases; both are monocotyledons, which do not form true wood.

But whereas a mature balga can be transplanted, a mature kingia cannot. Despite their visual similarities, kingia and balga are not closely related, and belong to separate families.

The flowering stems of kingia differ from those of balga. Balga's 'spear' arises from the tip of the plant's growing shoot, so each shoot can produce only one flowering stem. Kingia's 'drumsticks' — globular or egg-shaped heads of flowers on stout stems — arise from the sides of the shoot. Each shoot can therefore produce more than one, and they can number up to 100!

Whereas balga is one of several species in the genus *Xanthorrhoea*, kingia has no close relatives and is classed as a genus by itself. It has several special features, including aerial roots.

Kingia belongs to the family Dasypogonaceae, which contains the pineapple bushes (genus *Dasypogon*) and a few other genera. Botanists have differing views on exactly which genera the family comprises. Genetic studies have shown that it is most closely related to the southern rushes, in the family Restionaceae.

Ecological notes

Kingia's aerial roots are most unusual, since such roots are normally found only on plants growing in very moist environments. This suggests that kingia once grew in rainforests but adapted to the present drier conditions.

The roots are produced by the growing shoot each winter, at the beginning of the growing season. They descend down the trunk underneath the leaf-bases and are not visible. They grow about 2 cm a month during the plant's growing season, squeezing between the leaf-bases and the existing roots from previous years, and sending out many lateral roots. Some eventually enter the soil; they then grow almost vertically downwards, and do not spread along the surface.

This system of roots is thought to help the plant in several ways. The fine roots among the leaf-bases probably absorb water that collects there after summer or autumn showers that wet the trunk but barely penetrate the soil. Organic materials, from the decayed leaves and bird-droppings that collect in the leaf-bases, are probably absorbed by the roots too, which would assist plants growing in infertile soils. The aerial roots no doubt also take up oxygen; this could explain why kingia can thrive on swampy, waterlogged sites.

Kingia's stem is not strong, and the network of aerial roots helps prop up the plant. Moreover, after 300 or 400 years the trunk's soft core begins to die back from the base; the plant still survives, because the roots can carry up water and nutrients, prolonging the plant's life.

The aerial roots also protect the plant from fire and insects. The mass of long leaves protects the growing tissue, and the leaf-bases protect the trunk. When the leaf-bases eventually rot away at the trunk's base, the thick, compact mantle of roots protects the trunk. Thus kingia survives fire, and is little troubled by insects.

Fire induces kingia to flower. There are always flower buds in the leaf-axils waiting to burst into growth. After fire, they grow rapidly into 'drumsticks', and flowering begins within three weeks. Balga's flowering too is promoted by fire, but is delayed until the following spring. Although kingia's flowering is most prolific after fire, about two thirds of specimens produce a few 'drumsticks' each year, in winter.

The age of a specimen of kingia can be measured by removing its leaf-bases and aerial roots and examining the core of the trunk. (This kills the plant, and should be attempted only on sites where the vegetation is to be cleared.) The core's surface is slightly wavy; each wave and depression corresponds to a year's growth. The plants grow about 1½ cm a year, so a specimen with a stem 6 m long would be about 400 years old.

The trunk records environmental conditions during the plant's lifetime, which sometimes extends back well before European settlement. For instance, patterns left by prolific flowering indicate the years of fires. A study of specimens from jarrah–marri forest at Roleystone has shown that fire rarely occurred there in the 200 years before European settlement.

Growth habit

Kingia can grow up to 7 m in the Metropolitan Region. It normally has a single, unbranched trunk, but branches occasionally, if the growing tip (hidden among the foliage) is damaged.

Associated life

Various insects visit kingia's flowers, as do birds such as the silvereye.

A species of lucanid beetle (illustrated), with a metallic sheen, often shelters in the leaves. At the base of the crown of foliage the leaves are quite hairy and are massed together. This creates a humid environment, where many millipedes settle.

In the tight mass of dead leaves are black native cockroaches and many spiders' webs, and sometimes mantid egg-cases or spiders' egg-sacs.

Distribution

Kingia is confined to Western Australia. It occurs chiefly in the lower South-West, but extends eastwards to Cape Riche, east of Albany, and northwards to Mt Lesueur, near Jurien.

In the Metropolitan Region, kingia occurs mostly on the clayey flats of the eastern side of the coastal plain. It also grows in a few places in the Darling Scarp.

Human uses

In the past, kingia trunks were used to make floors for barns, stables and sheds, where they proved quite resistant to termites.

Collection and naming

Collected by Robert Brown in 1801 at King George Sound. Specific name, from the Latin *australis* 'southern', refers to the southern hemisphere, or perhaps to the southern part of the Australian continent, where the specimen was collected.

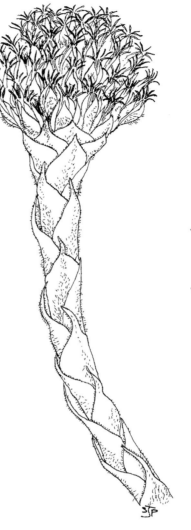

∧ *Leaf, with part of its base attached.*

< *Part of flowering 'drumstick'.*

∨ *The lucanid beetle* Lamprima *sp.*

Distinctive features

Kingia can be distinguished from balga (p. 208) as follows.

Leaves silky and bluish or bluish-green; if pulled out they reveal broad leaf-bases, up to 2½ cm across.

Flowers located at the tips of 'drumsticks' (stout stalks covered with silky bracts); in heads 4-7 cm across.

Unlike balga, kingia rarely branches; and its trunk is straighter and smoother than balga's.

Spearwood, pondil

∧ *Carbolic long-horned (or longicorn) beetle, whose larvae burrow in the branches of spearwood.*

Spearwood provides some of the best habitat for orchids in the Metropolitan Region. In undisturbed areas it forms thickets on low-lying sites, where orchids benefit from the moist soil, the shade and the absence of small shrubs. Such orchids include beak, bunny, donkey, flying duck, hare, spider and sun orchids, several species of greenhood, and species of hammer orchid, including two that are now rare.

Spearwood is a large shrub, common on the coastal plain, particularly south of the Swan River. Its foliage is soft, especially the new growth, which is on flexible stems and thickly covered in hairs. It grows in moist, but not waterlogged, soil, and often marks the transition between wetland and dryland vegetation.

Kunzea glabrescens has been confused in the past with *K. ericifolia*, which has a similar distribution in the south-west corner of Western Australia. *K. glabrescens* is distinguished by its much shorter leaves and by the round shape of its bracteoles (small leaf-like structures associated with the flowers).

There are about 36 species in the genus *Kunzea*, which belongs to the myrtle family. All are shrubs and occur in southern or eastern Australia, about 25 of them in Western Australia.

Growth habit

Although spearwood grows to 4-5 m tall it is a shrub, since it splits near the base into a large number of near-equal branches. These are straight and almost vertical, and continue to divide, with a very narrow angle of branching. The name 'spearwood' refers to the straight and slender stems.

Ecological notes

Spearwood is killed by fire. The even-aged stands often seen result from the growth of the subsequent seedlings.

Human uses

The stems are used as beanpoles in market gardens, and for making craypots and sometimes fences. Unfortunately they are sometimes cut illegally in reserves. This, and the associated access by vehicles, causes much damage.

Spearwood is now used in many projects to rehabilitate wetlands. To maintain the natural zones of vegetation, it should be planted at the outer edge of the wetland vegetation, where it gives way to dryland vegetation.

Associated life

Spearwood's flowers are a good source of food for insects such as jewel beetles and ants. Long-horned beetles bore into the branches of larger specimens, sometimes killing them by ringbarking.

In thickets, spearwood provides not only habitat for orchids but also cover for birds and other animals. New Holland honeyeaters nest in these thickets at Jandakot.

Distribution

Spearwood grows in the State's south–west corner, stretching from the Moore River to near Albany.

Collection and naming

Collected in 1981 at the southern end of Lake Goollelal, Kingsley, by H.R. Toelken, senior botanist at the State Herbarium of South Australia. Specific name from the Latin *glaber* 'without hair' and *–escens* '–ish', meaning 'almost without hairs', probably referring to the leaves.

< *Side view of flower (x 2).*

v *Cluster of fruits.*

Distinctive features

Erect shrub to 5 m, growing mostly in low-lying areas. Young growth hairy and soft to the touch.

Bark rough and grey.

Leaves 3-10 x ½-1½ mm.

Flowers yellow, mainly in spring, grouped into globular heads about 1½ cm across.

Fruits in globular clusters.

Tall labichea

Labichea lanceolata

∧　*Hoverfly (x 2).*

Tall labichea is an erect shrub commonly seen in wet gullies and near granite rocks. In winter and spring its green foliage is dotted with bright yellow flowers.

Tall labichea belongs to the legume family. All of the 14 species of *Labichea* are confined to Australia. Eight of them occur in southern Western Australia, and the rest in Queensland and the Northern Territory, on the opposite side of the continent. This species is the tallest.

Ecological notes

In wet gullies tall labichea grows among other tall shrubs, and usually reaches 3 m or more. On shallow granite soils it is often less than 3 m.

Tall labichea is killed by fire, but its usual habitats are less prone to fire than elsewhere.

The seeds of some plants in the legume family are spread by birds. They swallow the seeds and digest the seed-stalk, but excrete the seed. This is probably true of tall labichea, as its seed's stalk is prominent and fleshy.

Associated life

Any seeds that have not been eaten by birds and have fallen to the ground are probably collected by ants.

Small insects visit the flowers, including hoverflies and tiny, black colletid bees. Numerous thrips may be seen on the petals, where they suck juices.

The foliage does not appear to support many insects. Here and there leaves can be found sewn together, probably by a moth larva. Swellings along the woody stems are inhabited by the larvae of a wasp, probably a gall-wasp in the family Cynipidae.

Occurrence and distribution

Tall labichea occurs widely in south-western Australia, from the Murchison River to Cape Arid, east of Esperance. It appears, however, not to occur in the extreme south-west corner, between Bunbury and Albany.

In the Metropolitan Region, tall labichea grows in the valleys of many rivers and streams in the Darling Range. It can be found, for example, where O'Brien Road crosses Wooroloo Brook (just east of Walyunga National Park), by the Helena River below Mundaring Weir, and by the Serpentine River in Serpentine National Park.

Collection and naming

Collected by Baron von Huegel in 1833 at King George Sound and the Swan River. The specific name is Latin for 'shaped like a lance-head', and refers to the leaves.

∧ *Typical leaves, with three leaflets.*

< *Stem with leaves, flowers and pods.*

Distinctive features

Erect shrub 2-3½ m tall, growing in valleys or on granite in the Darling Range.

Leaves green, shiny, comprising either one leaflet or three, with the central one by far the largest; solitary or central leaflet 4-12 cm long and ½-1½ cm wide, with a sharp point up to 3 mm long.

Flowers yellow, comprising four petals, each of them 1-1½ x ½-1½ cm; red markings at the base of one. Produced in winter and spring and arranged in a group of 2 to 12 along the stem.

Pods 2½-4 cm long and about 1 cm wide, ending in a narrow beak.

Seeds dark brown, elliptic in outline, 5 x 3½ mm, with prominent fleshy attachment.

Roadside tea-tree

Leptospermum erubescens

∧ *Anchor jewel beetle (x 2).*

Leptospermums are commonly called tea-trees. It is said that the crew of Captain Cook's ships made a 'tea' from the leaves of one of the common leptospermums of the east coast.

The genus *Leptospermum* extends from south-eastern Asia to New Zealand. Nineteen species occur in Western Australia, but the genus is best represented in eastern Australia, where most of the world's 79 species occur. One of these is well known here: coast (or Victorian) tea-tree, which used to be commonly grown in Perth as a hedge. It is now naturalised and a troublesome weed, and can be found growing in many remnants of vegetation, particularly near the coast.

Associated life

A tea-tree in flower is one of the most rewarding places for viewing insects. The flowers attract large numbers of native bees and flies, wasps, ants, beetles, butterflies, moths and thrips. Most take pollen or nectar; others chew the petals. A few, notably assassin bugs, wait on the flowers to capture other insects.

In spring, about a dozen species of jewel beetle, belonging to five or more different genera, can be found on the flowers. Few other plant species attract as wide a range.

On the stems of some specimens of roadside tea-tree are abundant small globular swellings, or galls. These are caused by a gall-forming wasp. The female lays an egg on the stem. The larva feeds inside the stem, and secretes a chemical that causes the plant cells to multiply.

Distribution

Roadside tea-tree is distributed widely in the southern part of Western Australia. It extends from the Darling Range in the Perth Metropolitan Region through the Wheatbelt and the Great Southern into the Goldfields.

Occurrence in the Metropolitan Region

In the Metropolitan Region, roadside tea-tree is recorded from a number of sites on the Darling Scarp and Darling Plateau. It is commonly encountered along back roads through the forest in the Mundaring area, particularly in the patches of lighter soils.

Ecological notes

Roadside tea-tree thrives on road verges in the Mundaring area and in the Wheatbelt. It likes sunny, open sites; plants shaded on one side noticeably seek light by growing out at an angle towards it. It also seems to like the periodic disturbance of soil along roadsides. It reproduces well on bare ground, and the seedlings compete well with weeds.

By resprouting from the base, roadside tea-tree is able to survive at least mild fires.

Appearance

Roadside tea-tree is a shrub usually 3 m tall, although occasional specimens reach 4 m. It commonly divides at the base into a dozen or more branches, which on old specimens can be up to 12 cm thick.

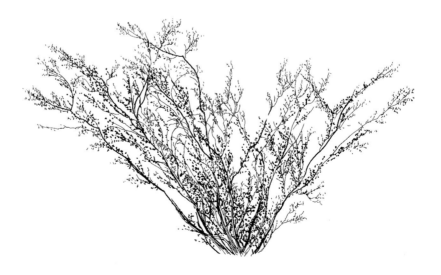

The sombre colouring of the bark and foliage is enlivened in spring by the plant's white or pinkish flowers, borne in profusion. After flowering there is a burst of new growth. The young shoots are long and supple, and often bend downwards.

Collection and naming

Collected by Preiss in 1840 in woodland on gravelly soil near St Ronans Well, west of York, and near the Gordon River, south of Katanning, in woodland on gravelly, somewhat muddy, sterile soil. Also collected in 1840 or 1841 by Molloy near the Vasse River. Specific name is Latin for 'reddening' or 'blushing', and refers to the flowers, which may be pinkish when they first open.

White spray

Logania vaginalis

In spring, white spray produces small, pure white flowers on the ends of its branching stems, like clusters of bright stars.

It belongs to a family of about 500 plant species (the Loganiaceae), most of which occur in tropical regions outside Australia. The genus *Logania*, however, is largely confined to Australia, where 31 of its 34 species occur, chiefly in the temperate, southern parts. Twenty-one species occur in Western Australia. Most are woody shrubs, but some are soft plants that shoot each year from a woody underground rootstock.

Occurrence and distribution

White spray grows on the coast, from Leeman, north of Jurien, round to Esperance and the Recherche Archipelago.

In the Perth Metropolitan Region, it grows only on limestone. Like many other limestone species, such as coast hop-bush, Yanchep mallee, Fremantle mallee and rock mallee, it is not common.

At Star Swamp, North Beach, white spray can be found round the swamp's eastern and northern sides. At Reabold Hill, it grows in places along

Scenic Drive, on the hill's southern and eastern slopes. It used to grow on some of the limestone slopes bordering the lower Swan River, for example between Chidley Point and Point Roe, and on the west side of Freshwater Bay.

Ecological notes

The steep slopes at Reabold Hill and by the Swan River contain many sites where moisture collects. The surrounds of Star Swamp, where the densest stands of white spray occur, are particularly moist. Thus, in the Metropolitan Region at least, white spray appears to need both limestone and moisture, and usually occurs among a dense vegetation of wattles and other large shrubs.

In such shrubby vegetation there are two contrasting habits of growth. Vigorous species, such as white-stemmed wattle and two-leaf hakea, are round and bushy, and spread into whatever space is available. Others, such as white spray, are sparse and slender. White spray produces far less mass than the vigorous wattles with which it associates, but keeps pace with them upwards, and thus ensures it gets enough light.

White spray seems to need other shrubs for support. Many isolated specimens fall over, although most of them survive. This species survives mild fires by resprouting from a small rootstock.

Growth habit

This slender, upright shrub can grow to 4 m tall in thick vegetation at Star Swamp, and the specimens that grew by the lower Swan River reached at least 3½ m. On Reabold Hill, however, where it occurs among lower vegetation, many specimens are less than 2 m tall. Young plants usually have a single stem, but most mature specimens have several stems arising from the ground.

Associated life

Native bees visit the flowers. The sewing of clusters of buds together is probably the work of a moth larva.

Leaf-eating beetles of the species illustrated have been taken from several plants at Star Swamp. Some leaves have blisters, probably caused by a moth larva that eats the tissue between the leaf's outer layers. Black scribbles found on some leaves are probably made by the larvae of a tiny fly or moth.

Collection and naming

Collected by Labillardière in September 1792 from near Esperance. Specific name, from the Latin *vagina* 'sheath', refers to the slight swelling of the stem that connects each pair of opposite leaves.

∧ *A leaf-eating beetle.*

Distinctive features

A slender or sparse shrub to 3½ m or more, growing on limestone.

Leaves in opposite pairs, 4½-8½ cm long and 1 or 2 cm wide, pointed.

Flowers produced in late winter and spring, small, white, in dense clusters on branching stems.

Fruits 7-9 mm long, splitting into 4 parts at the ends.

Saltwater paperbark

Melaleuca cuticularis

Saltwater paperbark is one of several paperbark trees natural to the Metropolitan Region. As its name implies, it occurs near salt or brackish water. Thus it can be found round Lake Coogee; in places near the Swan Estuary, such as Pelican Point and Mt Henry; and on saline clay flats east of Forrestdale Lake.

The Swan Estuary is near the northern limit of its occurrence. On the coastal plain it also grows beside the Leschenault Estuary, but its main distribution is the south coast from Walpole to Israelite Bay, where it borders estuaries, inlets and coastal swamps. Further inland, it grows around some salt lakes in the Great Southern.

Ecological notes

Saltwater paperbark is tolerant of waterlogging, and also of salt in the soil or the air.

Wherever it and freshwater paperbark (p. 182) occur together, saltwater paperbark grows nearer the water. At Salter Point on the Canning River only saltwater paperbark grows, but only freshwater paperbark grows on the opposite bank. Salter Point is low-lying and, being a peninsula, exposed to salt winds blowing off the river from several directions. The opposite bank is less exposed and steeper; thus the soil-water is fresher. Saltwater paperbark survives fire, resprouting along its branches or from its rootstock.

∧   *Nankeen night-heron.*

Appearance

At Lake Coogee saltwater paperbark is a tree to about 5 m, but by the Swan Estuary it often grows as a shrub to only 3 m. The Forrestdale specimens are even smaller: few are more than 2 m tall. On the south coast, however, saltwater paperbark is much larger, reaching about 7 m.

It is a gnarled, somewhat irregular tree with much character. It has whiter bark than the other Perth paperbarks, and dull green foliage, which carries abundant white flowers in the spring.

Associated life

The canopy of saltwater paperbark is used by waterbirds for nesting, roosting and resting. The nankeen night-heron commonly roosts here during the day. Saltwater paperbark does not split into several trunks as commonly as freshwater paperbark, and therefore offers fewer hollows at the base to nesting ducks.

Two types of gall on saltwater paperbark's foliage, both of which appear to be derived from the leaf-buds, are made by the larvae of gall-wasps. One is pinkish and appears as a cluster of succulent galls; the other is pale brown and narrowly conical in shape. The first type attracts tiny thrips and mites on its outside.

At Lake Coogee the yellow admiral has been seen at saltwater paperbark's flowers, which are probably also attractive to other butterflies.

Collection and naming

Collected by Labillardière in 1792 near Esperance. Specific name, from the Latin *cuticula* 'thin external skin', refers to the deciduous, papery bark.

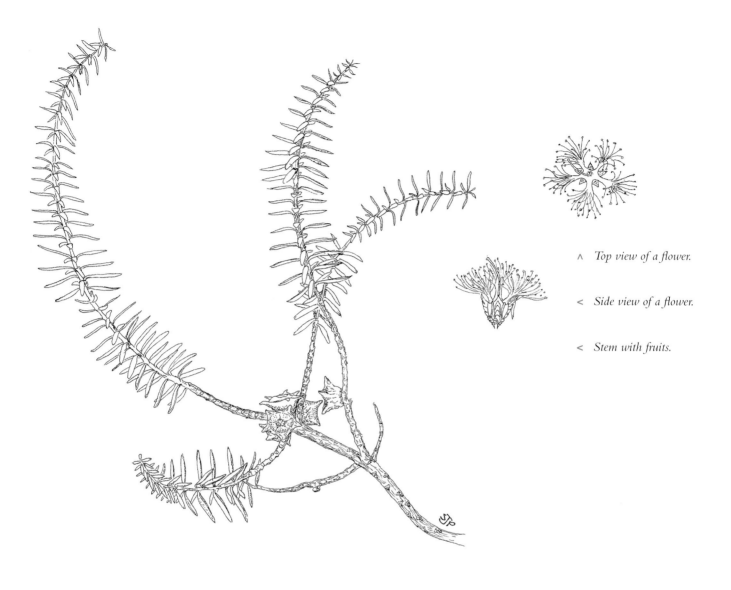

∧   *Top view of a flower.*

<   *Side view of a flower.*

<   *Stem with fruits.*

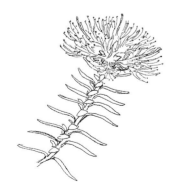

∧   *Stem with cluster of flowers.*

Distinctive features

Small tree or large shrub growing in salty wetlands.

Bark white and papery.

Leaves in opposite pairs, 7-11 x 2½-4½ mm.

Flowers white or cream, in small clusters at the end of the stem, produced in spring.

Fruits cup-shaped, 6-7 mm long, with 5 protrusions around the rim.

Chenille honey-myrtle

Melaleuca huegelii

∧   *Marbled xenica.*

Chenille honey-myrtle, prized for its showy flower-spikes, is probably the most commonly planted of Perth's melaleucas. It is grown in Perth and also in many other parts of the world, particularly California.

Associated life

Chenille honey-myrtle's flowers are produced in late spring and early summer, when adult insects are abundant. They are very attractive to insects, including several species of jewel beetle, as well as butterflies and moths, native bees, wasps and small flies.

The butterflies include the Australian painted lady, a fast-flying nomadic and migratory species. The marbled xenica, an orange-brown butterfly with darker brown markings, frequently visits the flowers of chenille honey-myrtle in bushlands where the butterfly still occurs. Moths in large numbers visit the flowers at night. Dragonflies are abundant in this season, and often set up territories near the honey-myrtle to prey on the small insects it attracts. The ladybird, another predatory insect, is found too. Less common, and more cryptically coloured, is the praying mantis.

The branches of chenille honey-myrtle are used by wood-boring insect larvae; the shapes of abandoned holes suggest both long-horned beetles and jewel beetles. Other insects are associated with the foliage.

Chenille honey-myrtle's flowers seem less attractive to birds, although the red wattlebird and brown honeyeater have been seen drinking nectar from them.

Distribution

Chenille honey-myrtle is distributed along the west coast from Dirk Hartog Island to Augusta.

Occurrence in the Metropolitan Region

Chenille honey-myrtle is a fairly common shrub of coastal limestone. In the shrubland vegetation that grows where the soil is too shallow for trees, it is often either the dominant species or the co-dominant with white-stemmed wattle. It also occurs as an understorey shrub of the tuart forest.

As well as the Cottesloe sands, it occurs in places on the Quindalup, particularly at Woodman Point, Garden Island and east of Rockingham.

Interestingly, chenille honey-myrtle can also be found to some extent on the eastern side of the coastal plain; for example, in Cardinal Drive Bushland, the Vines. Here it is grows on the Muchea Limestone, scattered deposits associated with former lakes or springs, along a line from Muchea to Benger, west of the Darling Scarp.

Growth habit

Chenille honey-myrtle is like a mallee eucalypt: it has a well developed rootstock from which a number of stems often grow. Isolated specimens form bushes up to 5 m tall, with a spread of up to

10 m. In stands, its curving branches combine in an intertwining thicket.

In the shade of the tuart forest it grows sparser and taller, sometimes reaching 8 m. It also grows taller than usual in the cypress thickets at Woodman Point, where it needs to grow as high as the cypresses to receive enough light.

Chenille honey-myrtle varies in form from place to place. Some cultivated specimens are northern forms, much smaller than the local ones.

Ecological notes

Chenille honey-myrtle's bark protects it from mild fires. In the bush it is affected by intense fires, fuelled by the dense scrub in which it grows, but its rootstock enables it to resprout from below the ground. Since it takes 20 years or more for the regrowth to develop into a full-sized shrub, it is often seen as less than fully developed.

On the north side of Reabold Hill, this species is the last in a plant succession. The first spring after a fire, annuals such as blue lace-flower ('Rottnest daisy') grow in profusion. Shining fanflower (*Scaevola nitida*), which germinates in abundance, dominates for the next few years, until the much larger white-stemmed wattle asserts its presence. All the while the seedlings and suckering regrowth of chenille honey-myrtle are developing at a slower pace. The honey-myrtle eventually dominates, when the wattles die of old age.

Seasonal growth

Chenille honey-myrtle begins its new growth in mid spring. Pink buds form in the leaf-axils of the new shoots, and open to produce white flowers in spikes 1-10 cm long in late spring and early summer. The flower-spikes are almost terminal — 'almost', because the tip of the shoot continues to grow during flowering, and over the rest of summer. Occasionally a few more flowers are produced later in the summer.

Human uses

Apart from cultivation, the main use of chenille honey-myrtle is in beekeeping: although not found in large concentrations, it is useful for its nectar and pollen.

Collection and naming

Collected by Baron von Huegel in 1833 at Fremantle, and named after him.

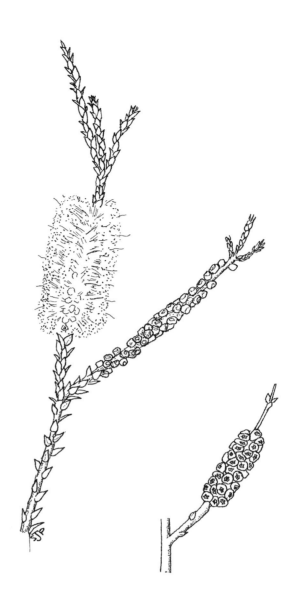

Distinctive features

Shrub or small tree growing near the coast, particularly on limestone.

Bark rough and grey.

Leaves 3-10 mm long, without leaf-stalks, attached to stem by broad base, 2½ -4½ mm across, and narrowing to a point. Held at an acute angle to the stem, the leaves usually overlap.

Buds pink or red.

Flowers white, in late spring or early summer, arranged in cylindrical clusters, near the end of the stem.

Fruits held in dense clusters along the stem, up to 10 cm long.

Moonah, Rottnest tea-tree

Melaleuca lanceolata

Many visitors to Rottnest Island will know moonah, which is common round the developed areas at the island's east end.

Ecological notes

Moonah is a hardy coastal species whose habit of growth helps it survive near the ocean. Isolated individuals branch repeatedly at wide angles, developing a dense dome-shaped canopy that often extends to the ground. In undisturbed conditions moonah often occurs in close stands, with a continuous, smooth canopy that comes down to the ground round the stand's edges. Thus, whether it grows by itself or in a group, moonah develops a dense, almost continuous, dome of foliage that protects it from salt winds and sandblast. If salt kills part of the foliage, a dense network of dead twigs remains to protect the foliage behind.

Although the large, spreading branches often touch the ground, they rarely grow roots (one specimen on Bald Island, off the coast east of Albany, is known to have re-rooted in this way).

Moonah tolerates salt not only in the air but also in the soil. It grows very near the lakes on Rottnest, which are saltier than sea water. It also tolerates dry conditions, and is able to grow on the dry tops of coastal dunes. Nevertheless, moonah is now almost entirely absent from Perth's coastline. This is probably because it is killed by fire. Although afterwards it regenerates

∧   *Stand of moonah.*

well, a second fire before the saplings bear seed will eliminate it from the area. On Rottnest Island, past fires, together with the eating of moonah's seedlings by quokkas, have greatly reduced moonah's occurrence.

Colour

Although moonah's foliage (dull bluish-green to olive-green) and its bark (brownish mid grey) are not particularly dark, moonah always *looks* dark, probably because of its closed canopy and the dense shade it casts. (The illustration is lightened to show the detail and texture.)

Associated life

On Rottnest Island, moonah forest is the habitat of birds such as the fan-tailed cuckoo, red-capped robin, golden whistler and western gerygone, and lizards such as the spiny-tailed gecko.

Although few insects can be found on the heavily shaded ground under moonah's dense canopy, moonah's foliage supports many insects. One of the very few species of native Australian aphid, a species of *Taiwanaphis*, is found on moonah, in colonies on the new growth.

Many insects are also attracted to the flowers, from mid summer to early autumn, including wasps, native bees and the pea-blue butterfly. Birds such as the singing honeyeater and silvereye visit them too.

The grubs of a large, dark species of longicorn beetle tunnel in moonah's wood. Holes commonly seen at the base of trees on Rottnest are probably where the adult beetles emerge.

On Garden Island moonah supports moonah mistletoe, on which a butterfly recorded from the island, the spotted jezebel, probably breeds.

A pale blue lichen can be seen on the trunks and lower branches of some of the trees on Rottnest.

Occurrence and distribution

As might be expected of such a hardy plant, moonah has a wide range. It occurs in all the

Australian mainland states except the Northern Territory. (The name 'moonah' originates from eastern Australia.) In Western Australia it occurs near the coast from Dirk Hartog Island to the South Australian border, with scattered occurrences well inland, especially near salt lakes.

One of moonah's few occurances on the Swan Coastal Plain is a small population in Yalgorup National Park, on an island in Lake Preston. Its protection there from fire is probably the reason why it has survived there but nowhere else in the vicinity.

Occurrence in the Perth area

Moonah's main occurrences in the Perth area nowadays are on Garden and Rottnest islands. It is abundant on the north end of Garden Island and round the settlement on Rottnest.

One of the few mainland occurrences in the Perth area is in the dunes at City Beach. About 120 m south of the car park opposite the southern groyne is a small clump of moonahs. Old aerial photographs suggest that the clump is just two merging specimens, which until the 1960s were part of a larger group. The 100 or more stems that now emerge from the ground are the upper parts of these two trees, the lower parts having been covered by moving sand. In 1990 their combined canopy measured 30 m by 18 m. By conserving moisture, the mass of sand that has half buried these specimens will probably have increased the trees' vigour. And by supporting their branches, it has probably extended their lives. By 2008, some of the branches on the trees' northern side had died, suggesting that they were beginning to succumb to disease or old age.

Human uses

Moonah has been planted fairly extensively. It is useful as a windbreak and shade tree near the coast. Its surface roots can cause problems, however, in disturbing any curbs or paving slabs near by. On Rottnest Island, moonah and Rottnest cypress (p. 84) are the chief species in plantations, fenced to exclude quokkas, to restore the original tree cover.

Collection and naming

Collected in 1820 from a plant in cultivation in Berlin. The specific name is Latin for 'shaped like a lance-head', and refers to the leaves.

< *Red-capped robin.*

Distinctive features

Densely foliaged small tree of the coast and offshore islands, growing as an individual to about 5 m, with a dome-shaped canopy, or in dense stands up to 10 m.

Bark fissured, brownish mid grey.

Leaves held at wide angle to stem, usually bent downwards, about 1-2 cm long and 1-2 mm wide.

Flowers white to pale yellow, produced in summer and early autumn, arranged in cylindrical clusters 1-5 cm long, interspersed with leaves, near the end of the stem.

Fruits along the stem in clusters with spaces between them.

Gorada

∧ *Blotched dusky-
blue (underside).*

Gorada is rare in Perth, where it is currently known only from the Cannington area. It was found in Jandakot when the area was developed, and perhaps still occurs there.

Outside the Metropolitan Region, however, gorada occurs widely, from Kalbarri to the south coast, and inland to east of Kalgoorlie. It is more typical of the Wheatbelt than the lower South-West, but penetrates the South-West as far as Ludlow.

Appearance

Gorada is a large, rather open, shrub to 3½ m tall. It usually has several stems, which spread and twist; often one or more sprawls to the ground. The decorative, grey to white bark is papery and stringy.

Ecological notes

In the Perth area, gorada grows on clay flats. It occurs as scattered individuals, unlike the other paperbarks, which form dense stands.

Gorada's several stems can be well spaced apart, suggesting a massive rootstock that will have developed over many years. The species is clearly long-lived.

Associated life

Gorada's foliage supports numerous booklice and mirid bugs, and small weevils are frequently found. Other insects include beetles and moth caterpillars. The insects support numerous spiders, mostly tiny species.

Shoots tied together and bent to one side are commonly seen in spring, the work of a tiny cream-coloured moth larva. Spherical galls attached to the stems contain thrips, as well as wasp maggots that probably feed on them.

Gorada's flowers attract various wasps and native bees. A small butterfly seen at the flowers at Kenwick, the blotched dusky-blue, breeds on dodders.

At least two species of orange lichen grow on the lower branches. A suitably humid environment for lichens would be created by the damp, swampy environment in which gorada grows, together with the trapping of moisture by gorada's dense foliage.

Common name

'Gorada' is an Aboriginal word meaning 'little' or 'short', and refers to the small size of this species compared to Perth's other paperbark species, particularly freshwater paperbark and modong.

Collection and naming

Collected by James Drummond in the 1840s from Western Australia. Specific name, from the Latin *latus* 'side' and *flos* or *floris* 'flower', refers to the position of the flowers, on the sides of the old wood.

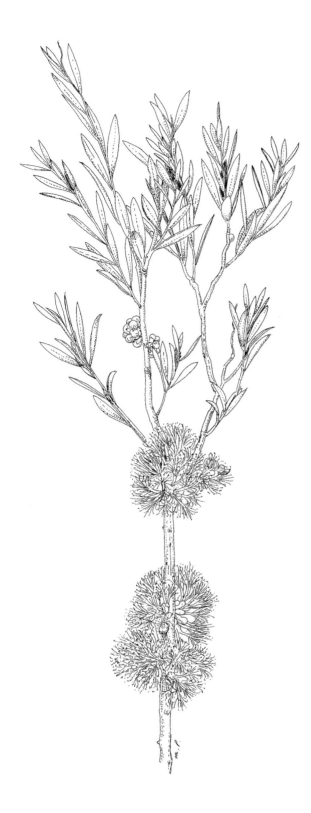

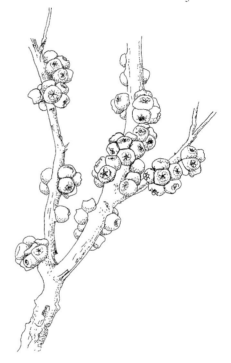

< *Stem with leaves, buds and flowers.*

v *Stem with clusters of fruits.*

Distinctive features

Shrub, usually broader than tall, up to 3½ m, with several stems, growing in clay swamps.

Bark grey to white, papery, stringy.

Leaves pointed, 1-3 cm long and 1-3 mm wide, broadest towards the tip, and narrowing to the stem.

Flowers white, produced in summer, grouped in globular clusters of 5-20, in leaf-axils or on leafless older stems.

Fruits about 5 mm broad.

Modong, stout paperbark

Melaleuca preissiana

Modong is Perth's largest paperbark, reaching up to 15 m. It is picturesque, with its irregular shape and thick, wavering branches. Its detailed crown is fairly open, and its branches and puffs of foliage make a pleasing silhouette. Well developed specimens have thick trunks and are probably quite old.

Modong occurs widely in the Metropolitan Region, but is commoner on the coastal plain than in the Darling Range. It grows chiefly in shallow winter-wet depressions, and is particularly abundant in the Bassendean soils, where there are many such wetlands.

It is often confused with the better-known freshwater paperbark (p. 182). With practice the two species can be distinguished at a distance by their habit of growth. Freshwater paperbark is usually more regularly shaped than modong: compare the illustration on page 182 with the one below. Close up, the two species can be distinguished by the shape and size of their leaves. Where they occur together, modong grows further back from the water than freshwater paperbark. It commonly associates with swamp banksia or flooded gum. It is also often found with Christmas tree, the summer flowers of the two combining to mark the approach of Christmas.

∧   *White-faced heron.*

Common name

'Modong' is recorded as an Aboriginal word for a large tea-tree or paperbark that grows on swampy plains, probably this species. The alternative, 'stout paperbark', refers to the thick trunk and branches.

Flora of the Perth Region calls this species 'moonah', but probably in error.★ Other sources, such as Edna Walling's *Country Roads: The Australian Roadside,*★★ use 'moonah' for Rottnest tea-tree.

Associated life

In early summer the blossoms' copious nectar attracts many beetles, wasps, bees and other insects. Modong also supports many wood-boring insects; fallen branches bear numerous tunnels and holes made by the larvae of jewel beetles.

Waterbirds such as white-faced herons, black ducks and hardheads use modong for breeding, particularly when the trees are standing in water. Modong is less important to waterbirds, however, than freshwater paperbark, which is more regularly inundated.

Human uses

Modong is useful to beekeepers, producing good pollen and copious nectar for about three weeks in December-January. The individual trees apparently flower all together, since the species is noted for the abrupt start and finish of its nectar-flow.

Modong grows slowly but is hardy in cultivation. It should be grown much more in Perth's parks for its picturesque appearance.

Distribution

Modong occurs widely in the wetter South-West, from Eneabba southwards, and east to Fitzgerald River National Park.

Collection and naming

Collected by J.A.L. Preiss in 1840 near Perth. Specific name after Preiss.

★ The mistake probably arose from a confusion in the first edition of Blackall and Grieve's *How to Know Western Australian Wildflowers*, Part I, p. 301 (1974; first published 1954).

★★Victoria, 1985; first published in 1952.

Distinctive features

A medium-sized tree with thick branches, growing in swampy depressions.

Bark whitish, papery.

Leaves pointed, 1-1½ cm long and 1-2 mm wide, held at wide angle to stem.

Flowers white, in summer, in loose clusters interspersed with leaves; arranged in groups of one to three, in leaf-axils.

Fruits 3-4 x 3-4 mm.

Freshwater paperbark

Melaleuca rhaphiophylla

This is Perth's commonest paperbark. Many people believe it to be the only one, but there are also modong (p. 180) and saltwater paperbark (p. 172) — and both gorada (p. 178) and banbar (p. 184) have somewhat papery bark too. Modong, which is quite common, is often mistakenly believed to be freshwater paperbark. Their differences are mentioned on page 180.

Freshwater paperbark is typically found bordering Perth's rivers and permanent lakes. It occurs near both fresh and saline water, but is less adapted to saline conditions than saltwater paperbark (p. 172).

Freshwater paperbark has a fairly extensive range in the South-West, occurring in wetlands from Kalbarri round the coast to the Fitzgerald River National Park, and inland to York.

Growth habit

Where it borders rivers or coastal lakes, freshwater paperbark grows as a small tree, rarely more than 10 m tall. It also occurs in swampy places on the alluvial soils of the eastern side of the coastal plain, where it is lower and shrubbier.

It is more regularly shaped than Perth's other paperbarks, being a good example of the splitting habit of growth (see p. 2). Its canopy of foliage is fairly dense.

Associated life

No other tree or shrub in the Metropolitan Region is as well used by waterbirds. Specimens that split into several trunks often have hollows at the base, and older specimens sometimes have hollows higher in the trunk. In these hollows nest coots, dusky moorhens and various ducks, including the rare freckled duck. Horizontal forks in branches provide nest-sites for birds such as darters, cormorants, herons, egrets, ibises and spoonbills. Most importantly, freshwater paperbark is usually inundated in spring. Since waterbirds like trees standing in water, they prefer this species to modong, which grows on slightly higher ground.

Freshwater paperbark regenerates prolifically under the right conditions, and waterbirds also make use of the thickets of saplings.

The flowers, in spring to early summer, are often prolific. They attract myriads of insects, as well as birds such as the western spinebill and brown honeyeater.

Ecological notes

Freshwater paperbark now has to compete with bulrush (*Typha orientalis*), introduced from Asia. Bulrushes dry out in summer, when they are readily set alight. The fires burn fiercely.

Paperbark seedlings and even some mature specimens are killed, and those that survive are often severely damaged. To make matters worse, the new growth produced for the paperbarks' recovery does not produce seed for about five years — so if there is a fire in the meantime there is little or no regeneration. The regular burning of bulrushes, therefore, can decimate paperbark stands.

If fire can be prevented, however, or greatly reduced in frequency, the process can be reversed. In the absence of fire, paperbark seedlings will survive and eventually form dense stands that largely exclude the bulrush.

Human uses

Freshwater paperbark is of value to beekeepers, especially in conjunction with flooded gum, which on many sites occurs alongside it.

It is now being used in many projects to revegetate cleared wetlands, in order to improve their biological and aesthetic value.

Collection and naming

Collected by J.A.L. Priess in 1839 from sandy plains near Perth. Specific name, from the Greek *rhaphis* 'needle' and *phyllon* 'leaf', refers to the shape of the leaves.

< *Freckled duck.*

^ *Stem with buds, flowers and fruits.*

Distinctive features

A small to medium-sized tree growing beside a lake or river or in a swamp.

Bark white and papery; strips off in papery sheets.

Leaves 2-4 cm long, slender (up to 1 mm wide), round in cross-section.

Flowers produced in spring or early summer, white to cream, in dense clusters 1-4 cm long, at or near end of stem.

Fruits 5-6 mm broad, in small clusters.

Banbar

Melaleuca teretifolia

∧ *Little black cormorant.*

'Banbar', the common name, is an Aboriginal word meaning 'round and cylindrical'. It is suitable in describing the unusual leaves of this species, which are long, thin and cylindrical. Up to 8 cm in length, they are far longer than those of any other melaleuca in this book. Freshwater paperback's leaves are similarly shaped, but much smaller and finer.

Ecological notes

Banbar tolerates flooding well, perhaps better than any other Perth tree or shrub. It can survive continuous flooding for several years, but not permanent flooding. In the rings of vegetation around a lake it is often the innermost woody plant; a typical sequence is banbar, freshwater paperbark, flooded gum, and modong with swamp banksia.

Appearance

Banbar is a spreading shrub, branching at fairly wide angles. It is usually 2-3 m high, with up to a dozen or more slender stems; old specimens can grow to 5 m and have stems up to 25 cm thick. As an individual it looks rather sparse, but it typically grows in a group, where the branches intermingle in a dense tangle.

In spring to early summer the clusters of flowers along the stems combine in 'beads' or long 'brushes', and make quite a display among the narrow, spaced leaves. They are usually white or pale yellow, sometimes pink.

Associated life

Where it grows in water and forms tall thickets, banbar is particularly valuable for waterbirds. At Booragoon Lake it is used by breeding colonies of great cormorants, little black cormorants, little pied cormorants and white ibises. There are also many other waterbirds that breed or rest in it.

Feral bees and many native insects are attracted to the flowers, in spring to mid summer.

Occurrence and distribution

Banbar extends from Boyanup, south of Bunbury, to Mogumber.

In the Metropolitan Region it can be found in several lakes and swamps on the coastal plain, such as Booragoon, Bibra (especially the swampy south-eastern part) and Manning Lakes.

Collection and naming

Collected by Baron von Huegel in 1833 from a marsh by the Swan River. Specific name from the Latin *teres* or *teretis* 'round in cross-section' and *folium* 'leaf'.

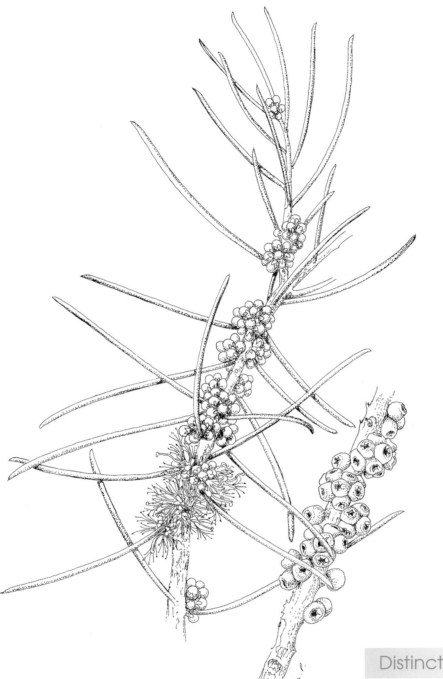

< *Stem with leaves, buds and flowers.*

< *Stem with clusters of fruits.*

Distinctive features

A shrub or small tree occurring in swamps.

Bark grey, papery or rough.

Foliage bluish-green.

Leaves 3-8 cm long, narrow and round in cross-section, 1-2 mm wide, ending in a point; usually held at a wide angle to the stem.

Flowers produced in spring to mid summer; white, pale yellow or pink; up to 30 in clusters on flowering stems.

Fruits 4-5 mm across.

Mohan

Melaleuca viminea

Perth's wetlands are quite varied. There are lakes, swampy depressions, estuaries, rivers and streams. Some lakes and swamps are situated in the belts of coastal sands; others are in the alluvial soils at the foot of the Darling Scarp. Still others occur on the Darling Plateau. Some river valleys have steep sides; others have flood plains.

Associated with those various wetlands are 20 or so of Perth's trees and tall shrubs. Each has its own particular environment, or niche. Some species, such as albizia, prefer rivers to lakes or swamps. Saltwater paperbark and salt sheoak, as their names suggest, prefer salty soil. Banbar tolerates severe flooding. Flooded gum likes wetland soils for their fertility, and also grows away from wetlands in the fertile soils of the Darling Scarp.

Some species dominate; others combine with other species. Freshwater paperbark grows in dense stands and crowds out other wetland trees and shrubs. Modong and swamp banksia, on the other hand, are often found together. They like the same conditions but do not compete strongly with one another. Some smaller wetland species, such as river pea, grow quite well in the shade of other species.

Mohan (pronounced with a silent 'h') is one of the smaller species of wetland melaleuca, and is probably outcompeted by the larger species. It grows in several different kinds of wetland habitat: it does not appear to be fussy about conditions, and may be exploiting sites unfavourable to the larger species.

Appearance, common name

Mohan splits repeatedly into equal branches, fanning out to produce an unbroken canopy. In the open, it forms a neat, round shrub of 3 m or more. In stands, or among taller vegetation, it spreads less and grows to about 7 m.

Mohan's colouring is dull: its foliage is a dark grey-green and its bark rough and grey. This is reflected in the common name, an Aboriginal word meaning 'dark-coloured'. In spring mohan's white flowers, grouped into short brushes at or near the ends of the stems, are conspicuous.

Occurrence in the Metropolitan Region

Mohan occurs in several places by the Swan and Canning estuaries, such as Alfred Cove and Salter Point. In the Darling Range it grows along Wooroloo Brook, where there is a good population at the O'Brien Road crossing; and at Lake Leschenaultia, especially at the southern end and along the south-east shore.

As well as these riverine habitats, it commonly occurs in clay-based swamps on the eastern side of the coastal plain. It is rarely found, however, round lakes or swamps in the sandy soils on the western side of the plain.

Associated life

Mohan often forms thickets. These are useful to the black swan, black duck, musk duck, coot and dusky moorhen as shelter and for breeding.

In spring, the abundant blossoms attract bees, flies, wasps, beetles and other insects.

Distribution

Mohan extends from Kalbarri to Israelite Bay, east of Esperance. It occurs commonly near the coast, in forested areas and in the western Wheatbelt, with more scattered occurances further inland.

Collection and naming

Collected by James Drummond in 1839 near Perth. Specific name, from the Latin *vimineus* 'rush-like', refers to the long, flexible shoots.

∧ *Musk duck (male).*

Distinctive features

Shrub or small tree growing in wetlands.

Bark coarse, fibrous.

Leaves up to 2 cm long and 1-2 mm wide, often curved downwards.

Flowers white, usually produced between late winter and mid spring, in clusters at the ends of the stems.

Fruits 3-4 mm across, in clusters.

Prickly mirbelia

Mirbelia dilatata

∧ *Assassin bug (x 2).*

Mirbelias have bright, showy flowers, in yellows, oranges, reds and purples. The genus, belonging to the legume family, is entirely Australian, with 32 species. Twenty-nine of these occur in Western Australia, mostly in the southern half of the State.

Ecological notes

Legumes, being both abundant and nutritious, are important as food for animals such as kangaroos and wallabies. Many protect themselves from being eaten: some are poisonous; others spiny or prickly. This species has prickly, spreading leaves with three to seven sharp points.

Prickly mirbelia is killed by fire, but regenerates afterwards in dense stands. The thin stems of dead and aging specimens suggest that it is short-lived.

Appearance

Prickly mirbelia is adapted to growing in dense stands in a forest: it is upright and spindly, with a single stem. It is typically 3 m or more tall, sometimes 5 m.

In spring and early summer, pink or purple flowers are brightly displayed on its prickly green or bluish-green foliage. Young growth is bright green.

Occurrence and distribution

Prickly mirbelia grows on moist, heavy soils. It is concentrated in the extreme South-West, extending through the Darling Range as far north as Perth. It is found also in the Porongurup and Stirling ranges, at Albany and at Esperance. There are some outlying populations inland, such as at Lake Grace, and further north, such as at New Norcia.

In the Metropolitan Region, prickly mirbelia is largely confined to moist, swampy areas in the Darling Range, particularly in the south. It occurs round Karnet, south of Serpentine Dam, and is especially abundant along North Road, just south of Karnet.

Associated life

Pale patches on prickly mirbelia's leaves result from the sucking of numerous psyllid bugs; the foliage also supports tiny weevils. Preying on these insects are numerous spiders.

Some small specimens of prickly mirbelia show stems that have been bitten off, probably by kangaroos. The eaten portions may have comprised soft new growth, less prickly than when fully formed.

Small halictid bees and other native bees visit the flowers. Assassin bugs can sometimes be found there, ambushing the bees or other small insects.

The larvae of weevils or other beetles eat the seeds. Holes in the pods are made by the females, in order to lay their eggs, or by the emerging adults.

Collection and naming

Collected by Peter Good in 1801 or 1802 at King George Sound. Specific name, from the Latin *dilatatus* 'enlarged' or 'widened', refers to the leaf, which widens towards the end.

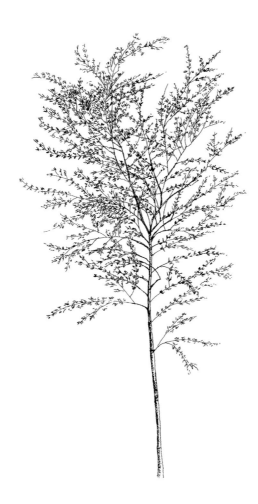

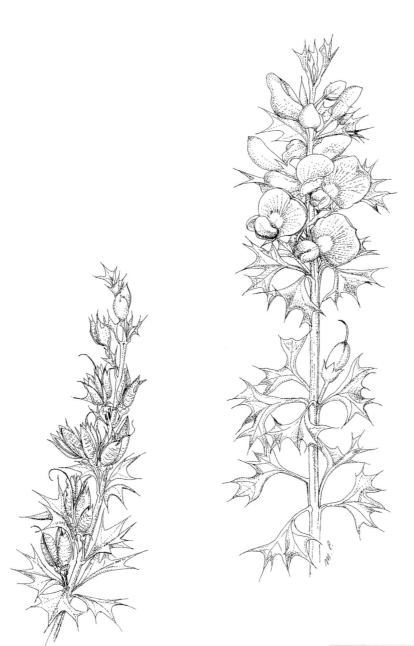

Distinctive features

An erect, spindly shrub 3-5 m tall.

Leaves green or bluish-green, not flat, roughly triangular in shape, dividing into 3 to 7 lobes, each with a sharp point; arranged in whorls of 3 or 4 along the stem, or scattered.

Flowers pea-shaped, pink, violet or purple, with a yellow 'eye', produced from mid spring to early summer.

Pods about 1 cm long and 3-5 mm wide, stalked; when open they can be seen to be divided lengthways into two cells.

Christmas tree, mooja

Nuytsia floribunda

Christmas tree's dense masses of brilliant orange flowers contrast strongly with its bluish–green foliage. When the bark is blackened by fire the colours are particularly striking. The tree indeed has a festive look. Flowering in Perth from late spring to early summer, it marks the approach to Christmas.

Botanically, Christmas tree is most unusual. It has no close relatives, and is classed as a genus by itself, in the mistletoe family. In growing from the ground as a tree, it is unlike other members of the family, which grow on the branches of trees.

Ecological notes

Christmas tree is semi–parasitic. Its roots make rings around those of nearby trees, and suckers within the rings extract water from them. Christmas tree is the only mistletoe with dry, winged fruits, dispersed by the wind. From a tree of good size, the fruits usually land 2½ to 10 m away, sometimes as far as 35 m. They are shed between early autumn and mid winter. The single seed of each fruit germinates after being soaked by autumn or winter rains.

∧ *Rainbow bee-eater.*

The seedlings remain shrubby for several years, often dying back in summer. Seven to 20 years after germination, they send up a single stem that grows strongly and develops into a tree. At this stage flowering begins.

Christmas tree reproduces also by suckering: new plants sprout from a large network of underground stems. Groups of saplings are thus often seen round mature specimens.

The trunk of a Christmas tree is not true wood, but starchy tissue. In paddocks horses often chew right through the trunk, killing the tree (this can be prevented with a wire guard). They also eat the young suckering plants and dig up the underground stems.

Growth habit

Christmas tree has a bizarre and appealing habit of growth.

It usually has a well developed trunk, which becomes very thick relative to the tree's size. The branches too are thick, but not strong. They bend under the weight of the foliage and terminal flowers; the branchlets, and even the major branches, often have a downward curve. Major branches often break off the tree, leaving gaps that contribute to its irregular outline.

Associated life

During its short period of flowering, Christmas tree is one of the richest sources of pollen and nectar for insects such as bees, wasps, ants and nectar-eating beetles, and is particularly favoured by the spotted jezebel butterfly.

The flowers also attract birds such as the red wattlebird, little wattlebird, brown honeyeater, western spinebill, New Holland honeyeater and silvereye. The yellow-rumped thornbill, black-faced cuckoo-shrike and bee-eater eat insects attracted to the flowers. Up to six bee-eaters have been seen congregating at a single tree. They perch near by and dart out to catch the insects in the air.

Christmas tree's foliage is more nutritious than that of the banksia species with which it associates, and appears to support more insect species. On the tree's trunk, particularly where it is protected from the sun and hot winds, lichens may be found.

Human uses

The Aboriginal people used to dig up the suckers and peel back the pale yellow outer bark to eat the moist, brittle centre, which tastes like candy.

Christmas tree is useful to beekeepers for building up broods. The honey, however, is of poor quality.

Only rarely is Christmas tree cultivated. As explained above, seedlings take a long time to develop and flower. In cultivation they also need generous watering over the first few summers. Christmas tree would be a lovely addition to many parks and gardens, well worth the time and effort needed to grow it. Transplanted specimens can be used to enable earlier flowering.

Occurrence and distribution

Christmas tree is common in almost all the soil-types on the coastal plain, particularly in low-lying areas. In the Darling Range it grows chiefly in rocky or damp places. It ranges from Kalbarri to Israelite Bay.

Collection and naming

Collected by Labillardière in 1792 from the Esperance area. Specific name from the Latin *flos* or *floris* 'flower' and *abundus* 'abounding in'.

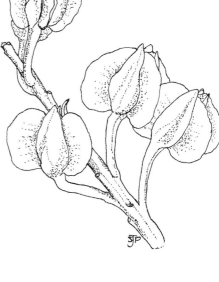

∧ *Fruits.*

< *Stem with leaf, buds and flowers.*

∧ *Shoots with young leaves.*

Albizia

Paraserianthes lophantha

The slender branches and feathery, well spaced leaves give albizia a light, airy look. From its appearance it might be mistaken for a tropical plant, and indeed the other three of the world's four species of *Paraserianthes* are tropical. Two of them occur in regions north of Australia, the remaining one in Queensland. Albizia's common name is derived from the genus *Albizia*, in which this species was formerly included.

Albizia is in the same family as the wattles. Like them it bears pods, in which hard-coated seeds develop, and is fast-growing and short-lived. Of seedlings that germinated after a fire in the Helena Valley, some grew to 7 m in four years.

Albizia's leaves, like those of wattle seedlings, are doubly divided. But rather than having one pair of pinnae (the leaf-stalks containing the leaflets), the large leaves of albizia have eight to 10 pairs.

Associated life

Albizia often harbours large numbers of sap-sucking bugs, which are eaten by ladybirds and their larvae. Ants cultivate the bugs for honeydew. Excess honeydew provides the medium for a black smut-fungus to develop, which reduces the plant's vigour. With the plant weakened, swift-moths lay their eggs on it. The larvae burrow and feed in the stems, and grow into large grubs up to 9 cm long (similar to the wichetty grubs eaten by Aboriginal people) before emerging.

The larvae of cossid moths, also called wood moths, tunnel in the stems of albizia too. Before they pupate, in the plant's thicker stems, they produce for their protection an elliptical area of frass, about 4 cm long, covering their emergence hole. The frass can readily be seen, and comprises faecal pellets stuck together in a mass of silk.

Albizia plants can die young as a result of the effects of the smut-fungus or the moth larvae, but the plants' rapid development ensures that they produce many seeds.

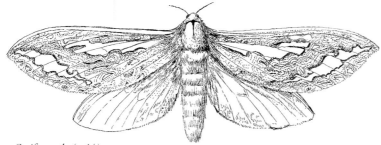

∧ *Swift-moth (x ½).*

The flowers attract the silvereye and other honey-eating birds, and insects such as carpenter bees and honeybees. Young plants are readily eaten by kangaroos.

Growth habit

This small tree up to 10 m has a well defined pattern of growth. With a prominent central stem, it is a good example of the shaft habit. Where the tree has room, the side-branches grow long and curve upwards.

Ecological notes

Albizia likes moisture, and therefore often occurs among dense vegetation. Its habit of growth helps it to find its way up to the light. Like many wetland species, and many vigorous colonisers, it is killed by fire.

The pods remain closed. When shed, they float away on the wind, being broad and light. They decay rapidly on the ground, and expose the seeds, which are further dispersed by ants. Albizia regenerates prolifically, sometimes producing 'carpets' of seedlings.

Occurrence and distribution

In its natural distribution, albizia extends southwards from Gingin to the State's south-west corner, and eastwards near the south coast to east of Esperance, including islands of the Recherche

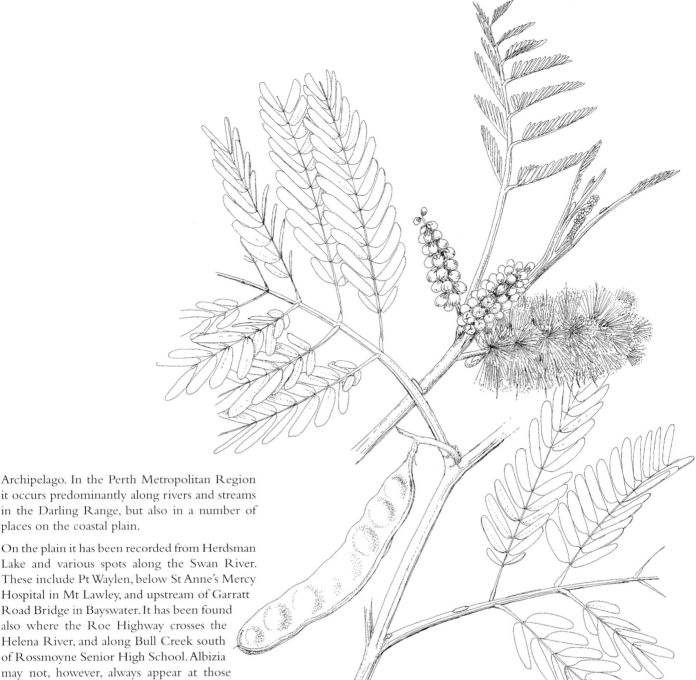

Archipelago. In the Perth Metropolitan Region it occurs predominantly along rivers and streams in the Darling Range, but also in a number of places on the coastal plain.

On the plain it has been recorded from Herdsman Lake and various spots along the Swan River. These include Pt Waylen, below St Anne's Mercy Hospital in Mt Lawley, and upstream of Garratt Road Bridge in Bayswater. It has been found also where the Roe Highway crosses the Helena River, and along Bull Creek south of Rossmoyne Senior High School. Albizia may not, however, always appear at those places, since it tends to die out but then later pop up again where the soil has been disturbed.

Since the European settlement of Australia, albizia has greatly extended its distribution by becoming naturalised in many places, including parts of South Australia, Victoria, New South Wales and Tasmania. In Perth it is now found here and there on dry sites, well away from the rivers or swamps to which it was formerly restricted. By this means it has become established, in low numbers, in Kings Park, and occasional specimens may be found also in Bold Park.

Collection and naming

Collected by Felix de Lahaie in 1792 on Labillardière's voyage, probably at Geographe Bay. Specific name from the Greek *lophos* 'crest' and *anthos* 'flower'.

Distinctive features

A small, erect tree up to 10 m, growing beside rivers or other drainage-lines.

Leaves large, about 20 cm or more long and 15 cm wide, doubly divided, with 8-10 pairs of pinnae.

Flower-spikes 3-6 cm long, borne two to three together in leaf-axils; flowers greenish-yellow, produced in late winter or early spring.

Pods almost flat, oblong in outline, about 7 cm long and 1 cm wide, straight or slightly curved.

Seeds transverse in pod, black with red stalk.

Spreading snottygobble

Persoonia elliptica

With its bright green foliage, this small, spreading tree stands out in the forest. Its branches curve and wander in all directions. Its plain grey bark peels easily off the trunk in small crumbly pieces.

Spreading snottygobble and upright snottygobble (p. 196) are the best-known of the Western Australian persoonias, or snottygobbles. Both have great appeal. Botanically, they are as distinctive as they look. Persoonias are shrubs or small trees that belong to a primitive sub-family of the banksia family. Most of the members have fleshy fruits, rather than the woody fruits typical of the family as a whole. A persoonia fruit is a drupe (like a plum or cherry): the seed is enclosed in a stone embedded in soft, fleshy tissue.

There are about 90 species of *Persoonia*, all of which are confined to Australia, with 43 occuring in Western Australia. A related species, *Toronia toru*, previously thought to be a persoonia, occurs in New Zealand. In eastern Australia, persoonias are called 'geebungs'.

Occurrence and distribution

Both snottygobbles are typical of the jarrah forest. In the Metropolitan Region spreading snottygobble is found chiefly on the Darling Plateau, but also in gravelly soils at the foot of the Darling Scarp. It ranges from Perth to Albany.

Ecological notes

The ripe fruits fall to the ground, and used to be eaten by the Aboriginal people. They are probably eaten also by kangaroos, wallabies and other mammals, as well as the emu. An old name for the two snottygobbles is 'emu-bush'. The seeds would be well distributed by these means. They are difficult to germinate artificially, and passing through the gut of an animal may trigger their germination.

Spreading snottygobble survives fire well. Its rough bark, which extends to the twigs, is an effective shield.

Associated life

The common bronzewing often nests in spreading snottygobble's horizontal forking branches.

The inconspicuous flowers, hidden among the foliage, are almost odourless in the daytime but strongly scented at night. Moths, or nocturnal beetles, are probably the main pollinators.

∧ *Common bronzewing.*

Large holes are sometimes found in the branches, but it is not known what type of insect is responsible.

Lichens commonly grow on the bark.

Cultivation

Some of the eastern Australian persoonias are grown in cultivation, but the Perth snottygobbles are seldom cultivated. To induce the seeds artificially to germinate requires special techniques, and even then the results are often unreliable.

Collection and naming

Collected by Robert Brown in 1801 or 1802 from the Albany area. Specific name, from the Greek *elliptikos* 'elliptical', refers to the shape of the leaves.

∧ *Leaf and fruit.*

Distinctive features

Small, spreading tree up to 6 m, in jarrah forest on the Darling Plateau or at the foot of the Darling Scarp.

Bark grey, corky.

Leaves bright green, an inverted egg-shape or narrower, 2-11 cm long; soft and flexible.

Flowers greenish-yellow, produced from mid spring to late summer.

Fruits smooth, elliptical, slightly flattened, 10-15 x 6-10 mm.

Upright snottygobble

Persoonia longifolia

The casual observer would not guess that this species and spreading snottygobble (p. 194) are related, so different are they in bark, leaves and general appearance. But their flowers and fruits are very similar.

The leaves too, although very different in shape, do have similarities. In both species they are soft and flexible, and mostly held edge-up (like those of most eucalypts). They are also arranged in the same way on the stem, being either alternate or crowded (rather than in whorls or opposite pairs).

Spreading snottygobble captures the attention by its colour and habit of growth. Upright snottygobble is striking too. Its bark is coarse, flaky and colourful. Peel a bit off, and the inside layers are reddish-purple. The leaves are long and somewhat sickle-shaped, and combine in shaggy clumps.

Upright snottygobble has a much simpler form than its relative. It is an erect small tree or shrub 1-5 m high, with few branches.

Occurrence and distribution

Like spreading snottygobble, upright snotty-gobble grows in the jarrah forest, and in the Perth area is confined to the Darling Plateau. It extends from Bickley to Albany.

Ecological notes

This species too drops its fruits. After several days on the ground, they change from green to yellow-green, which may increase their visibility.

Like the other species, upright snottygobble survives fire. It resprouts afterwards from the twigs or from an underground rootstock.

Associated life

Many native bees visit the small, yellow flowers in summer, and are probably the main pollinators. Another insect to visit the flowers is the western brown. The sexes of this butterfly have quite different markings, especially on the forewings; but what is more unusual is that they appear at slightly different times of the year. The first males are seen in October, but it is several weeks before any females appear. At the end of the season, in April, only females are present.

Cultivation

This appealing plant would no doubt be cultivated if only that could be done easily! As with the previous species, the germination of the seeds is probably triggered by their passing through the gut of an animal. Germinating them artificially requires special techniques, with no guarantee of success.

Collection and naming

Collected by Robert Brown in 1801 or 1802 from the Albany area. Specific name from the Latin *longus* 'long' and *folium* 'leaf'.

∧ *Western brown (female).*

Individual plant species

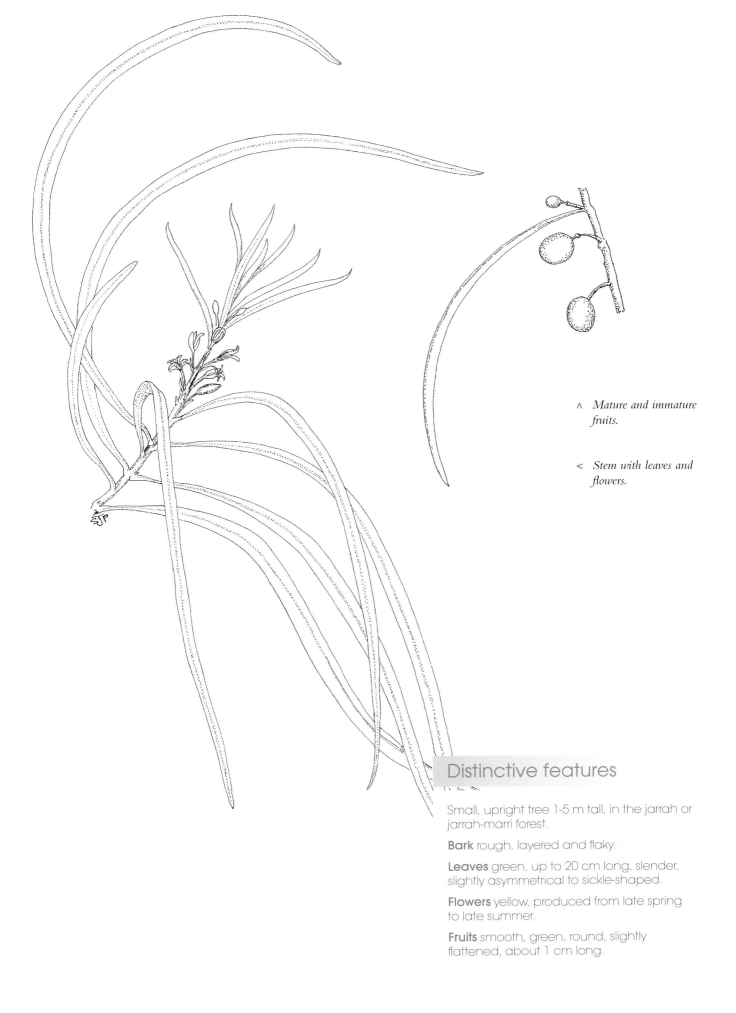

∧ Mature and immature fruits.

< Stem with leaves and flowers.

Distinctive features

Small, upright tree 1-5 m tall, in the jarrah or jarrah-marri forest.

Bark rough, layered and flaky.

Leaves green, up to 20 cm long, slender, slightly asymmetrical to sickle-shaped.

Flowers yellow, produced from late spring to late summer.

Fruits smooth, green, round, slightly flattened, about 1 cm long.

Coast pittosporum

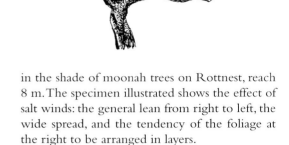

Pittosporum ligustrifolium

The genus *Pittosporum* is named from the Greek *pittos* 'pitch' (in the sense of a sticky substance), and *sporum* 'seed'. The ripe fruits split open to reveal seeds immersed in a sticky resin. About 150 species are recognised. Eleven species occur in Australia, six of them in Western Australia.

Coast pittosporum was previously considered a form of *Pittosporum phylliraeoides*, which is now recognised as three separate species. One of these, weeping pittosporum (*P. angustifolium*), has a wide distribution across southern Australia. Coast pittosporum, the Perth species, is a close relative, with broader leaves and a denser, spreading-erect habit. The remaining species, *P. phylliraeoides*, occurs in the Shark Bay area and has leaves with a covering of white hairs on their undersides.

In this book's original edition, coast pittosporum was called 'cheesewood'. This is actually an alternative common name for weeping pittosporum. Now that the species has been split, it is better to use a separate name.

Occurrence and distribution

Coast pittosporum is a species of the coast and offshore islands, extending from Northampton to Dunsborough.

A good place to see it is Rottnest Island, where it is associated with limestone round the salt lakes. Well developed specimens grow on the golf course. The species is also fairly common on Garden Island.

On the mainland, however, only a few scattered groups of specimens remain. A few plants survive in Yanchep National Park, and on limestone bordering the lower Swan River at Blackwall Reach. A small group grows on the western slope of the lookout hill at Pt Peron. Some of the mainland specimens are low shrubs, because of either shallow soil or frequent burning.

Appearance

The striking difference in form between coast pittosporum and weeping pittosporum reflects coast pittosporum's adaptation to the salt winds of coastal environments. Weeping pittosporum has pendulous branches and dispersed foliage. Coast pittosporum has erect or spreading branches, its foliage arranged in a dense dome or 'umbrella', typical of coastal trees and shrubs. Like weeping pittosporum, coast pittosporum is a small tree. It is normally about 4 m tall, but occasional specimens, in the shade of moonah trees on Rottnest, reach 8 m. The specimen illustrated shows the effect of salt winds: the general lean from right to left, the wide spread, and the tendency of the foliage at the right to be arranged in layers.

Coast pittosporum is pleasantly coloured. Its foliage is quite a bright, fresh green, and its bark light to medium grey. Over most of the tree the bark is fairly smooth, but on old specimens it is rough and tessellated at the base.

Associated life

Brown blotches on the leaves are caused by the pittosporum bug, a small insect that sucks the sap. It exudes a sticky, waxy substance, on which fungi sometimes grow.

Native bees, wasps and butterflies visit coast pittosporum's flowers. On 26 August 2005, a specimen near Vlamingh Lookout, Rottnest Island, was observed attracting yellow admirals and painted ladies.

The flowers are visited also by birds, such as the silvereye and the singing honeyeater. The latter also eats the seeds, digesting their surrounding sticky resin but excreting the seeds themselves.

Ecological notes

By ingesting the seeds, the singing honeyeater greatly assists coast pittosporum's regeneration on Rottnest Island. The seeds are thus dispersed. Moreover, the absorption of the resin when the seeds pass through the bird's gut removes chemicals that would otherwise inhibit their germination.

Seedlings that germinate among clumps of prickle lily are protected from grazing quokkas, and some survive to grow into new trees.

Conservation concern

Whereas coast pittosporum thrives on Rottnest and Garden islands, it does not propagate itself so readily on the mainland. Being uncommon on the mainland, it may disappear, unless measures are taken to help it.

∧ *Silvereye.*

Human uses

The Aboriginal people ate the gum exuded from coast pittosporum.

Unlike weeping pittosporum, coast pittosporum is seldom cultivated, apart from its use in some of the revegetation plantations on Rottnest Island. To help ensure it does not die out, it should be cultivated on the coastal plain. Its small size, erect habit and shady canopy, as well as its tolerance of sea winds and limestone soils, would make it very useful. It could also be a very good street tree, except that its slow growth would make it vulnerable to vandalism in the early stages.

Collection and naming

Collected by A. Cunningham in 1822 from Rottnest Island. Specific name from the Latin *ligustrum* 'privet' and *folium* 'leaf'.

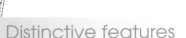

Distinctive features

Small tree or erect shrub growing on coastal limestone (now almost entirely restricted to offshore islands).

Bark grey, fairly smooth.

Foliage green.

Leaves narrowly elliptical, 2-8½ x ½-1½ cm, flat and leathery.

Flowers small, white to yellow, singly on stalks or in small groups on branching stems, produced in winter.

Fruits orange or red when ripe, heart-shaped or egg-shaped, 1-2½ x 1-2 cm, containing 4 to 24 red, irregularly shaped seeds.

Quandong

Santalum acuminatum

∧ *Stone.*

Quandong belongs to the same genus as the famous sandalwood, which was one of Western Australia's major exports in the late 19th and early 20th century. Sandalwood's wood and roots contain a volatile oil with an attractive scent. They were used in Asia to make carved ornamental objects and to prepare incense for burning in temples.

Members of this genus are root-parasites. There are about 25 species, in Australia, Indonesia and nearby areas. Four species occur in Western Australia. The genus belongs to the sandalwood family, which also includes broom ballart (p. 140).

Appearance

Quandong is a small, upright tree growing to about 4 m. Its pale yellow-green foliage contrasts with the dull green of other species. On old specimens the dark brown bark develops an attractively coarse texture.

The fleshy fruits are 2-4 cm across. They form in spring, and ripen in late spring and summer into a rich red. They are drupes: each contains a single seed embedded in a stone.

∧ *Spotted jezebel (female).*

Associated life

Quandong's fruits are an important food for the emu. The fleshy part is digested, and the stone is passed through the bird. Where emus are present they are the major dispersers of the seeds. The flesh of the fruits is eaten also by nitidulid beetles and moth larvae.

The leaves are eaten by the larvae of a butterfly, the spotted jezebel, as well as by a species of soldier beetle. The beetles betray their presence by crescent-shaped nicks, a few millimetres deep, in the leaf's edge.

Human uses

The Aboriginal people ate the fleshy part of the drupes and also the kernel. Besides being eaten raw, the flesh can be used to make distinctive jams and jellies.

Occurrence and distribution

Many members of the sandalwood family have wide distributions that include arid inland regions. Quandong is no exception: it is one of Australia's most widespread plants, occurring in all the mainland states. In Western Australia it grows along the coast southwards from Carnarvon, and ranges widely through the inland.

In the Metropolitan Region, quandong favours the coastal dunes and limestone. On the coastal dunes it is found in places such as Woodman Point and Trigg Bushland. On limestone it can be found in various places, including limestone slopes bordering the Swan River, such as between Chidley Pt and Pt Roe. It occurs also in places in the Darling Scarp, such as in Kalamunda National Park, on the upper slopes of the Helena Valley.

Ecological notes

Quandong is burnt to the ground by fire and recovers by shooting from a rootstock. The regrowth takes 20 years or so to form a well

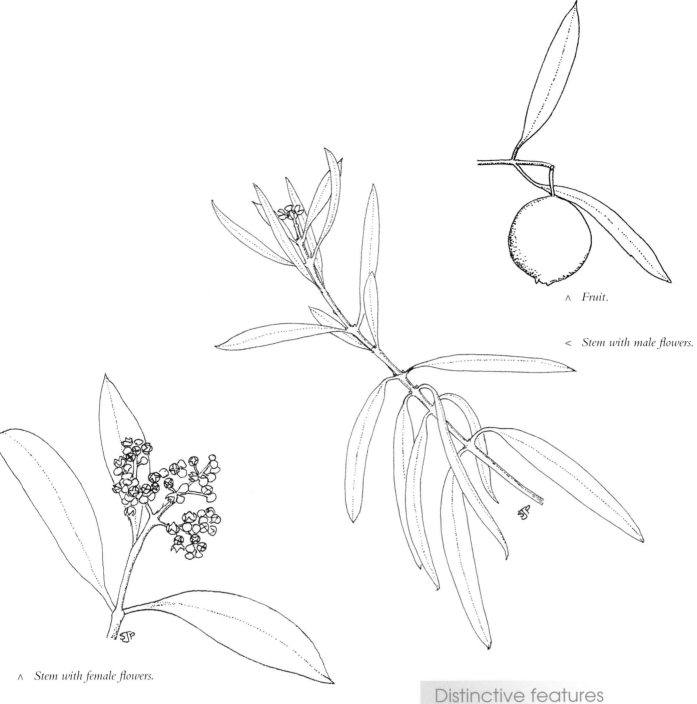

∧ *Fruit.*

< *Stem with male flowers.*

∧ *Stem with female flowers.*

developed specimen. Since bushfires round Perth usually now occur at intervals of much less than 20 years, well developed specimens are rare, except in places protected from fire.

As well as reproducing by seed, quandong also forms new plants by shooting from underground runners. It is thus often seen in groups.

Collection and naming

Collected by Robert Brown in 1802 from Fowlers Bay, South Australia. Specific name, from the Latin *acuminatus* 'sharpened' or 'pointed', refers to the shape of the leaf.

Distinctive features

Upright shrub or small tree growing on coastal sand or limestone or in the Darling Scarp. Pale green foliage.

Leaves in opposite pairs, leathery; leaf-stalk ½-1 cm long; leaf-blade 4½-11½ x ½-2 cm, tapering.

Flowers tiny, 2-3 mm across, arranged on branching stems that are usually not as long as the leaves, produced from late spring to early autumn.

Fruit a drupe (stone-fruit), globular in shape, 2-3 cm in diameter; green when unripe; red when ripe, in late spring or summer. Stone hard, densely pitted.

Basket bush

Spyridium globulosum

Basket bush is typical of maritime environments. It occurs along the coast in a narrow strip; also by estuaries, such as the Swan; and on offshore islands, such as Rottnest, Garden and Penguin. It ranges from Geraldton and the Abrolhos Islands to Israelite Bay.

The genus *Spyridium* is confined to the temperate parts of Australia. There are about 30 species, 16 of which occur in Western Australia.

Ecological notes

Basket bush is killed by fire, and has declined in abundance since European settlement. Its decline has been less marked than that of some of the larger species killed by fire, such as moonah and Rottnest cypress. Seedlings develop rapidly and may begin flowering and seeding when two or three years old. Thus basket bush can tolerate fairly short intervals between fires. Moreover, on sites close to the ocean it often grows in an open shrubland, which does not carry fire as readily as taller or denser vegetation.

In areas of tuart forest where fires have not been too frequent (e.g. Woodman Point and Yanchep National Park), basket bush often grows thickly as a dominant understorey shrub. It probably used to dominate the understorey in many areas of tuart forest where it is no longer common (for example, parts of Bold Park and Star Swamp Bushland).

Basket bush is much longer-lived than might be inferred from its rapid early growth. In Wembley Downs a few specimens retained in gardens when houses were built in the early 1960s survived until at least the 1990s.

Appearance

Close to the ocean, basket bush grows tall only where it is protected from salt winds by other tall shrubs. Among low shrubs it spreads wide but keeps low, often growing to less than 2 m.

Further from the ocean it grows much taller, and in the shade of the tuart forest it is seen as a sparse shrub with a delicate tracery of slender stems, 4 or 5 m tall.

Two colour-forms can be found in Perth. The leaves of the common form are glossy and dark green or mid green above, and pale, almost white, below, where they are densely covered in minute hairs. Occasional bright yellow dead leaves stand out among the live ones. By the Swan Estuary — where basket bush occurs in places such as Peppermint Grove, the limestone scarp at Kings Park, and the west side of Aquinas Bay in Salter Point — there is also a form with pale grey-green foliage. It has minute, velvety hairs on both sides of the leaves.

Associated life

In spring the larvae of a species of geometer moth eat the foliage. The caterpillars of moths in this family are known as 'measure-worms' or 'loopers'. They hold on to the plant with the claspers at their rear end, and stretch forward with their front end. They then loop their body to bring their rear end against their front end. Thus they progress by a combination of 'measuring' and looping. The caterpillars are active at night, when they can be seen with the aid of a torch. They will usually be feeding, or hanging from a

thread fastened to a leaf, to avoid predators. In the daytime they remain motionless and resemble a bit of dead stem.

In winter the minute, strongly scented flowers attract hoverflies and other kinds of fly.

Collection and naming

Collected by Labillardière in 1792 near Esperance. Specific name, from the Latin *globosus* 'globular', *–ul–*, a diminutive, and *-osus* 'abounding in', refers to the shape, size and abundance of the flower heads.

∧ *Looper caterpillar, attached to stem.*

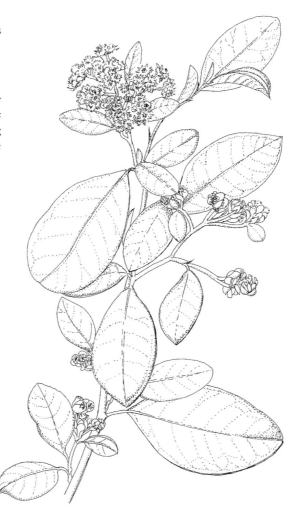

Distinctive features

Large shrub growing on coastal sand or limestone or near the Swan Estuary.

Leaves either glossy mid green to dark green or silky grey-green above, pale below, elliptical, 1½-5 x 1-2½ cm.

Flowers tiny, whitish, in clusters at the ends of branching stems, produced in winter.

Brook peppermint

*Taxandria
linearifolia*

∧ *Scorpion fly.*

Brook peppermint can be recognised from a distance as a uniform mass of foliage marking a drainage-line or a wetland. In spring and early summer, its small white flowers are produced in great profusion, and its mass of foliage turns a dusty white.

Brook peppermint was formerly in the genus *Agonis*. However, it has 10 stamens, one opposite each petal and each sepal, rather than the 20–30 stamens that characterise *Agonis*, and is now placed in the genus *Taxandria*.

Occurrence and distribution

Brook peppermint occurs along streams and in swamps in the Darling Range and on the adjacent part of the coastal plain. It occurs in the south-west corner of Western Australia, southwards from Muchea, and extends along the south coast as far as Cape Arid National Park.

Common name

In this book's first edition, this species was called 'swamp peppermint'. Since, however, it occurs along streams more typically than in swamps,

'brook peppermint' should be preferred. It is also called 'creek peppermint'. The original meaning of 'creek' is a small inlet. In this country, 'creek' is commonly used in a very different way, to denote a small stream. This is particularly so in eastern Australia and in the drier, inland parts of Western Australia. In the Darling Range and elsewhere in this State's south-west corner, the watercourses smaller than rivers are named as brooks, for example Bennett Brook, Wungong Brook.

Ecological notes

Brook peppermint has a well developed rootstock, which can send up vigorous shoots after the plant is damaged by a flood. As a result, it is less easily destroyed by burning or clearing than most other shrubs along streams in the Darling Range. It is often the only remaining shrub species along streams that run through farms. It forms dense thickets, which help to control erosion along watercourses.

Associated life

Thickets of brook peppermint are an important habitat for wildlife. In the jarrah forest southwards from Perth, they are the main places where the quokka survives, offering protection from the introduced fox.

By shading pools along watercourses, the thickets create a cool, damp habitat for frogs and aquatic life. They are also important to birds. The red-eared firetail, a finch that feeds on sedge and sheoak seeds, uses brook peppermint for cover. This bird, which formerly occurred on the coastal plain, is now confined in the Metropolitan Region to densely vegetated gullies of the Darling Range. Other bird species that use brook peppermint for food or cover include the inland thornbill, the splendid fairy-wren, the red-winged fairy-wren, the white-browed scrub-wren and the western spinebill.

The occurrence of brook peppermint also indicates the habitat where one may find Western Australia's largest dragonfly, the western petaltail. This primitive species is very scarce, and is unusual in that its nymphs do not live in water but in holes they dig in damp ground. It formerly bred at Bull Creek but nowadays is found chiefly in the Darling Range.

The flowers, produced all year round, are rich in nectar, and attract tiny insects such as native flies, native bees and beetles of the families Dermestidae, Nitidulidae and Buprestidae (jewel beetles).

Scorpion flies and robber flies are sometimes seen round brook peppermint hunting these smaller insects. They capture the prey in their legs, pierce it with their proboscis and suck its juices. The capture of prey is an essential part of the scorpion fly's mating behaviour. The male holds the food out in front for the female and copulates with her while she eats.

Collection and naming

Collected from the west coast of Australia in 1815. Specific name from the Latin *linearis* 'linear' and *folium* 'leaf'.

∧ *Stem with fruits.*

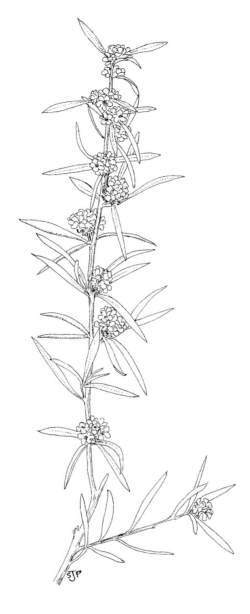

∧ *Top and side views of a flower (x 3).*

Distinctive features

Slender-branched shrub up to 6 m, occurring along streams or in winter-wet depressions.

Leaves 1½-3½ cm long.

Flowers about ½ cm across, with 5 white petals; numerous along stems, produced over much of the year.

Swishbush, golden spray, koweda

Viminaria juncea

∧ *The jewel beetle* Melobasis lathami.

This species has some colourful common names. 'Swishbush' refers to the sound its branches make when swaying in the wind, and 'golden spray' to the yellow and orange flowers held on branching stems above or outside the foliage. 'Koweda' is Aboriginal.

Swishbush is the only species in the genus *Viminaria*, in the legume family. The seedlings have leaves made up of one to three leaflets, but in mature plants the leaves are replaced by thread-like phyllodes (leaf-stalks) up to 30 cm long.

Appearance

The flexible phyllodes and stems of swishbush give it a willowy look, like green stinkwood (p. 160). It is of similar size to the stinkwood, but does not grow quite so tall (up to 5 m). Young specimens have a more regular habit than the stinkwood, and are particularly flowing and graceful. In mid spring to early summer, swishbush can be readily distinguished from green stinkwood by the grouping of its flowers.

Occurrence and distribution

Swishbush is one of the few plant species of Australia's higher-rainfall zones to occur in both eastern and western Australia. It is very widely distributed, occurring in all the mainland states except the Northern Territory. In Western Australia it extends from the south-west corner north to Kalbarri and east to Ravensthorpe. It prefers winter-wet sites or clayey soils.

In the Metropolitan Region it occurs chiefly in the Darling Scarp and the clay flats on the eastern side of the coastal plain. In the Darling Plateau it is largely restricted to valleys. On the western side of the coastal plain it is confined to the Swan and Canning rivers and to some of the larger lakes, such as Herdsman Lake, Thomsons Lake and Loch McNess.

Ecological notes

Few other species can grow on such wet sites as swishbush. The soil contains little oxygen, and waterlogging makes it difficult for plants to take up phosphorus, an essential nutrient. Swishbush overcomes these problems by means of a specialised root system. It has clusters of roots like the proteoid roots of banksias and their relatives (see p. 16), which absorb phosphorus efficiently. Where it is standing in water, swishbush develops

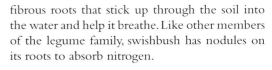

fibrous roots that stick up through the soil into the water and help it breathe. Like other members of the legume family, swishbush has nodules on its roots to absorb nitrogen.

Swishbush is very vigorous, especially when young. Like many vigorous shrubs, it is fairly short-lived and is killed by fire. It produces abundant seed, and regenerates readily.

Associated life

Native bees and a species of jewel beetle (*Cisseis* sp.) visit the pea-flowers of swishbush. Another jewel beetle (illustrated) eats the phyllodes. Leafhoppers suck sap from the stem and secrete a sweet honeydew attractive to ants. The ants return the favour by protecting colonies of leafhoppers from predators. Other sucking insects include shieldbugs. Moth caterpillars eat the surface of the green stems, and wood-boring insect larvae tunnel in the base of the trunk.

Human uses

The Aboriginal people used the branches of swishbush, along with ferns and bark, for building shelters.

It is now used in many projects to restore wetland vegetation.

Collection and naming
Collected about 1795 from a specimen cultivated in Hanover, Germany. Specific name from the Latin *junceus* 'rush–like'.

Distinctive features

Large open shrub, often with pendulous branches, occurring on clayey soil or near swamps or watercourses.

Leaves absent; phyllodes up to 30 cm long, slender, and round in cross-section.

Flowers pea-shaped, yellow with orange-red keel, in large sprays above the foliage, produced in mid spring to early summer.

Pods brown or black, 4-6 mm long and 2½-3½ mm wide.

Balga

Xanthorrhoea preissii

∧ *Section of spike, with opened fruits.*

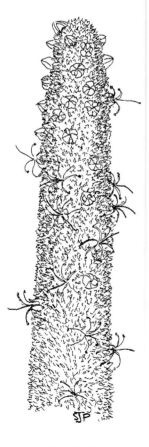

∧ *Top of spike.*

Balga is one of several different grasstrees that occur in Perth. This species is widespread and common. It develops an impressive trunk and is the only one that grows taller than 3 m. Its flowering spear is impressive too, being up to 3 m or more long. It comprises: the scape, the spear's non-flowering stem; and the spike, the upper, flowering section. In balga the spike, packed with thousands of white flowers, occupies the spear's top two thirds.

Grasstrees without visible trunks, growing in banksia or jarrah-banksia country on the coastal plain, are likely to be another species very common in Perth, *Xanthorrhoea brunonis*. When in flower it can be distinguished from balga by its shorter spear, 1-1½ m long, with only the top 10-30 cm covered in flowers. A third and uncommon species, *X. acanthostachya*, has a very prickly-looking spike, and grows in the Darling Scarp and adjacent coastal plain. Least like the others is *X. gracilis*, which in Perth is restricted to the Darling Plateau and has comparatively small clumps of foliage and a very slender spear.

Kingia (p. 162), which is of similar appearance to balga, belongs to a different genus in a different family, and has a number of different features.

Plants in the genus *Xanthorrhoea* are indeed not closely related to those in any other: *Xanthorrhoea* is the only genus in its family, Xanthorrhoeaceae. The genus is confined to Australia, where there are over 30 species, of which 10 occur in Western Australia.

Growth and appearance

Balga's impressive display of flowers occurs in mid to late spring. After flowering, the spike produces beak-like capsules, which release shiny black seeds in summer and autumn. After a year or two the spear crashes to the ground. Only one spear is produced on each crown of foliage. If two spears appear to spring from the one crown, it is a sign that it is beginning to divide.

Balga's trunk is bumpy and often crooked, and in older specimens often branches, sometimes producing up to a dozen crowns of foliage. It contrasts with kingia's trunk, which is straight or smoothly curving, and rarely branches. Kingia's drumsticks grow from buds in the leaf axils, on the sides of the shoot. As the tip of the shoot produces only leaves, the plant grows smoothly upwards.

Balga, however, produces its spear from the tip of the shoot, so subsequent leaf growth must begin from new shoots in the leaf axils. Many shoots are

produced, but often one dominates and the rest die; this change in the stem's angle of growth produces a wiggle. Sometimes two shoots survive, and the stem forks. More than two shoots seldom survive: a balga that forks into three or more is unusual.

Associated life

Balga supports a rich associated life. Insects, including a species of jewel beetle, eat the leaves, and other insects and small lizards shelter in them. When disturbed, many of these animals drop into the mass of foliage, where they are well protected.

The flowering spears attract honey-eating birds, such as the red wattlebird, brown honeyeater and singing honeyeater, and large numbers of insects, including bees, wasps, ants, moths and butterflies. Two butterfly species that particularly like to feed at balga spears are the Australian painted lady and the yellow admiral.

When the spears begin to fruit, the larvae of weevils and other beetles burrow in and eat the forming seeds. Ringneck parrots pluck out the young green fruits.

Other insect larvae burrow into the trunks of older balgas. These include the bardi grub (the cream, legless larva of a long-horned beetle) and the scarab larva (which has legs and a black abdomen).

Balga's dense mass of live and dead leaves can shield the ground underneath from the rain and from falling leaves and twigs. The resulting dry, bare patches of sand are favoured by antlions for digging their sandpit traps.

Where the skirt of dead leaves actually reaches the ground a persistently moist environment may be created. Lifting up the leaves may reveal at times many hundreds of tiny, semi-translucent white fruiting bodies of decomposer fungi such as *Marasmius* or *Mycena*. In Perth's seasonally hot and dry climate it is only in such microclimates that these tiny fungi may thrive. On old, charred stems of balgas, particularly near the ground, one may also find a good display of several species of moss or lichen.

When a balga dies, fungi and the larvae of native flies enter the trunk and cause it to rot. Eventually the core disintegrates, leaving a cylinder of leaf-bases. This 'shell' makes an excellent home for snakes and lizards.

Ecological notes

It is commonly believed that balgas grow only an inch in a hundred years. This is a gross underestimate, but they do grow slowly. The average rate of growth is similar to that of kingia: about 1½ cm a year. Thus a balga 5 m tall would be about 300 years old.

The slowness of balga's growth is understandable: its trunk, like that of kingia, is built from layers of flat leaf-bases. One and a half centimetres of growth represents about 580 new leaves.

The flowering of balga is stimulated by fire — although specimens will flower some years, or even most years, in its absence. Balga survives fire well. Its trunk is well protected by the tightly packed leaf-bases, and each growth-point by a dense crown of long leaves. It recovers rapidly.

A balga is a store of information about the environment. It cannot, however, provide as long a history as kingia: it does not live as long; and the core in the lower part of the trunk thickens and obscures the annual growth-waves.

Human uses

The Aboriginal people made torches from balga spears, which they used when hunting fish at night. They ate the bardi grubs in balga trunks, and made the gum of balga into cakes. The gum was used also by Europeans, to make varnish.

Today balga is used in horticulture. Some nurseries sell seedlings or mature specimens. Some people grow their own. The seeds are easily collected in autumn, and germinate readily. If planted where there is much competition from surrounding plants, the seedlings may take many years to develop a good mass of foliage, and it may be 20 years before they flower. If they are planted in an open, sunny spot, free from competition, however, they will develop much more quickly and flower much sooner.

Occurrence and distribution

Balga is found in the western part of the South-West, from north of Geraldton to Walpole, where it grows on a wide range of soils.

Collection and naming

Collected by J.A.L. Preiss in 1840 at York. Specific name after Preiss.

∧ *Yellow admiral.*

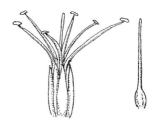

< *Single flower (x 2).*

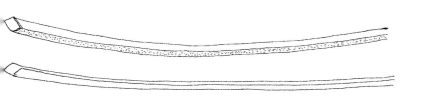

∧ *Sections of leaves.*

Woody pear, forest pear, danja

Xylomelum occidentale

∧ *Wingless, female thynnid wasp.*

The woody, pear-shaped fruit of this species is probably Australia's largest woody fruit. Appropriately, *Xylomelum* is derived from the Greek *xylon* 'wood' and *melon* 'fruit'. This genus, in the banksia family, is confined to Australia, where there are two species in the east and two in the west.

The alternative common name 'forest pear' (or 'forest woody pear') is used to distinguish this species from the other Western Australian species, which occurs in the northern sandplains and parts of the Wheatbelt.

Associated life

The flowers, in summer, attract many bees, wasps and flies. Since, however, they are cream and produced in masses, they are comparatively visible at night, and may be designed for pollination by nocturnal animals.

The leaves do not appear to support many insects. Leaf-blades bent over and fastened with silk suggest moth larvae. The foliage is, however, very suitable for spiders in making their webs, since they can attach bits of web to the spines on many of the leaves. Many spiders' webs may be found in woody pear's foliage in late spring, when bush flies and hoverflies provide abundant prey.

The red-capped parrot eats the seeds.

Ecological notes

Protected by its bark, woody pear survives fire and resprouts from its twigs. The large fruits take several years to mature. The large seeds they contain are winged. They spiral as they drop, and can be carried a short distance in the wind.

Appearance

This slow-growing tree is irregularly shaped, but tends to be fairly upright. Old specimens have a woody look. It grows up to 9 m, much the same height as the banksias with which it associates. Its green foliage is brighter than that of the surrounding banksias and sheoaks.

Occurrence and distribution

Woody pear grows in sandy or sandy-gravelly soils, from Perth to Augusta. In 1965 it was collected from somewhere west of Wanneroo, where it is likely to have since been destroyed by clearing. All other known locations are further south.

In the Perth Metropolitan Region it is largely confined to sandy-gravelly (Forrestfield) soils on the eastern side of the coastal plain. There are, however, some specimens on the Murdoch University campus, where they will be protected if possible from further developments — and augmented by the planting of seedlings in suitable spots, from seed collected from the specimens.

On the plain to the south of Perth, woody pear is quite common.

Cultivation

Woody pear grows slowly but appears to be hardy and able to survive under varying conditions. To help preserve this species in Perth, it should be grown in parks near where it occurs naturally.

Collection and naming

Collected by Charles Fraser in 1827 at Geographe Bay. Specific name from the Latin *occidentalis* 'western'.

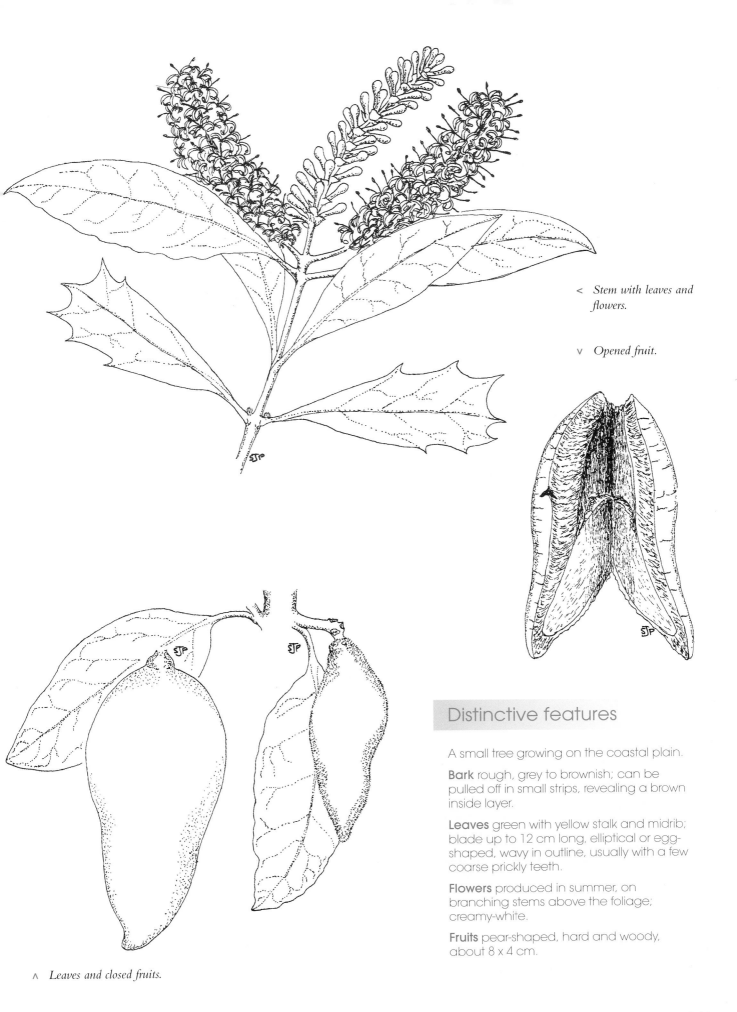

< *Stem with leaves and flowers.*

∨ *Opened fruit.*

Distinctive features

A small tree growing on the coastal plain.

Bark rough, grey to brownish; can be pulled off in small strips, revealing a brown inside layer.

Leaves green with yellow stalk and midrib; blade up to 12 cm long, elliptical or egg-shaped, wavy in outline, usually with a few coarse prickly teeth.

Flowers produced in summer, on branching stems above the foliage; creamy-white.

Fruits pear-shaped, hard and woody, about 8 x 4 cm.

∧ *Leaves and closed fruits.*

Part three
Activities

Cultivation

Which of Perth's trees and tall shrubs should we cultivate? All of them! They are all beautiful, as this book's first chapter aims to show. And by supporting many of our local insects, they make an important contribution to maintaining our biodiversity. This is particularly so if they are naturally occurring specimens, or are planted on sites where they occur or used to occur naturally. The word 'local' is used to refer to such plants. Jarrah, for example, is local to Kings Park but not to the coastal dunes in Swanbourne. Local plants have further value in reflecting our natural environment, and giving us a sense of place.

In the past, nearly all the trees and shrubs planted in Perth were non-locals, and indeed not even Perth species, being from overseas or from other parts of Australia. Today we are planting our local species a lot more — but not nearly as much as they deserve to be.

There are, however, some practical limitations to cultivating the species in this book. Nearly all are easy to propagate, but some are unsuitable for particular sites or uses. The larger banksias will not grow in places heavily irrigated or fertilised, and very few of the species in this book are ideal as street trees. In practice, therefore, we should grow in suitable places every Perth species we can propagate.

Places for planting Perth's trees and tall shrubs

Despite the above limitations, there are many places where Perth's trees and tall shrubs can be grown, which include the following.

Parks and open spaces

Perth's parks and open spaces offer many excellent opportunities for planting local trees and shrubs, particularly in places not irrigated, or where irrigation can be modified or discontinued.

Some open spaces contain or border lakes, rivers or drains. A most valuable use of our local trees and shrubs can be made in revegetating such areas (see 'Rivers, lakes, swamps, streams and drains', page 216).

Parks containing sports fields often have room round their edges for local trees. In golf courses, the use of local trees and shrubs to separate their fairways can provide a relaxing 'bush' setting.

∧ *Fig. 46*
The saplings and seedlings of marri in this park have germinated naturally within a garden bed, from seeds from the mature trees near by.

Highways, railways and dual carriageways

The broad verges of freeways, highways and railways are excellent places to establish local trees and shrubs, and some median strips are suitable too. Because these verges are often almost continuous and traverse large areas, their associated vegetation can provide valuable habitat corridors.

Many dual carriageways through urban areas have only narrow street verges, but have median strips suitable for planting with local trees or shrubs.

Minor roads

There are many requirements for street trees, such as the need for adequate visibility under their crown of foliage to allow road traffic and pedestrians on the footpath to be readily seen. The shrubby species in this book are therefore unsuitable. Other species grow too large. To survive vandalism, newly planted street trees generally need to have been grown in tubs to a height of at least one and a half metres. Some species will not readily grow so large in a tub, or may be vulnerable to vandalism by growing too slowly thereafter. Some, if trained to grow to a shape suitable for a street tree, will later become top-heavy and fall over. And species such as moonah, with its surface roots, can cause problems by lifting up paving or curbing.

One of Perth's trees, peppermint, has been used widely as a street tree. Several additional species have been used to some extent, including saw-tooth banksia, marri, limestone marlock, jarrah, flooded gum and pricklybark. Moonah has been used where the verges are wide, and salmon white gum could be considered for its hardiness and very moderate size. All of these species are better used where there are no overhead wires.

Educational institutions

Growing local trees or shrubs in school grounds can provide an opportunity for students to study and become familiar with their local species. Some universities have large grounds, where local trees and shrubs can be accommodated.

Private gardens

An excellent way of getting to know your local plants is to grow them in your garden. If their environment is made as natural as possible — by not fertilising them or giving them any more watering than they need — there is more opportunity to witness their natural behaviour.

In many gardens there may not be room for the trees in this book, or even the shrubs. But these are just a few of Perth's plants. The vast majority are much smaller. Of the 1,500 species native to the Perth Metropolitan Region, four fifths are shrubs or herbs (non-woody plants) less than a metre tall. Many can readily be fitted into even a tiny garden. For advice on determining which Perth plants are local to your area, see *Growing Locals*[1].

Getting the best out of our trees and tall shrubs

In using our local trees and shrubs, with thought we can get the best out of them. We can make the most of their benefits to biodiversity, as well as allowing their beauty to be well displayed. We can

produce an effect that is natural and informative. The following advice is given with these aims in mind.

Natural regeneration

Is planting necessary? That should be our first question when revegetating a reserve, park or garden. If mature trees or shrubs are already present on the site, there is the possibility of allowing or encouraging them to regenerate naturally. The result is far more natural and beautiful than planting (see p. 8).

Natural regeneration often goes unnoticed. Wherever we see remnants of vegetation or planted local trees or shrubs, we should make a point of looking for seedlings or saplings. If a tree or shrub is not regenerating there is a good reason. The plant may not be producing seed — or more usually the seedlings may be being killed when very young by mowing, hoeing, burning or trampling, or by competition from a heavy growth of weeds. A minor change in management may allow regeneration to succeed. In grassed parks, trees or shrubs can often be allowed to regenerate if we create garden beds round or near them.

∧ *Fig. 47*
A planted garden bed three years old, modelled on the natural vegetation of Perth's coastal limestone: one-sided bottlebrush (left), two-leaf hakea (centre), parrotbush (behind), grey cottonheads (in front) and Fremantle mallee (extreme right).

Local forms of local species

It is best to grow not only the local species but their local forms, by collecting seed or cuttings (with permission: see below) from specimens occurring at the site or as near by as possible. Care should be taken to ensure that the materials are collected from naturally occurring specimens and not planted ones, since planted specimens may be of a non-local form — or indeed the wrong species altogether. For example, in projects involving flooded gum or salt sheoak, river gum or swamp oak are often planted by mistake, by collecting the seeds from planted specimens. Non-local species or forms are of less ecological value, and moreover can cause problems by outcompeting the local species or forms, or interbreeding with them.

The local forms of local species are essential in any project to restore a degraded bushland — and the body responsible for managing the area will usually require this.

Habitat links

As explained in the conservation chapter, links between areas of habitat, in the form of 'corridors' or 'stepping-stones', are extremely important for biodiversity, to help the survival of plants, animals and fungi. Many of the corridors defined in the *Bush Forever* report[2] are splendid 'greenways', providing pathways for walkers and cyclists. In addition to those links, many more can be provided by establishing plants along other routes between habitat areas.

Because of their habitat value, local plants are the most useful for this purpose. The trees and tall shrubs local to the site, being the largest such species, are particularly important.

Rivers, lakes, swamps, streams and drains

The Swan Estuary and the associated Swan and Canning rivers are not only a marvellous scenic and recreational feature but also a wonderful habitat for aquatic and terrestrial wildlife. The river system traverses the coastal plain, and its banks and floodplains provide some of the most important of Perth's greenways. The State's Healthy Rivers Program seeks to maintain the environmental health and community benefit of the rivers by improving the quality of their water. As part of the program, the State and local governments are re-establishing vegetation along the rivers' shores.

Tree species that occur naturally along the rivers, such as flooded gum, freshwater paperbark and salt sheoak, are an important part of this revegetation.

Like the rivers, Perth's lakes and swamps are significant features and important for their wildlife. They comprise not only natural wet areas but also artificial ones. Many artificial lakes are created in the landscaping of low-lying areas. And many artificial swamps are constructed for treating runoff water from highways or urban areas. They act to purify the water, filtering out some of its sediments, nutrients and pollutants, before it finds its way into natural wetlands.

The revegetation of these various wetlands with local trees and shrubs, together with rushes and understorey plants, is important for a number of reasons. The trees and shrubs help stabilise the soil and purify the water. They also provide shade, keeping the water cooler and discouraging algal blooms. And they enhance biodiversity. They provide cover, and sites where birds and bats can nest or roost, as well as support a great many insects.

A further reason for using local plants is because their shed leaves provide the conditions to which the aquatic invertebrates are adapted. By contrast, the soft leaves from many exotic trees form a jelly-like slush in the water, harmful to aquatic life. An important aspect of the leaves of many of Perth's wetland trees — such as flooded gum and the various paperbark species — is that they provide chemicals called tannins, which stain the water dark brown. By thus reducing the penetration of light, they help prevent algal blooms. The staining is greatest for wetlands in the infertile Bassendean sands, in the central and eastern parts of the coastal plain. Nearer the coast, the tannins are bound up in lime in the soil.

As with lakes and swamps, streams and drains can benefit greatly from revegetation with local plants. Many form useful corridors. Drains on the coastal plain are numerous, and some offer scope for not only revegetation but also engineering works. At various places along their routes, broad pools may be created, as well as floodplains, islands and riffles, providing greatly improved habitat for fishes, frogs, aquatic invertebrates and waterbirds — as well as greatly enhancing their aesthetic value.[3]

The natural vegetation that fringes rivers, lakes, swamps or streams comprises a number of zones, corresponding largely to the height of the water-table. Revegetation will be most informative and aesthetically pleasing if the trees, shrubs and rushes are planted in their natural zones (see 'Maintaining natural zones', below).

Planting to control weeds

Many revegetation projects, such as disturbed areas within or on the edges of bushlands, aim to re-establish as much as possible of the original vegetation, from the largest trees to the smallest herbs. Planting the local trees and tall shrubs first can help to some degree in controlling weeds. Once they develop it is then easier to re-establish the smaller shrubs and herbs.

On some wetland sites, however, some of the smaller plants, such as centella, slender knotweed and tassel sedge, grow rapidly and readily colonise disturbed sites, forming a dense ground cover that outcompetes annual weeds. It is useful to plant these first. Perennial weeds will still need other means of control.

Spacing and mixing for more natural effects

Many Perth woodlands comprise an upper and a lower layer of trees, as well as many different shrubs and herbs. The dominant, larger trees, in the upper layer, are usually eucalypts, often with banksias and common sheoak in the lower layer.

The upper layer needs to be given particular attention, if planting is to achieve a natural effect. In a natural woodland the spacing between the dominant trees varies enormously, with some in tight clumps and others many metres away from their nearest neighbours. The human tendency when planting trees, however, is to space them apart almost equally, even when that is not the intention! Such trees readily betray themselves as a plantation (see Fig. 15, p. 8).

To achieve anything like a natural effect, one must make an exaggerated effort to plant some pairs or groups of trees very close together (to within a metre of one another) and others out by themselves. The result will be a more natural variety, not only of spacings but of the trees' forms. Those in groups will grow up slender, or lean out away from their neighbours (see Fig. 10, p. 5, and Fig. 48, this page), whereas those by themselves will be more branched and spreading. In nature many seedlings germinate and survive beside logs, where they receive some protection, or in small ruts or depressions, where they get more moisture. Such features on the site can be used to concentrate the plantings and make

< *Fig. 48*
Five yarris, near Gidgegannup. Tight groups of trees are common in nature, and have great beauty.

the spacing more irregular and natural. Planting the trees when quite small will further help them develop in more individual ways. Planting too few of them will help too. By thus allowing spaces for natural regeneration, this will in time result in a mix of older and younger trees, providing an even more natural effect.

Fill in the open spaces with short-lived shrubs, such as coojong. It does not matter if too many coojongs are planted, since in 10 to 20 years most will have died, and a more natural distribution will result from their natural reproduction. This and other short-lived wattles, such as red-eyed wattle, provide quick cover and support many insects, contributing to biodiversity. Some should be planted close to or within groups of planted eucalypts, to induce variety in their form. The wattles grow very quickly and develop a broad mass of foliage. To seek light, some of the eucalypts will find their way up through the wattles without branching, and others will grow out at angles.

Maintaining natural zones

Few bushlands contain uniform vegetation: it usually changes from spot to spot, reflecting changes in the physical environment. A bushland a few kilometres from the coast, for example, may be dominated in different places by jarrah, marri or tuart, reflecting subtle differences in the soil. The effect can easily be spoilt by planting, say, tuart in a jarrah area.

An even more marked zonation can be seen in wetland vegetation. Banbar may occur in the innermost strip, where there is most flooding, with freshwater paperbark, flooded gum, modong and swamp banksia, and spearwood occurring progressively further from the water.

Similarly, a zonation will be seen in the natural vegetation of a limestone hill, corresponding to the decrease in the depth of the soil towards the summit. Much of the vegetation is often shrubby, with large trees, such as tuart, occurring only at the base, where the soil is sufficiently deep.

Regardless of the site, the likely variability of its original vegetation should be considered, noting the occurrence or positions of any remnant trees or shrubs. By taking care with planting to reflect the natural zones, we can produce a result that is more informative and beautiful.

Excluding non-locals

In revegetating with local plants, it is best not to include any non-locals among them. The growth of the local species is slowed by the many insects they support. Many non-local trees, such as eastern Australian eucalypts, are very vigorous. They typically grow larger and faster than our local species, outcompeting them by overshadowing them, or by reproducing prolifically. They dominate visually too, because of their size and their masses of bright, unblemished foliage.

At any site chosen for revegetation with local plants there will often, of course, be specimens of non-local trees or shrubs already present. After the locals are established, any seedlings of the non-locals that appear should be removed, with consideration given to the eventual removal of the parent trees.

Allowing enough room

In our crowded city, space is often limited by powerlines overhead, or by roads or buildings near by. In order not to plant trees or shrubs that will subsequently be lopped or pruned, consider the space available and choose species whose size will not exceed it. The space *above* a tree is particularly important. Side-branches can be removed with less effect on the tree's beauty than lopping (see Fig. 52, p. 225, and Fig. 16, p. 9).

In the coastal suburbs most trees and shrubs are asymmetrical: they lean away from the south-west, the main direction of salt-bearing winds. Both in public parks and in private gardens, this is usually forgotten! Trees are often planted immediately to the west of buildings or powerlines. They are also planted in the centre of a median strip, when it would be better to plant them nearer the western side.

To gauge the effect of salt winds on a particular species at a particular site, it is sometimes possible to examine specimens of that species in a nearby park or bush reserve.

If you are growing the plants in your garden, bear in mind that the shape of plants depends also on what light they receive. Those growing in an open, sunny position tend to be round and compact and to spread out, whereas those in the shade of other vegetation are usually sparser, more open and taller. A plant that receives sunlight from one side only will grow out towards it. Trees such as eucalypts need plenty of light, and will not grow well if in too shady a position.

Remember that trees and shrubs do sometimes drop branches, and that their roots can interfere with foundations. Plant the larger trees well away from buildings. Eucalypts and toobada should not be planted near septic systems.

Friends groups: how you can contribute

As mentioned in the conservation chapter, many community groups, generally known as 'friends' groups, have formed for particular bushlands or wider areas. Their work often involves planting, in order to restore degraded portions of bushlands, or to establish habitat links.

Some groups collect their own seed; others use grants of money to employ suitable seed collectors. The plants are usually grown in an accredited nursery for planting by the group.

An excellent way to learn about plants and nature, and do useful conservation work, is to join one of your local groups and become involved in its activities. For more information, contact the Urban Nature group at the Department of Environment and Conservation (DEC), or visit its website.

Growing your own

Another way to learn about Perth's trees and tall shrubs is to collect your own seed or cuttings and grow some of them.

All plants native to Western Australia are protected. A licence from DEC[4] is required to collect seeds or cuttings from such plants on Crown land, or to sell the plants you grow. No licence is needed to collect from plants for your own use from private land, if you have the permission of the owner or occupier (unless the plant concerned is declared rare flora, in which case Ministerial approval is required).

∧ *Fig. 49*
Examples of different types of fruit: (a) POD *of red-eyed wattle, (b)* CONE *of dune sheoak, (c)* NUT *of woollybush (x 2), (d) cluster of* CAPSULES *of toobada, (e)* FOLLICLE *(in cone) of firewood banksia, (f)* FOLLICLE *of harsh hakea, (g)* SCHIZOCARP *of corkybark, (h)* DRUPE *of quandong.*

Growing plants from seed

Seeds of some of Perth's trees and tall shrubs can be bought from seed-suppliers, but some of these may be from cultivars or non-local forms of the species. If you collect them from naturally occurring plants in your own district, you will be using the form best suited to the local conditions.

Types of fruit

The different types of fruit found on the different plant species in this book are illustrated in Fig. 49 and listed in Table 3, overleaf. Some species retain their seed, which can be collected at any time of year. Others release it at a particular time, and it can be collected only then (see Table 3). Most species with capsules retain their seed for several years, sometimes until the branch dies. Others, such as the peppermints, marri and balga, release it. Collect fruits when they are mature but unopened. Mature eucalypt fruits may still be slightly green, but most mature fruits will have changed colour from green to brown. If a tree carries fruits of several ages, select the oldest unopened ones, but check for insect damage. Place them in a paper (not plastic) bag until they dry and open. Then shake the seeds into a container and store in jars until it is time to plant them.

The collecting method for balga, kingia, basket bush and the hop-bushes differs from the above (see Table 3).

Pods are the fruits of legumes, such as wattles and pea-plants. These split open to expose or release the seeds, usually in late spring or summer. Collect the seeds when ripe, at the time the pods are dry and brittle and split easily.

Some species with follicles retain their seed. Snip off the fruits with secateurs and extract the seeds after the fruits have opened, in a few days. The fruits of other species open at a given time of year and release the seed. At the time specified in the table, collect the seeds from ripe fruits, or from the ground soon after the fruits have split open.

The follicles of Perth's larger banksia species are joined together in a cone. Most release some seed in autumn, but seed can be collected at any time of year by the method described in the table.

The seed of the other species that bear cones — the cypresses and sheoaks — can be collected at any time of year. Snip them off and place them in paper bags to open and release their seeds.

Drupes and berries must be collected when ripe. For some species, such as broom ballart, the whole drupe can be planted. The stone of quandong should be extracted from the flesh.

Table 3 – Trees and tall shrubs of Perth: seed collection and propagation

Common name	Botanical name	Type of fruit	Time of year to collect seed	Comments
red-eyed wattle	*Acacia cyclops*	pod	late Nov., Dec., Jan.	Scarify seeds or immerse in hot water.
summer-scented wattle	*A. rostellifera*	pod	Nov., Dec.	
coojong	*A. saligna*	pod	mid Dec.	
white-stemmed wattle	*A. xanthina*	pod	mid Jan.	
swamp cypress	*Actinostrobus pyramidalis*	cone	all year	
woollybush	*Adenanthos cygnorum*	nut	Nov., Dec.	Difficult to grow from seed; easier from cuttings.
peppermint	*Agonis flexuosa*	capsule	April	
common sheoak	*Allocasuarina fraseriana*	capsule	all year	Seeds lose their viability, so plant soon after extraction.
rock sheoak	*A. huegeliana*	cone	all year	
dune sheoak	*A. lehmanniana*	cone	all year	
candle banksia	*Banksia attenuata*	follicle in cone	all year	Burn cone until follicles crack open, then immerse in cold water. Then put cone in dry place; about two weeks later the seeds will drop out. Plant soon after, since seeds lose their viability.
bull banksia	*B. grandis*	follicle in cone	all year; autumn best	
holly-leaf banksia	*B. ilicifolia*	follicle in cone	all year; autumn best	
swamp banksia	*B. littoralis*	follicle in cone	April, May	
firewood banksia	*B. menziesii*	follicle in cone	all year; autumn best	
saw-tooth banksia	*B. prionotes*	follicle in cone	all year; autumn best	
parrotbush	*B. sessilis*	follicle	Jan.	
pingle	*B. squarrosa*	follicle	all year	Pluck out follicles and heat them in a frying pan until they open. Soak them in water for 20 minutes then dry them in the sun, or in an oven at 40°C (105°F). Follicles will release their seeds in 6-8 hours.
wonnich	*Callistachys lanceolata*	pod	late Dec., early Jan.	Scarify seeds or immerse in hot water.
toobada	*Callistemon phoeniceus*	capsule	all year	
Rottnest cypress	*Callitris preissii*	cone	all year	
mouse-ears	*Calothamnus rupestris*	capsule	all year	
salt sheoak	*Casuarina obesa*	cone	all year	Seeds lose their viability, so plant soon after extraction.
tree smokebush	*Conospermum triplinervium*	nut	early Dec.	Sow whole nut as soon as collected. Leave pots in sun, and wait until May before watering them. Smoked water stimulates germination.
marri	*Corymbia calophylla*	capsule	Feb., March	
lesser bloodwood	*C. haematoxylon*	capsule	Feb., March, April	

Table 3 – Trees and tall shrubs of Perth: seed collection and propagation (continued)

Common name	Botanical name	Type of fruit	Time of year to collect seed	Comments
coast hop-bush	*Dodonaea aptera*	capsule	early Oct.	Rub capsules in hands to extract the black, spherical seeds.
Perth hop-bush	*D. hackettiana*	capsule	early Dec.	
sticky hop-bush	*D. viscosa*	capsule	Oct.	
powderbark	*Eucalyptus accedens*	capsule	all year	
Yanchep mallee	*E. argutifolia*	capsule	all year	
limestone marlock	*E. decipiens*	capsule	all year	
Fremantle mallee	*E. foecunda*	capsule	all year	
tuart	*E. gomphocephala*	capsule	all year; autumn best	
buttergum	*E. laeliae*	capsule	all year	
salmon white gum	*E. lane-poolei*	capsule	all year	
jarrah	*E. marginata*	capsule	all year	
bullich	*E. megacarpa*	capsule	all year	
yarri	*E. patens*	capsule	all year	
rock mallee	*E. petrensis*	capsule	all year	
flooded gum	*E. rudis*	capsule	all year	
pricklybark	*E. todtiana*	capsule	all year	
wandoo	*E. wandoo*	capsule	all year	
broom ballart	*Exocarpos sparteus*	drupe	late Dec.	Difficult to propagate.
heart-leaf poison	*Gastrolobium bilobum*	pod	Dec.	Scarify seeds or immerse in hot water.
river pea	*G. ebracteolatum*	pod	Dec., Jan., Feb.	
valley grevillea	*Grevillea diversifolia*	follicle	all year	Only a few mature fruits available at any given time.
smooth grevillea	*G. manglesii*	follicle	Dec.	
corkybark	*Gyrostemon ramulosus*	schizocarp	Nov.	Smoked water stimulates germination.
snail hakea	*Hakea cristata*	follicle	all year	
harsh hakea	*H. prostrata*	follicle	all year	
two-leaf hakea	*H. trifurcata*	follicle	Dec.	
grey stinkwood	*Jacksonia furcellata*	pod	Dec.-April	Scarify seeds or immerse in hot water.
green stinkwood	*J. sternbergiana*	pod	Dec.-April	
kingia	*Kingia australis*	capsule	Feb.	Sow whole papery seeds.
spearwood	*Kunzea glabrescens*	capsule	March, April	
tall labichea	*Labichea lanceolata*	pod	Dec., Jan.	
roadside tea-tree	*Leptospermum erubescens*	capsule	Oct.-Nov.	
white spray	*Logania vaginalis*	capsule	Oct.-Nov.	
saltwater paperbark	*Melaleuca cuticularis*	capsule	all year	
chenille honey-myrtle	*M. huegelii*	capsule	all year	
moonah	*M. lanceolata*	capsule	all year	
gorada	*M. lateriflora*	capsule	all year	
modong	*M. preissiana*	capsule	all year	
freshwater paperbark	*M. rhaphiophylla*	capsule	all year	
banbar	*M. teretifolia*	capsule	all year	
mohan	*M. viminea*	capsule	all year	

Table 3 – Trees and tall shrubs of Perth: seed collection and propagation (continued)

Common name	Botanical name	Type of fruit	Time of year to collect seed	Comments
prickly mirbelia	*Mirbelia dilatata*	pod	late Jan.-Feb.	Scarify seeds or immerse in hot water.
Christmas tree	*Nuytsia floribunda*	nut	Feb., March	Sow whole nut: press into soil with open end down, to about a third its depth. Water plants frequently in summer for the first 5 years.
albizia	*Paraserianthes lophantha*	pod	late Dec.	Scarify seeds or immerse in hot water.
spreading snottygobble	*Persoonia elliptica*	drupe	June, July	Difficult to propagate.
upright snottygobble	*P. longifolia*	drupe	June, July	
coast pittosporum	*Pittosporum ligustrifolium*	capsule	Dec.-April	Seeds lose their viability, so plant soon after collecting.
quandong	*Santalum acuminatum*	drupe	Oct., Nov.	Water plants frequently in summer for the first 2 years.
basket bush	*Spyridium globulosum*	capsule	Dec.	Rub capsules between hands to extract the small, red seeds. Smoked water stimulates germination.
brook peppermint	*Taxandria linearifolia*	capsule	March, April, May	
swishbush	*Viminaria juncea*	pod	Dec.	Scarify seeds or immerse in hot water.
balga	*Xanthorrhoea preissii*	capsule in spike	Feb.-May	Extract seeds from the capsules with tweezers or collect them from the ground.
woody pear	*Xylomelum occidentale*	follicle	all year	Put fruits out in the sun in summer to induce them to open.

Storing and treating seeds

Empty the seeds into jars with screw-top lids, and store them in a cool, dry place. Labelling is important; include the name of the species and where and when the seed was collected.

Most seeds need no treatment. Some, such as those of wattles and pea-plants, have hard coats, which delay germination; these need to be treated (see Table 3). One possible treatment, scarification, is the removal of a small part of the seed-coat with a scalpel. Be careful not to damage the seeds by inserting the scalpel too deeply. Alternatively, pour very hot or boiling water over them and leave them to soak for 12 to 24 hours. Fertile seeds will swell.

Sowing

Large seeds, such as those of quandong, marri, banksias and hakeas, may be sown direct into the ground in late autumn or winter. Plant them to a depth one to two times their thickness. Marking their positions with stakes will help prevent the seedlings from being trodden on. Sowing in pots is generally more successful than sowing direct, because it enables the seedlings to be looked after until they are larger and less vulnerable. Spring is the best season for sowing, but autumn and winter are suitable too. Some species, such as eucalypts, honey-myrtles and wattles, will germinate in summer if you stand the pots in a tray of water in a cool spot; then you can plant them out that autumn. Use fine washed sand that is not salty. Pouring boiling water over the soil first should kill most weed seeds. Water the filled pots and leave the soil to drain and settle. Do not use soil likely to contain the root-rot water-mould.

For fine seeds, margarine tubs or ice-cream containers are suitable, with a few drainage holes poked in the bottom (with a heated piece of thick wire). Mix the seed with an equal amount of sand and sprinkle the mixture thinly on the soil. Water with a fairly fine spray to settle the soil.

Larger seeds too can be planted in these containers. Alternatively, to save yourself the trouble of separating seedlings later, plant them singly in pots 10 cm tall. Place seeds on the surface and cover with sand to a depth of one to two times their thickness.

Keep the pots moist (but not wet), either in the rain or by watering lightly every day. Most species will germinate within a month, but banksias and other species with large seeds may take longer. Fig. 50 shows what various seedlings look like soon after they germinate.

Smoked water

Many Australian plant species regenerate best after fire, and the germination of many of these is stimulated by smoke. Smoked water (or smoke-water), produced by bubbling smoke through water, can have the same effect. It is usually available from some specialised nurseries. The seeds of many of the species in this book will germinate well without the use of smoked water. Those of tree smokebush, corkybark and basket bush, however, do not normally germinate readily, and are greatly helped by smoked water. For more information, contact the Botanic Gardens and Parks Authority, Kings Park.

Growing plants from cuttings

Plants grown from cuttings are unlike seedlings. Seedlings are produced by sexual reproduction, and are genetically different from one another, even if all the seed is taken from the one parent plant. Cuttings are genetically identical to the parent plant, and therefore to each other, if taken from the one parent. Genetic variability aids survival, so growing plants from seed rather than cuttings will do more to conserve that species.

Moreover, plants grown from seed are better equipped for survival: they develop a taproot, which quickly goes deep, and helps the plant survive our hot, dry summers. A cutting develops several, more fibrous roots, which probably do not grow down so rapidly.

Growing from seed is also more rewarding, since one can follow the plant's development through a number of stages, starting with the seed-leaves and finishing with the mature plant. The juvenile stages are omitted if the plant is grown from a cutting. Cuttings are useful, however, when growing plants that are difficult to grow from seed, such as woollybush (and smaller species such as hibbertias and leschenaultias).

Autumn to late spring is the best time of year to take cuttings. The cutting can either be 'soft wood' (shoots not more than a few weeks old) or semi-hard wood (material about three months old).

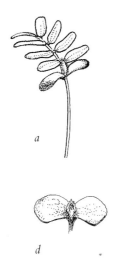

a

b

c

d

f

e

< *Fig. 50*
Newly germinated seedlings, with seed-leaves and young shoots: (a) red-eyed wattle, (b) common sheoak, (c) candle banksia, (d) saw-tooth banksia, (e) tuart, (f) jarrah.

∧ *Fig. 51*
Six-month-old seedling of coast pittosporum, in early summer; by late autumn it will be ready to plant out. The pot is 10 cm high.

A good medium for cuttings is rock wool, a type of mineral wool available at hydroponics shops. Put it into cell-packs or a small tray or punnet. Remove two thirds of the leaves from the cutting, then insert the cut end into hormone powder or hormone gel. A powder or gel designed for semi-hard wood will do for soft cuttings as well. To ensure that the hormone is not rubbed off when the cutting is planted, first make a hole in the mixture with a round-ended pencil.

Until they root, cuttings need plenty of moisture, and daylight, but avoid sunlight. Retain moisture by keeping them in a greenhouse, or by making a polythene or fibre-glass frame for them. Alternatively, individual cuttings can be placed under inverted glass jars. Two-litre plastic cool-drink bottles can be used too: dip the bottom of the bottle in hot water and screw off the glued base. Then the bottle (with its top screwed on) can be placed over the cutting.

Water cuttings once every few days, often enough to keep them moist. Check them at least twice a week, and remove any dead cuttings or rotting leaves to discourage fungi.

Looking after seedlings and cuttings

When seedlings have two or three pairs of leaves (more for small seedlings, such as melaleucas), separate them into individual pots, containing a regular potting-mix. Do the same for cuttings when they have formed roots.

If seedlings have germinated close together, place the container in a bucket of water and shake the soil and seedlings out. If the seedlings are well separated, dig each out with a knife leaving some earth around it. Dig out cuttings in the same way. Cuttings should be kept in humid conditions for a week after being separated.

Plant the individual seedlings or cuttings in pots 10 cm or more tall. The taller the pot the deeper the roots can grow, and the hardier the plant when it is planted out. Tin cans are less suitable because they rust; aluminium cans (with drainage holes) are good, but need to be cut to remove the seedling.

Keep the seedlings and rooted cuttings in pots over the first summer. Place them where they get sun for a third to half of the day. Do not stand them on earth, or their roots may grow into it. Water every second day in winter and spring, and once a day in summer; do not allow the pots to dry out.

It is best not to use any fertiliser. Local plants are adapted to infertile soils. Fertilising a plant in a pot may kill it or make it grow too vigorously and become pot-bound.

Planting

The best time for planting is after good rains in late autumn or early winter. The plants may then be able to develop deep roots in winter and spring. They should be only 15–30 cm tall and will be less pot-bound and better able to establish themselves than if kept in pots for longer.

Make a saucer-shaped hollow for each plant, to help catch rainwater without flooding it. In the hollow's centre dig a hole to the depth of soil in the pot, but wider. Water the pot to bind the soil and snip off any roots that emerge through holes in the bottom. Place your fingers either side of the plant, invert the pot and tap the edge firmly on a solid object to make the plant come out. Gently tease out visible roots until they hang down. Transfer the plant to the hole without breaking the ball of earth. Press earth in to fill the rest of the hole, water well and press in more soil if it subsides.

If it is still dry at this time of year, water the plants every few days until good rains begin to fall.

The plant once established

The plant species in this book are natural to the Perth area, and adapted to Perth's infertile soils. Fertiliser should be avoided: it can harm many species, especially banksias. Digging or hoeing adversely affects some species. It is best to leave the soil undisturbed; this also later allows the plants to reproduce.

The plants are also adapted to Perth's dry summers — although global warming is now making our climate hotter and drier. If planted in late autumn or early winter the plants should, if there have been reasonable winter rains, develop a good root-system by summer. Some, like some natural seedlings, may survive through the summer. It is much better, however, to water weekly or fortnightly in the first summer, to help a greater proportion survive.

Now that global warming is pronounced, it is possible that some watering may be needed at times thereafter. A good time to water may be in June, if it is dry. Our plants are adapted to wet conditions then, which may help them last through the following summer. Alternatively, water them in late summer and autumn, when they are under most stress. Such watering should not be too frequent, but fortnightly at most.

If the natural ground litter of leaves, twigs and bark is left around the plants, it will help retain moisture in the soil, and re-cycle plant nutrients. In moderate amounts it suppresses weeds but still allows seedlings of native plants to germinate.

If you have misplanned the placing of a tree or shrub and it grows too large for the space available, you may have to prune it. With thought, you can minimise the effect on the plant's beauty. By cutting off only those branches that are in the way, you can preserve the rest of the plant's structure. Do not leave any protruding stumps: remove the whole branch. The plant will be less likely to regrow at that point, and it will not show the sort of ugliness illustrated in Fig. 16 (p. 9).

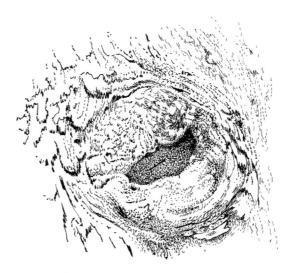

∧ *Fig. 52*
If a branch is cut where it joins the parent branch, new bark will eventually grow completely over it, and the pruning will become almost invisible.

[1]Powell, Robert, and Jane Emberson. *Growing Locals: Gardening with Local Plants in Perth*. Perth, 1996.
[2]State of Western Australia. *Bush Forever: Keeping the Bush in the City: Volume 1, Policies, Principles and Practices; Volume 2, Directory of Bush Forever Sites*. Perth: Western Australian Planning Commission, 2000.
[3]For further advice, see the following. Pen, Luke J. *Managing Our Rivers: A Guide to the Nature and Management of the Streams of South-West Western Australia*. Perth, 1999.
[4]Department of Environment and Conservation, 17 Dick Perry Avenue, Technology Park, Western Precinct, KENSINGTON, W.A. (tel. 9334 0333).

The trees and tall shrubs in this book offer a lifetime of enjoyment. There is so much to know about them, such as: where they occur; at what times of the year they grow, flower or fruit; how they disperse their seeds; what animals or fungi associate with them; and whether they are coping with their changed environment.

The more we get to know our local trees or shrubs, the better we can appreciate their beauty. Then there is the joy of simply looking at them — or sometimes the pain, where their appearance sorrowfully reflects environmental changes to which they are struggling to adjust.

In getting to know these trees and shrubs, the first step is of course to identify some of them, and perhaps some of the many smaller plants associated with them.

Identifying plants

This book is intended to enable the reader to identify Perth's trees and some of its larger shrubs. Several other books enable the identification of all or most of the smaller plants. *Perth Plants*[1] is a field guide to the native and naturalised plants that occur in Kings Park or Bold Park, and includes many of the species that may be found in bushlands on the western side of the coastal plain. *Wildflowers of the West Coast Hills Region*[2] contains pictures or descriptions of many of the plant species native to the Darling Scarp or Darling Plateau within the Perth Metropolitan Region. In addition, a field key for identifying Perth's eucalypts is available from the Department of Environment and Conservation (DEC).

The standard work on the flora of the Perth Metropolitan Region and beyond used to be *Flora of the Perth Region*[3], published in 1987 by the Department of Conservation and Land Management (now DEC). It is now out of print — and also out of date, since many of the plants' botanical names have since changed. It is still, nonetheless, a useful reference for its plant descriptions. For identifying species, the best reference now is *FloraBase*, a website maintained and updated by DEC as the authoritative source of information on Western Australian plants. The site includes an interactive key, which uses descriptions, pictures and maps, to allow plants to be identified in different ways, depending on the material one has available.

A further way to identify plants is to visit DEC's Public Reference Herbarium, of Western Australia's native and naturalised plants. It is housed in DEC's Western Australian Herbarium, 17 Dick Perry Avenue, Technology Park, Western Precinct, Kensington. A reference library with botanical keys, species descriptions, reference specimens and other information is open to the public on weekdays. Leaflets are available on how to collect plant specimens (with the necessary permits and approvals), and the conditions under which specimens may be taken into the herbarium.

Locating and mapping plants

Once you can identify a plant species, you will begin to notice where it occurs, and build up a mental picture of its distribution. For students, it is a useful exercise to map the occurrences of plant species within a suburb or neighbourhood, or a particular patch of bush. Results from different students can be combined to produce an atlas of plant distribution (as in the Melville atlas[4]), which can be compared with the distribution of soils or various physical features. A street directory or the global positioning system can be used to record where each plant species occurs.

Students can also map plants along a line, or transect. DEC has a brochure explaining how this may be done.

Keeping a diary

A good way to learn about plants is to keep a diary. Diaries make interesting records of the past and present; seasonal patterns and general trends can emerge. Schools as well as individuals can keep diaries, with different students observing different species.

Select as your subject a nearby remnant of bush, or one or more plant species. Local plants are of particular interest. If not watered, they will show their adaptations or responses to the broader environment. They will also have their associated insects and other animals to observe. If you grow local plants in your garden you can study them on the spot.

You do not have to write the diary every day or even at regular intervals, but do record the date of each entry. You may want to record anything you notice (something apparently trivial may become important later) or confine your observations to one particular interest: the natural reproduction of plants, perhaps, or the marks made on leaves by insects.

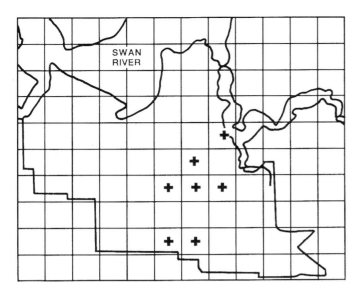
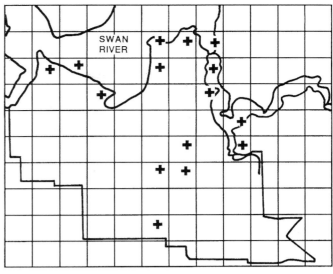

Two maps from the Melville atlas (see Note 4 on p. 229), showing the occurrences of two wetland plant species: banbar (left) and freshwater paperbark (right). Whereas banbar is almost entirely restricted here to the chain of lakes south of the Swan estuary, freshwater paperbark grows by the estuary as well.
(Reproduced by permission of the School of Biological and Environmental Sciences, Murdoch University.)

< Fig. 54
Entries from a garden diary. Underlining the names of plants, animals and fungi makes them easier to find for future reference.

14·6·09 (Sun.)
Basket bush in front is now well out in flower & is attracting hoverflies & other small insects.
Balga seeds in pot, planted 14·5, are beginning to germinate.
Lizard caught in mulch this afternoon. Released at same spot.
abt 8cm long
brown above, white
undern., neat black line along
side. 4 fingers & toes.
nasals in contact. Probably the skink Lerista elegans.

20·6·09 (Sat.)
Counted 26 new seedlings of parrotbush, mostly near southern path.
Flock of black cockatoos arrived abt midday.
Visited neighbouring tuart trees then our mature tuart in back. Eventually were 14 birds in our tree, walking in outer branches tearing off bits of bark (probably looking for borer grubs). Abt 3 p.m. they suddenly flew off in a group.

An unfamiliar insect or fungus can be photographed for later identification. Or you can make a drawing of it, noting its features.

Photographing plants

Because Perth's trees and tall shrubs are such an important part of our landscape, many people will have included them in photographs of outdoor scenes, perhaps as part of the setting for outdoor events. But they are also rewarding subjects in themselves. They make fine photographs or drawings, as individuals or in groups, and as wholes or in parts — trunks, branches, bark or flowers.

Early morning or late afternoon, when the sun is low, are often the best times for photographing trees. The effect is more atmospheric, and the tree will often stand out more boldly. Much of its trunk and lower branches may be lit up by the sun, rather than largely in the shadow of its canopy. Silhouettes at these times can make good pictures too.

Pictures can become valuable historical records, preserving the memory of scenes that have since been altered. One can set out deliberately to build a collection of such photographic records of the environment. A sequence of pictures taken over several years can document such things as how vegetation recovers after a fire, or how a garden develops by the growth and reproduction of its plants.

Joining a friends group

An excellent way to do something tangible for your local natural environment is to join a 'friends' group for one of your local bushlands, or some other community group for the protection of a wider area. The conservation chapter in this book refers to the valuable work done by such groups.

To find out which groups operate near you, contact Natural Resource Management, Perth Region (tel. 9374 3333), which can also advise on how you might start your own group, if none exists for your bush reserve. Another useful contact is Urban Nature, Swan Region, DEC (tel. 9368 4399).

Joining a nature-study group

There are various groups in Perth for the study of nature, such as the Wildflower Society of Western Australia, the Western Australian Naturalists' Club, Birds Australia and the Western Australian Insect Study Society. Further groups, such as the

> *Fig. 55*
> *View in the Darling Scarp. Naturally occurring trees — both living and dead — are important features of this scene. It would look very bare without them (and their shadows).*

Australian Association of Bush Regenerators and the Environmental Weeds Action Network, focus on particular actions to protect the environment.

Joining such groups provides the opportunity both to learn more about nature and to share one's interests with others.

Joining Land for Wildlife

If you have a block of land with bush on it, and intend to manage it for conservation, joining Land for Wildlife is an excellent way to learn how to do so. It need not be your own land: if you are part of a group managing bush or creating wildlife habitat on behalf of a school or local government, that group may apply to join. The block will need to be two hectares or larger.

Land for Wildlife is a voluntary scheme to encourage and assist landowners or land managers in Western Australia to maintain or increase the habitat value of their property, even though it may be used primarily for other purposes. More than 2,000 properties have been registered with the scheme since its inception. They are scattered throughout the State's south-west corner, with many in the Perth Metropolitan Region.

On joining the scheme, you will be visited by a Land for Wildlife officer, for an inspection of the land concerned and a discussion about its management. You will receive a copy of the officer's report, together with other information, including lists of references and the contact details of useful organisations.

If the land contains a bushland, or other good habitat, you may be eligible to join the scheme as a full member, and be given a Land for Wildlife sign to erect on your property (Fig. 56). If your

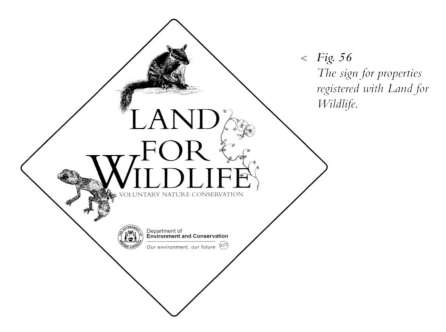

< *Fig. 56*
The sign for properties registered with Land for Wildlife.

property is cleared, you will become an interim member, until your revegetation develops enough to begin to provide some habitat. A second visit will be made to your property at this time; if it is assessed as providing wildlife habitat you will become a full member, eligible for the Land for Wildlife sign.

As a full or interim member of Land for Wildlife, you will receive copies of the very informative magazine *Western Wildlife*. You can also attend field days and other activities organised by the scheme. You will thus be able to learn from instruction and direct observation, and by sharing your experiences with others in the scheme.

For further information, or to apply to join the scheme, contact the Land for Wildlife Coordinator, Wildlife Branch, Department of Environment and Conservation, Locked Bag 104, Bentley Delivery Centre, W.A. 6983 (tel. 9334 0530; fax 9334 0278).

[1]Barrett, Russell, and Eng Pin Tay. *Perth Plants: A Field Guide to the Bushland and Coastal Flora of Kings Park and Bold Park, Perth, Western Australia*. Perth, 2005.
[2]Marshall, John, and other members of the Darling Range Branch of the Wildflower Society of Western Australia. *Wildflowers of the West Coast Hills Region: Field Guide*. [Western Australia], [199-?].
[3]Marchant, N.G., & others. *Flora of the Perth Region: Parts One and Two*. Perth, 1987.
[4]Bridgewater, P.B, and J.R. Wheeler. *Atlas of the Distribution of Certain Plant Species in the City of Melville, Western Australia*. Perth, 1980.

Appendices

Works consulted

Abbott, Ian. 'Comparisons of Habitat Structure and Plant, Arthropod and Bird Diversity between Mainland and Island Sites near Perth, Western Australia'. *Austral Ecology*, 1, no. 4 (1976), 275–80.

Abbott, Ian. *Aboriginal Names for Plant Species in South-Western Australia*. Technical Paper No. 5, Forests Department of Western Australia (now DEC). Perth, 1983.

Abbott, Ian. 'Comparisons of Spatial Pattern, Structure, and Tree Composition between Virgin and Cut-Over Jarrah Forest in Western Australia'. *Forest Ecology and Management*, 9 (1984), 101–26.

Abbott, Ian. 'Emergence, Early Survival, and Growth of Seedlings of Six Tree Species in Mediterranean Forest of Western Australia'. *Forest Ecology and Management*, 9 (1984), 51–66.

Abbott, Ian. 'Rate of Growth of *Banksia grandis* Willd. (Proteaceae) in Western Australian Forest'. *Australian Journal of Botany*, 33 (1985), 381–91.

Abbott, Ian. 'Recruitment and Mortality in Populations of *Banksia grandis* Willd. in Western Australian Forest'. *Australian Journal of Botany*, 33 (1985), 261–70.

Abbott, Ian, and Robert Black. 'An Ecological Reconnaissance of Four Islands in the Archipelago of The Recherche, Western Australia'. *Journal of the Royal Society of Western Australia*, 60, no. 4 (1978), 115–28.

Abbott, Ian, and Owen Loneragan. *Ecology of Jarrah (*Eucalyptus marginata*) in the Northern Jarrah Forest of Western Australia*. Bulletin No. 1, Department of Conservation and Land Management (now DEC). Perth, 1986.

Barrett, Russell, and Eng Pin Tay. *Perth Plants: A Field Guide to the Bushland and Coastal Flora of Kings Park and Bold Park, Perth, Western Australia*. Perth, 2005.

Batini, F.E. *The Jarrah Leaf Miner*. 2nd impression. Information Sheet No. 8, Forests Department of Western Australia (now DEC). Perth, 1983.

Beard, J.S. (ed.). *West Australian Plants*. 2nd edition. Perth, 1970.

Bennett, Eleanor M. 'A Guide to the Western Australian She-oaks (*Allocasuarina* and *Casuarina* species)'. *The Western Australian Naturalist*, 15, no. 4 (December, 1982), 77–105.

Bennett, Eleanor M. *The Bushland Plants of Kings Park, Western Australia*. Perth, 1988.

Bhullar, Simrath, and Jonathan Majer. 'Arthropods on Street Trees: A Food Resource for Wildlife'. *Pacific Conservation Biology*, 6 (2000), 171–3.

Blackall, William E., and Brian J. Grieve. *How to Know Western Australian Wildflowers: A Key to the Flora of the Temperate Regions of Western Australia: Parts I-III*. Perth, 1954–65; reprinted 1974. *Part IV*, by B.J. Grieve and W.E. Blackall. Perth, 1975.

Blackall, William E., and Brian J. Grieve. *How to Know Western Australian Wildflowers: A Key to the Flora of the Extratropical Regions of Western Australia*. 2nd edition, restructured and revised by B.J. Grieve. *Part I*. Perth, 1988. *Part III*. Perth, 1980–81.

Blakers, M., S.J.J.F. Davies and P.N. Reilly. *The Atlas of Australian Birds*. Melbourne, 1984.

Boland, D.J., M.I.H. Brooker and J.W. Turnbull. *Eucalyptus Seed*. CSIRO. Australia, 1980.

Bootle, Keith R. *Wood in Australia*. Forestry Commission of New South Wales. Sydney, 1983.

Bougher, N.L. *Perth Urban Bushland Fungi Field Book: A Self-managed Format*. 3rd edition. Perth, 2007.

Bougher, N.L. 'Perth's Fungi Forever'. *Landscope*, 22, no. 3 (2007), 20–26.

Bougher, Neale L. *Fungi of the Perth Region and Beyond: A Self-managed Field Book*. Perth, 2009.

Braby, M.F. *Butterflies of Australia, their identification, biology and distribution: Volumes 1 & 2*. Collingwood, Victoria, 2000.

Braby, Michael F. *The Complete Field Guide to Butterflies of Australia*. Collingwood, Victoria, 2004.

Bridgewater, P.B., and J.R. Wheeler. *Atlas of the Distribution of Certain Plant Species in the City of Melville, Western Australia*. Perth, 1980.

British Broadcasting Corporation. *Life in the Undergrowth*. 2005 [a documentary television series narrated by Sir David Attenborough].

Brooker, M.I.H. '*Eucalyptus foecunda* Revisited and Six Related New Species (Myrtaceae)'. *Nuytsia*, 6, no. 3 (1988), 325-34.

Brooker, M.I.H., and S.D. Hopper. 'New Series, Subseries, Species and Subspecies of *Eucalyptus* (Myrtaceae) from Western Australia and from South Australia'. *Nuytsia*, 9, no. 1 (1993), 1-68.

Brooker, M.I.H., and D.A. Kleinig. *Field Guide to Eucalypts: South-western and Southern Australia*. Melbourne, 1990.

Brown, Liz. 'Biodiversity — the Other 99 Per Cent'. *Keeper No. 1, The West Australian*, Monday, February 8, 1999.

Burbidge, A.H., and S.D. Hopper. 'Checklist of Observations of Vertebrates Feeding at Flowers and on Fruits of Western Australian Plants'. Unpublished report. Department of Conservation and Land Management (now DEC). Perth, no date.

Bush, Brian, Brad Maryan, Robert Browne-Cooper and David Robinson. *A Guide to the Reptiles and Frogs of the Perth Region*. Perth, 1995.

Calaby, J.H. 'Observations on the Banded Ant-Eater *Myrmecobius f fasciatus* Waterhouse (Marsupialia), with Particular Reference to Its Food Habits'. *Proceedings of the Zoological Society of London*, 135, no. 2 (1960), 183-207.

Came, P.B., and others. *Scientific and Common Names of Insects and Allied Forms Occurring in Australia*. CSIRO. Australia, 1980.

Cayzer, Lindy W., Michael D. Crisp and Ian R.H. Telford. 'Revision of *Pittosporum* (Pittosporaceae) in Australia'. *Australian Systematic Botany*, 13 (2000), 845-902.

Chandler, Gregory T., Michael D. Crisp and Lindy W. Cayzer. 'Monograph of *Gastrolobium* (Fabaceae: Mirbelieae)'. *Australian Systematic Botany*, 15, no. 5 (2002), 619-739.

Christensen, Per. *The Tammar Wallaby and Fire*. Resource Notes No. 6, Department of Conservation and Land Management (now DEC). Perth, 1987.

Christidis, Les, and Walter Boles. *Systematics and Taxonomy of Australian Birds*. Collingwood, Victoria, 2008.

Cole, Rex Vicat. *The Artistic Anatomy of Trees: Their Structure and Treatment in Painting*. 2nd edition. New York, 1965.

Coleman, R.S. 'Bee Farming: The Honey Flora of Western Australia'. *Journal of Agriculture*, 3, no. 8 (1962), 649-64.

Common, I.F.B. *Moths of Australia*. Melbourne, 1990.

Common, I.F.B., and D.F. Waterhouse. *Butterflies of Australia*. Abridged edition. Sydney, 1981.

Conservation Commission of Western Australia. *Forest Management Plan 2004-2013*. Perth, Western Australia, 2004.

Cooney, S.J.N., D.M. Watson and J. Young. 'Mistletoe Nesting in Australian Birds: A Review'. *Emu*, 106 (2006), 1-12.

Crisp, M.D., and P.H. Weston. 'Cladistics and Legume Systematics, with an Analysis of the Bossiaceae, Brongniartieae and Mirbelieae'. In *Advances in Legume Systematics, Part 3*. Edited by C.H. Stirton. Royal Botanic Gardens, Kew, 1987, 65-130.

CSIRO. *The Insects of Australia: A Textbook for Students and Research Workers*. Melbourne, 1970.

Davidson, D.W., and S.R. Morton. 'Dispersal Adaptations of Some *Acacia* Species in the Australian Arid Zone'. *Ecology*, 65 (1984), 1038-51.

Davies, S.J.J.F. 'The Food of Emus'. *Australian Journal of Ecology*, 3 (1978), 411-22.

Del Marco, Andrew, Ryan Taylor, Karen Clarke, Kate Savage, Julia Cullity & Carla Miles. *Local Government Biodiversity Planning Guidelines for the Perth Metropolitan Region*. Perth, 2004.

Dell, Bernard, and Ian J. Bennett. *The Flora of Murdoch University: A Guide to the Native Plants on Campus*. Perth, 1986.

Dell, J. 'The Importance of the Darling Scarp to Fauna'. In *Scarp Symposium: Proceedings of a Meeting Held in Perth on 14th October, 1983*. Edited by J.D. Majer. Perth, 1983, 17-27.

Dell, J., and R.E. Johnstone. 'The Birds of Cockleshell Gully Reserve and Adjacent Areas'. *Records of the Western Australian Museum*, Supplement 4 (1977), 37-72.

Department of Conservation and Environment, Western Australia (now DEC). *Atlas of Natural Resources: Darling System: Western Australia*. Perth, 1980.

Department of Conservation and Environment, Western Australia (now DEC). *The Darling System — System 6: Conservation Reserves for Western Australia as Recommended by the Environmental Protection Authority — 1983: Parts 1 & II*. Report 13. Perth, 1983.

Department of Environment and Conservation, Western Australia. *Lands and Waters Managed by the Department of Environment and Conservation*. Perth, 2008.

Department of Environment and Conservation, Western Australia, no date. http://www.florabase.dec.wa.au [website].

Department of Conservation and Land Management (now DEC), Western Australia. *Native Seed Collection and Storage*. Information Sheet No. 5. Perth, 1987.

Department of Conservation and Land Management (now DEC), Western Australia. *Northern Forest Region Regional Management Plan, 1987-1997: Management Plan No. 9*. Perth, 1987.

Department of Fisheries and Wildlife, Western Australia (now DEC). 'Have Poisonous Plants Helped Save Some of Our Native Wildlife from Extinction?' *State Wildlife Authority News Service* (SWANS), 10, no. 1 (1980).

Dunlop, J.N., and Galloway, R. 'The Dispersal and Germination of Seed in the Weeping Pittosporum (*Pittosporum phylliraeoides* DC.)'. Report No. 7 (1984), Mulga Research Centre, 75-80.

Erickson, Rica, and others. *Flowers and Plants of Western Australia*. 3rd edition. Sydney, 1986.

Fairall, A.R. *West Australian Native Plants in Cultivation*. Rushcutters Bay, 1970.

Forests Department of Western Australia (now DEC). *A Primer of Forestry*. 2nd edition. Perth, 1925.

Forests Department of Western Australia (now DEC). *Forestry in Western Australia*. Revised edition. Perth, 1966.

Fox, J.E.D. 'A Review of the Ecological Characteristics of *Acacia saligna* (Labill.) H. Wendl'. *Mulga Research Centre Journal*, 12 (1995).

Froend, Ray. 'Impact of Groundwater Use and Decreased Rainfall on Banksia'. *Western Wildlife*, 12, no. 2 (April, 2008), 6-7.

Gardner, C.A. 'Trees of Western Australia: No. 3 — Tuart'. *The Journal of Agriculture of Western Australia*, 1 (Third Series), no. 2 (1952).

Gardner, C.A. *Wildflowers of Western Australia*. 11th edition. Perth, 1973.

Gardner, C.A., and H.W. Bennetts. *The Toxic Plants of Western Australia*. Perth, 1956.

George, Alexander S. *Flora of Australia, Volume 46: Iridaceae to Dioscoreaceae*. Canberra, 1986.

George, Alex S. *The Banksia Book*. Kangaroo Press. 2nd edition. [Kenthurst, N.S.W.], 1987.

George, A.S. 'New Taxa and a New Infrageneric Classification in *Dryandra* R. Br. (Proteaceae: Grevilleoideae)'. *Nuytsia*, 10, no. 3 (1996), 313-408.

Gill, Malcolm. '*Acacia cyclops* G. Don (Leguminosae — Mimosaceae) in Australia: Distribution and Dispersal'. *Journal of the Royal Society of Western Australia*, 67, Part 2 (1985), 59-65.

Grayling, Peter M. 'An Investigation of Taxonomy, Reproductive Biology and Hybridity in Four Taxa of *Eucalyptus* of Extreme Rarity'. Unpublished Dip. Sci. dissertation. University of W.A., 1989.

Grayling, P.M., and M.I.H. Brooker. 'Four New Species of *Eucalyptus* (Myrtaceae) from Western Australia'. *Nuytsia*, 8, no. 2 (1992), 209-18.

Green, J.W. *Census of the Vascular Plants of Western Australia*. 2nd edition. Perth, 1985.

Grieve, W.E. *See* Blackall, W.E., and B.J. Grieve.

Hall, Norman. *Botanists of the Eucalypts*. Melbourne, 1978.

Halse, Stuart. *Red-Capped Parrots, Marri and Apple Orchards — Adaptation and Pre-Adaptation*. Resource Notes No. 5, Department of Conservation and Land Management (now DEC). Perth, 1987.

Harden, Gwen (ed.). *Flora of New South Wales*. Sydney. Vol. 1, revised, 2000. Vol. 2, revised, 2002. Vol. 3, 1992. Vol. 4, 1993.

Hassell, E. *My Dusky Friends: Aboriginal Life, Customs and Legends and Glimpses of Station Life at Jarramungup in the 1880's*. Perth, 1975.

Hayward, Matt W., Paul J. de Tores, Michael J. Dillon and Peter B. Banks. 'Predicting the Occurrence of the Quokka, *Setonix brachyurus* (Macropodidae: Marsupalia), in Western Australia's Northern Jarrah Forest'. *Wildlife Research*, 34 (2007), 194-9.

Heddle, E.M., O.W. Loneragan and J.J. Havel. 'Vegetation Complexes of the Darling System, Western Australia'. In *Atlas of Natural Resources: Darling System, Western Australia*. Department of Conservation and Environment (now DEC). Perth, 1980, 37-72.

Hill, A.L., & C.J. Nicholson. *Water-Conserving Design for Gardens and Open Space*. Water Authority of Western Australia, Report No. WP 89. Perth, 1989.

Hill, K.D., and L.A.S. Johnson. 'Systematic Studies in the Eucalypts: 7. A Revision of the Bloodwoods, Genus *Corymbia* (Myrtaceae)'. *Telopea*, 6(2-3) (1995), 185-504.

Hopper, Stephen D., and others. *Western Australia's Endangered Flora and Other Plants under Consideration for Declaration*. Perth, 1990.

Houston, Terry F. '*Leioproctus* Bees Associated with Western Australian Smoke Bushes (*Conospermum* spp.) and their Adaptations for Foraging and Concealment (Hymenoptera: Colletidae: Paracolletini)'. *Records of the Western Australian Museum*, 14, no. 3 (1989).

Hussey, B.M.J., G.J. Keighery, R.D. Cousens, J. Dodd and S.J. Lloyd. *Western Weeds: A Guide to the Weeds of Western Australia*. 2nd edition. Perth, 2007.

Keighery, B.J., and V.M. Longman. *Tuart (*Eucalyptus gomphocephala*) and Tuart Communities*. Perth, 2002.

King, D.R., A.J. Oliver and R.J. Mead. 'The Adaptation of Some Western Australian Mammals to Food Plants Containing Fluoroacetate'. *Australian Journal of Zoology*, 26 (1978), 699-712.

Lamont, Byron. 'Availability of Water and Inorganic Nutrients in the Persistent Leaf Bases of the Grasstree *Kingia australis*, and Uptake and Translocation of Labelled Phosphate by the Embedded Aerial Roots'. *Physiologia Plantarum*, 52 (1981), 181-6.

Lamont, Byron. '"Proteoid" Roots in the Legume *Viminaria juncea*'. *Search*, 3 (1972), 90.

Lamont, Byron B. 'Tissue Longevity of the Arborescent Monocotyledon *Kingia australis* (Xanthorrhoe-aceae)'. *American Journal of Botany*, 67, no. 8 (1980), 1262-4.

Lamont, Byron. 'Morphometrics of the Aerial Roots of *Kingia australis* (Liliales)'. *Australian Journal of Botany*, 29 (1981), 81-96.

Lamont, Byron. 'Dispersal of the winged fruits of *Nuytsia floribunda* (Loranthaceae)'. *Australian Journal of Ecology*, 10 (1985), 187-93.

Lamont, Byron B., and Brian G. Collins. 'Flower Colour Change in *Banksia ilicifolia*: A Signal for Pollinators'. *Australian Journal of Ecology*, 13 (1988), 129-35.

Lamont, Byron B., and Susan Downes. 'The Longevity, Flowering and Fire History of the Grasstrees *Xanthorrhoea preissii* and *Kingia australis*'. *Journal of Applied Ecology*, 16 (1979), 893-9.

Lamont, Byron B., and John E.D. Fox. 'Spatial Pattern of Six Sympatric Leaf Variants and Two Size Classes of *Acacia aneura* in a Semi-Arid Region of Western Australia'. *Oikos*, 37 (1981), 73-9.

Lamont, Byron, and James Grey. 'Ants, Extrafloral Nectaries and Elaiosomes on a Pioneering Species'. In *Medicos IV: Proceedings of the 4th International Conference on Mediterranean Ecosystems*. Edited by B. Dell. Perth, 1984, 89-90.

Lamont, Byron B., and B.J. Lange. '"Stalagmiform" Roots in Limestone Caves'. *The New Phytologist*, 76 (1976), 353-60.

Lamont, Byron B., Catherine S. Ralph and Per E.S. Christensen. 'Mycophagous Marsupials as Dispersal Agents for Ectomycorrhizal Fungi on *Eucalyptus calophylla* and *Gastrolobium bilobum*'. *The New Phytologist*, 101 (1985), 651-6.

Linnean Society of London. 'An Update of the Angiosperm Phylogeny Group Classification for the Orders and Families of Flowering Plants: APG II'. *Botanical Journal of the Linnean Society*, 141 (2003), 399-436.

Long, J.L. 'Weights, Measurements and Food of the Emu in the Northern Wheatbelt of Western Australia'. *The Emu: Journal of the Royal Australasian Ornithologists Union*, 64 (1965), 214-19.

Mabberley, D.J. *The Plant-Book: A Portable Dictionary of the Vascular Plants*. 2nd edition. Cambridge, United Kingdom, 1997.

McDonald, Tim. 'Rock Sheoak'. *State Wildlife Authority News Service* (SWANS), 12, no. 2 (1982), 29-31.

McMillan, R.P. 'The Biology of *Iridomyrmex conifer*'. Unpublished M.Sc. dissertation. University of W.A., 1982.

McMillan, Peter. 'Fallen Timber: Fuel for Thought'. *Environment WA*, 6, no. 2 (1984), 17-19.

McMillan, R.P. 'Notes on a Mistletoe Weevil, *Metyrus albicollis* Germ.' *Western Australian Naturalist*, 17 (1987), 20-1.

Maiden, J.H. *The Useful Native Plants of Australia*. London & Sydney, 1889; reprinted Melbourne, 1975.

Majer, J.D. 'The Possible Protective Function of Extrafloral Nectaries of *Acacia saligna*'. *Annual Report 2* (1978), Mulga Research Centre. Perth, 1979, 31-9.

Majer, Jonathan D. 'Ant-Plant Interactions in the Darling Botanical District of Western Australia'. In *Ant-Plant Interactions in Australia*. Edited by R. Buckley. The Netherlands, 1982, 45-61.

Majer, Jonathan, and Roger Clay. 'Flooded Gum (*Eucalyptus rudis*) Decline in the Perth Metropolitan Area: A Preliminary Assessment'. *School of Environmental Biology Bulletin No. 19*, 2001.

Majer, J.D., R.D. Cocquyt & H.F. Recher. 'Powdery Bark in *Eucalyptus accedens* Deters Arthropods?: An Evaluation using Ants'. *Journal of the Royal Society of Western Australia*, 2004, 87, 81-83.

Majer, J.D., and H.F. Recher. 'Invertebrate Communities on Western Australian Eucalypts: A Comparison of Branch Clipping and Chemical Knockdown Procedures'. *Australian Journal of Ecology*, 13, no. 3 (1988), 269-78.

Majer, J.D., H.F. Recher & A.C. Postle. 'Comparison of Arthropod Species Richness in Eastern and Western Australian Canopies: A Contribution to the Species Number Debate'. *Memoirs of the Queensland Museum*, Vol. 36, Part 1 (1994), 121-31.

Majer, J.D., H.F. Recher, R. Graham and R. Gupta. 'Trunk Invertebrate Faunas of Western Australian Forests and Woodlands: Influence of Tree Species and Season'. *Australian Ecology*, 2003, 28, 629-41.

Marchant, N.G. 'The Western Australian Collecting Localities of J.A.L. Preiss'. In *History of Systematic Botany in Australasia: Proceedings of a Symposium held at the University of Melbourne, 25-27 May 1988*. Edited by P.S. Short. South Yarra, Victoria, 1990, 131-5.

Marchant, N.G., and others. *Flora of the Perth Region: Parts One and Two*. Perth, 1987.

Marshall, John, and members of the Darling Range Branch, Wildflower Society of Western Australia. *Western Australian Wildflowers: West Coast Hills: Field Guide*. [Perth], [1995].

Mast, Austin R., & Kevin Thiele. 'The Transfer of *Dryandra* R. Br. to *Banksia* L.f (Proteaceae)'. *Australian Systematic Botany*, 20, no. 1, 2007, 63-71.

Maslin, B.R. 'Studies in the Genus *Acacia* — 3: The Taxonomy of *A. saligna* (Labill.) H. Wendt'. *Nuytsia*, 1, no. 4 (1974), 332-40.

Mazanec, Z. 'The Jarrah Leaf Miner and its Natural Enemies'. *Journal of Agriculture*, 22, no. 2 (1981), 78-80.

Meagher, Sara J. 'The Food Resources of the Aborigines of the South-West of Western Australia'. *Records of the Western Australian Museum*, 3, part 1 (1974), 14-65.

Moore, George Fletcher. *A Descriptive Vocabulary of the Language in Common Use amongst the Aborigines of Western Australia*. London, 1842.

Moore, Susan A (ed.). *The Management of Small Bush Areas in the Perth Metropolitan Region: Proceedings of a Seminar held on 20 September 1983*. Department of Fisheries and Wildlife (now DEC). Perth, 1984.

Morcombe, M.K. *Australia's Western Wildflowers*. Perth, 1968.

Morley, B.D., and H.R. Toelken (eds). *Flowering Plants in Australia*. Adelaide, 1983.

O'Dowd, Dennis J., and A. Malcolm Gill. 'Seed Dispersal Syndromes in Australian *Acacia*'. In *Seed Dispersal*. Edited by David R. Murray. Sydney, 1986, 87-121.

Paap, T., T.I. Burgess, J.A. McComb, B.L. Shearer & G.E. St J. Hardy. '*Quambalaria* species, including *Q. coyrecup* sp. nov., implicated in Canker and Shoot Blight Diseases causing Decline of *Corymbia* Species in the Southwest of Western Australia'. *Mycological Research*, 112 (2008), 57-69.

Pate, J.S., and A.J. McComb (eds). *The Biology of Australian Plants*. Perth, 1981.

Pen, L.J. *Peripheral Vegetation of the Swan and Canning Estuaries, 1981*. Bulletin 113, Department of Conservation and Environment (now DEC). Perth, 1983.

Pen, Luke J. *Managing Our Rivers: A Guide to the Nature and Management of the Streams of South-West Western Australia*. Perth, 1999.

Pike, Douglas (general editor). *Australian Dictionary of Biography*. Melbourne, 1969.

Powell, Robert. *Re-Establishing Local Trees and Shrubs on Farms*. Department of Fisheries and Wildlife (now DEC). Perth, 1983.

Powell, Robert, and Jane Emberson. *Woodman Point: A Relic of Perth's Coastal Vegetation*. Perth, 1981.

Powell, Robert, and Jane Emberson. *Growing Locals: Gardening with Local Plants in Perth*. Perth, 1996.

Recher, H.F., J.D. Majer & S. Ganesh. 'Eucalypts, Insects and Birds: On the Relation Between Foliar Nutrients and Species Richness'. *Forest Ecology and Management*, 85 (1996), 177-95.

Rippey, Elizabeth, and Barbara Rowland. *Coastal Plants: Perth and the South-West Region*. 2nd Edition. Perth, 2004.

Robinson, Angus. 'The Importance of Marri as a Food Source to South-Western Australian Birds'. *The Western Australian Naturalist*, 7, no. 5 (July, 1960), 109-15.

Rooke, Ian. 'The Social Behaviour of the Honeyeater *Phylidonyris novaehollandiae*'. Unpublished Ph.D. dissertation. University of W.A. Perth, 1979.

Ross, J.H. 'A Revision of the Genus *Labichea* Gaudich. ex DC. (Caesalpiniaceae)'. *Muelleria*, 6 (1985), 23-49.

Rye, Barbara L. *Geographically Restricted Plants of Southern Western Australia*. Report No. 49, Department of Fisheries and Wildlife (now DEC). Perth, 1982.

Sargent, O.H. 'Relations Between Birds and Plants'. *The Emu: Journal of the Royal Australasian Ornithologists Union*, 27 (1928), 185-92.

Saunders, D.A. 'Distribution and Taxonomy of the White-Tailed and Yellow-Tailed Black Cockatoos *Calyptorhynchus* spp.'. *The Emu: Journal of the Royal Australasian Ornithologists Union*, 79 (1979), 215-27.

Saunders, D.A. 'Food and Movements of the Short-Billed Form of the White-Tailed Black Cockatoo'. *Australian Wildlife Research*, 7 (1980), 257-69.

Saunders, D.A. 'Subspeciation in the White-Tailed Black Cockatoo, *Calyptorhynchus baudinii*, in Western Australia'. *Australian Wildlife Research*, 1 (1974), 55-69.

Saunders, D.A., and C.P. de Rebeira. *The Birdlife of Rottnest Island*. Perth, 1985.

Schodde, R., B. Glover, F.C. Kinsky, S. Marchant, A.R. McGill and S.A. Parker. 'Recommended English Names for Australian Birds'. *The Emu: Journal of the Royal Australasian Ornithologists Union*, 77 (supplement) (1978).

Scott, John K. 'The Impact of Destructive Insects on Reproduction in Six Species of *Banksia* L.f. (Proteaceae)'. *Australian Journal of Zoology*, 30 (1982), 901-21.

Scott, John K., and Robert Black. 'Selective Predation by White-Tailed Black Cockatoos on Fruit of *Banksia attenuata* Containing the Seed-Eating Weevil *Alphitopis nivea*'. *Australian Wildlife Research*, 8 (1981), 421-30.

Seabrook, Joanna. *Seeds of the Future: How to Establish a Native Plant Seed Orchard and Revolutionise Revegetation*. Perth, 1987.

Seddon, George. *Sense of Place: A Response to an Environment: The Swan Coastal Plain, Western Australia*. Perth, 1972.

Sedgwick, Eric H. 'A Population Study of the Barrow Island Avifauna'. *The Western Australian Naturalist*, 14, no. 4 (1978), 85-108.

Serventy, D.L., and H.M. Whittel. *Birds of Western Australia*. Perth, 1976.

Sharr, F.A.. *Western Australian Plant Names and their Meanings: A Glossary*. Perth, 1978.

Shea, S.R., and others. 'A New Perspective on Jarrah Dieback'. *Forest Focus*, 31 (July, 1984), 3-11.

Shearer, Bryan, Ray Wills & Mike Stukely. 'Wildflower Killers'. *Landscape*, 7, no. 1 (spring, 1991), 28-34.

Smith, Francis G. *Honey Plants in Western Australia*. Bulletin No. 3618, Department of Agriculture of Western Australia (now the Department of Agriculture and Food). Perth, 1969.

Specht, R.L. 'Vegetation'. In *The Australian Environment*. Edited by G.W. Leeper. 4th edition. CSIRO. Melbourne, 1970, 44-67.

Spencer, Rachel, and Naomi Hellriegel. 'Constructed Ephemeral Wetlands on the Swan Coastal Plain — the Design Process'. *River Science*, 26 (September, 2007).

State of Western Australia. *Bush Forever: Keeping the Bush in the City: Volume 1, Policies, Principles and Practices; Volume 2, Directory of Bush Forever Sites*. Perth: Western Australian Planning Commission, 2000.

Storr, G.M. 'The Avifauna of Rottnest Island, Western Australia: III. Land Birds'. *The Emu: Journal of the Royal Australasian Ornithologists Union*, 64 (1965), 172-80.

Tassone, R.A., and J.D. Majer. 'Abundance of Arthropods in Tree Canopies of *Banksia* Woodland on the Swan Coastal Plain'. *Journal of the Royal Society of Western Australia*, 80 (1997), 281-6.

Taylor, A., and S.D. Hopper. *The Banksia Atlas*. Australian Flora and Fauna Series No. 8, Australian Government Publishing Service. Canberra, 1988.

Taylor, Jan. *Flower Power in the Australian Bush and Garden: The Fascinating Interrelationships Between Insects and Plants*. Kenthurst, New South Wales, 1989.

Thomas, Jeremy. 'Tuarts of Kings Park'. *For People and Plants*, 55 (Spring, 2006), 24-5.

Tillyard, R.J. *The Insects of Australia and New Zealand*. Sydney, 1926.

Tingay, Alan, and Associates. *A Strategic Plan for Perth's Greenways: Final Report*. Perth, 1998.

Tingay, Susan, and Alan Tingay. *Eucalypts of the Perth Area*. Perth, 1976.

Tudge, Colin. *The Variety of Life: A Survey and a Celebration of all the Creatures that have ever Lived*. New York, U.S.A., 2000.

Van Delft, Ron. *Birding Sites around Perth*. 2nd edition. Perth, 1997.

Veneklaas, Erik, and Liz Manning. 'Wandoo Crown Decline: Linked to a Changing Environment?' *Landscope*, 22, no. 4 (2007), 17-22.

Walling, Edna. *Country Roads: The Australian Roadside*. Lilydale, Victoria, 1952; reprinted 1985.

West, J.G. 'A Revision of *Dodonaea* Miller (Sapindaceae) in Australia'. *Brunonia*, 7 (1984), 1-194.

Western Australian Museum. *Faunal Studies of the Northern Swan Coastal Plain: A Consideration of Past and Future Changes*. Perth, 1978.

Weston, Peter H. 'The Systematics and Biogeography of the Persooniinae (Proteaceae)'. Unpublished Ph.D. thesis. University of Sydney. Sydney, 1983.

Whelan, Robert J., and Allan H. Burbidge. 'Flowering Phenology, Seed Set and Bird Pollination of Five Western Australian *Banksia* species'. *Australian Journal of Ecology*, 5 (1980), 1-7.

Whittell, H.M. 'The Toxic Properties of the Bronzewing Pigeon'. *The Emu: Journal of the Royal Australasian Ornithologists Union*, 42 (1942), 56-7.

Williams, Andrew A.E. 'The Butterflies (Lepidoptera) of Garden and Rottnest Islands, Western Australia'. *Australian Entomologist*, 24, no.1 (1997), 27-34.

Zborowski, Paul, and Ross Storey. *A Field Guide to Insects in Australia*. Chatswood, N.S.W., 1995.

Zimmerman, Elwood C. *Australian Weevils: Volume 1*. Melbourne, 1994.

Index of living things

This index refers to all the plants, animals, fungi and other living things mentioned in this book. The page-references are given under the common name for those species that have one, otherwise under the scientific name. For plants, the common name and the scientific name, or at least the genus, are both listed, with cross-references from the scientific to the common name. For the trees and tall shrubs that are the subject of this book, the references given in **bold** type show where the main treatment can be found.

Since the common names of Western Australian birds are well defined, no scientific names of birds are given. For most other living things — apart from well known ones, such as 'cat' and 'pig' — the scientific name of the species, genus or family is added in brackets after the common name. For groups of the more obscure living things, such as booklice or southern rushes, the name of the family, or sometimes the order, is given, to help readers identify them. In some cases, however, no family name can be given; for example, the fungus beetles belong to three or more different families.

In most cases, two-word names are listed under the last word (e.g. 'banksia, bull'), with a few exceptions such as 'Christmas tree'.

The abbreviation 'sp.' denotes a single species; 'spp.' denotes more than one species.

basket bush (*Spyridium globulosum*) **202-3**, 219, 222-3, 227

bat(s) 21, 41, 45, 104, 131, 137, 216
  chocolate wattled (*Chalinolobus morio*) 21
  Gould's wattled (*Chalinolobus gouldii*) 21, 137, 139
  inland free-tailed (*Mormopterus planiceps*) 137
  south-western falsistrelle (*Falsistrellus mckenziei*) 112
  white-striped free-tailed (*Tadarida australis*) 21, 137

Beaufortia 82

bee(s) 19, 48-9, 50, 80, 90, 124, 126, 150, 154, 156, 158, 160, 168, 170, 176, 180, 188, 196, 205, 206
  carpenter (*Xylocopa* sp.) 160, 192
  colletid (family Colletidae) 90, 148-9, 166
  halictid (family Halictidae) 188
    black jacksonia 160
  smokebush (*Leioproctus* sp.) 90
  SEE ALSO honeybee

bee-eater, rainbow 20, 64, 190

bee-fly SEE fly, bee-

beetle(s) 19-20, 24, 29, 44, 48, 50, 52, 68, 70, 74, 78, 80, 92, 107-8, 111, 113, 120, 136, 146, 156, 160, 168, 178, 180, 187, 189-90, 194, 205, 208
  clerid (family Cleridae) 107, 140
    green wolf (*Eleale* sp.) 156
  Copidita sp. 78
  fungus 113
  jewel 48-9, 56, 58, 60, 80, 111, 158, 164, 168, 174, 180, 205-6, 208
    anchor (*Castiarina anchoralis*) 168
    Roe's (*Stigmodera roei*) 56
    southern fire-banded melobasis (*Melobasis sexplagiata*) 130
    SEE ALSO *Agrilus*; *Astraeus*; *Cisseis*; *Cyria*; *Melobasis*; *Stigmodera*
  lagriid (family Lagriidae) 146
  leaf (family Chrysomelidae) 118
  leaf-eating 118, 124, 170-1
  long-horned (family Cerambycidae) 18, 50, 58, 88, 92, 96, 118, 130, 134, 150, 158, 160, 164, 174, 208 SEE ALSO longicorn
  longicorn SEE longicorn; beetle, long-horned
  lucanid (family Lucanidae) 163
  nitidulid (family Nitidulidae) 154, 200, 205
  scarab (family Scarabaeidae) 208
  soldier (*Lagria* sp.) 200
  SEE ALSO weevil

biara SEE banksia, candle

bittern, black 21

blackbutt SEE yarri
  coastal SEE pricklybark

black-cockatoo(s) 24, 76, 113, 227
  Baudin's 20, 92
  Carnaby's 52, 64, 66, 92, 135, 154, 156

bloodwood(s) 42, 92, 96
  lesser (*Corymbia haematoxylon*) 30, 42, 92, **96-7**, 220

blowflies (Family Calliphoridae) 19

blue, wattle SEE butterfly

bobtail (*Tiliqua rugosa*) 21

boojak SEE parrotbush

booklice (order Psocoptera) 52, 98, 111, 148, 178

bottlebrush(es) 82-3
  Albany (*Callistemon glaucus*) 82
  lesser SEE toobada
  one-sided (*Calothamnus* spp.) 82, 86-7
    common (*Calothamnus quadrifidus*) 86, 215

bracket, scarlet SEE fungus

bronzewing(s) 55
  brush 21
  common 142, 194

broom (*Cytisus scoparius*) 140

buckthorn family (Rhamnaceae) 15

bug(s) 19, 48, 58-9. 102, 104, 118, 130, 140, 148, 192
  assassin (family Reduviidae) 19, 131, 140, 168, 188
  coccid (family Coccidae) 116
  crusader (*Mictis profana*) 19, 48, 160
  eriococcid (family Eriococcidae)
    Eriococcus sp. 108
    Apiomorpha spp. 116, 134
  harlequin (*Tectocoris* sp.) 19, 98, 100, 102
  heteropterans (suborder Heteroptera) 148
  jewel (*Coleotichus costatus*) 44
  mealy SEE scale insects
  mirid (family Miridae) 85, 178
  pentatomid SEE shieldbugs
  pittosporum (*Pseudapines geminata*) 198
  SEE ALSO lerp insects; shieldbugs

bullanock SEE kingia

bullich (*Eucalyptus megacarpa*) 3, 6, 30, 39, **124-5**, 221

bulrush (*Typha orientalis*) 182-3

butterfly(ies) 19, 48, 59, 82, 92, 156, 168, 172, 174, 198, 208
  Australian painted lady (*Vanessa kershawi*) 18, 120, 174, 208
  blotched dusky-blue (*Candalides acastus*) 178
  fiery jewel (*Hypochrysops ignita*) 48
  fringed heath-blue (*Neolucia agricola*) 160
  long-tailed pea-blue (*Lampides boeticus*) 160, 176
  marbled xenica (*Geitoneura klugii*) 59, 174
  satin azure (*Ogyris amaryllis*) 22, 82, 88
  silky azure (*Ogyris oroetes*) 22
  spotted jezebel (*Delias aganippe*) 22, 88, 176, 190, 200
  two-spotted line-blue (*Nacaduba biocellata*) 44, 48
  varied hairstreak (*Jalmenus inous*) 48
  wattle blue (*Theclinesthes miskini*) 48
  western brown (*Heteronympha merope*) 59, 92, 120, 196
  western jewel (*Hypochrysops halyaetus*) 160
  yellow admiral (*Vanessa itea*) 172, 198, 208-9

C

cadjeput (*Melaleuca leucadendra*) 43

Caladenia spp. SEE orchid, spider

Callistachys 15, 80
  lanceolata SEE wonnich

Callistemon SEE bottlebrush